NEW
WEAPONS
OLD
POLITICS

NEW WEAPONS OLD POLITICS

America's Military Procurement Muddle

THOMAS L. McNAUGHER

The Brookings Institution | Washington, D.C.

Copyright © 1989 by
THE BROOKINGS INSTITUTION
1775 Massachusetts Ave., N.W., Washington, D.C. 20036

Library of Congress Cataloging-in-Publication data

McNaugher, Thomas L.
  New weapons, old politics: America's military procurement muddle
  Thomas L. McNaugher.
    p.   cm.
  Includes bibliographies and index.
    ISBN 0-8157-5626-7 (alk. paper)—ISBN 0-8157-5625-9
  (pbk. : alk. paper)
    1. United States—Armed Forces—Procurement.   2. Munitions—
  United States.   I. Title.
  UC263.M36   1989
  355.8'2'0973—dc20   89-33215
                                                       CIP

9 8 7 6 5 4 3 2 1

Set in Linotronic Janson
Composition by Monotype Composition Co.
  Baltimore, Maryland
Printing by R. R. Donnelley and Sons Co.
  Harrisonburg, Virginia
Book design by Ken Sabol
Cover design by Richard Hendel

For my parents

Foreword

WEAPONS production has been big business for the United States since the Second World War. The need to arm large and far-flung military forces with technologically advanced weapons has given birth to huge industries that do little else but serve the Defense Department. It has also given rise to mammoth bureaucracies and an overarching political structure for ensuring that defense money is wisely spent. But the ramifications of this business go well beyond its contribution to defense. Funding for defense research has helped spawn high-technology industries that, at least earlier in the era, gave the nation a trade advantage. And because defense spending is far and away the largest single purchasing component of the federal budget, weapons procurement has given politicians new ways to direct federal spending to their constituents. Indeed, weapons procurement has become an intrusive element in American political and economic life.

In this book Thomas L. McNaugher highlights the extent to which strategies for developing arcane and uncertain technologies have come to be shaped more by the needs of American politics than by the needs of technology. The resulting acquisition process errs systematically in the way it chooses new technologies, develops them into weapon systems, and rushes them prematurely to the field. Worse, it operates largely beyond the control of policymakers and politicians charged with providing for the common defense. Repeated attempts to solve these problems with acquisition reform have not just failed, McNaugher suggests, but often have made things worse. He offers reforms that would fundamentally reorganize the way the defense sector intersects with American society.

The author thanks Norman R. Augustine, John Hamre, and Uri Reychav for long and thoughtful reviews of the manuscript. For help along the way he thanks Michael Brown, Douglas G. Hoecker, Andrew G. Mayer, Capt. Donald L. Pilling of the U.S. Navy, Frederic M. Scherer, and James E. Williams, Jr. Within Brookings, John D. Steinbruner, Michael K. MccGwire, Richard K. Betts, and Ed A. Hewett provided conceptual guidance and moral support. Theresa B. Walker edited the manuscript. Drew Portocarrero and Mark Thibault provided research assistance, Vernon L. Kelley and Andrew C. Scobell verified the book's factual content, and Susan E. Nichols, Annette D. Proctor, and Ann M. Ziegler typed the manuscript. Susan L. Woollen prepared the manuscript for publication, and Susan Lohmeyer compiled the index.

Brookings gratefully acknowledges funding for this project from the John D. and Catherine T. MacArthur Foundation, the Carnegie Corporation of New York, and the Ford Foundation.

The views expressed in this book are those of the author and should not be ascribed to the organizations that supported the project, nor to the trustees, officers, or other staff members of the Brookings Institution.

BRUCE K. MAC LAURY
President

May 1989
Washington, D.C.

Contents

CHAPTER 1

The Unhappy Accommodation

NOBODY LIKES the weapons acquisition process. Vocal critics of American weapons find them overly complex, expensive, and unreliable. Executive and legislative branch officials accuse the firms that produce these weapons of inefficiency, shoddy production practices, even dishonesty—hence the perennial cry of "fraud, waste, and abuse" in the defense sector. Defense industrialists and military procurement managers respond by citing countless congressionally imposed audits that undermine attempts to manage acquisition projects smoothly and efficiently. And almost everyone finds the overall acquisition process, the routines and procedures by which weapons are developed and produced, exasperating in its complexity. It is hard to find a government activity so thoroughly criticized as the way in which the United States develops, produces, fields, and supports weaponry.

Not all of this criticism is justified. The United States is not in serious danger of losing its technological lead over the Soviet Union. Frank Carlucci, former secretary of defense, has said, "Our average lead time over Soviet defense technologies is approximately ten years."[1] And in a world where everyone's weapons are growing more complex and expensive, U.S. weapons often stand out as top performers. The acquisition process seems to do tolerably well what it was established to do, namely, arm the nation's forces with weapons technologically superior to those of its chief adversary, the Soviet Union.

But tolerably well is not well enough. It would be foolish to demand perfect efficiency from an undertaking as large, complicated, and inherently uncertain as this one, which consumes roughly $140 billion a year; enlists the efforts of 30,000 firms and thousands of bureaucrats, politicians, engineers, and scientists; and explores increasingly sophisticated and expensive technologies. Yet precisely because of its size and central focus on esoteric technologies and complex weapon systems, even a little inefficiency can be very expensive. If perfect efficiency is too demanding a goal, unnecessary inefficiency is too expensive to incur.

And the United States tolerates a good deal of unnecessary inefficiency in its weapons acquisition process. Although the nation retains its lead over the Soviet Union, the process explores technology with a degree of inflexibility, haste, and unwarranted certainty that guarantees mistakes in choosing new technologies, designing new weapons, or updating fielded systems in a timely way. Although private defense firms develop most of the nation's weapons, these firms face questionable incentives for doing quality work. And although the Defense Department maintains an elaborate formal planning process, it organizes the nation's military forces haphazardly at best. The costs of such problems are measured not simply in dollars but also in the effectiveness of U.S. forces.

Moreover, those costs are growing. The acquisition process has become encumbered by political and bureaucratic strictures that prevent almost everyone involved with arms procurement—engineers, service project managers, defense planners, high-level policymakers, and members of Congress—from making sensible choices. Meanwhile the nation's forces and weapons have also grown increasingly complicated and sophisticated, reducing the margins for error all around. The acquisition process has grown less responsive as the challenge it faces has grown more demanding and less tolerant of error.

It may be impossible to describe in full a process that deals with everything from nuts and bolts to missile guidance systems and stealth bombers, from basic and applied science through sophisticated production equipment, from small high-tech firms to huge defense conglomerates. A book that sought to do so would be hopelessly arcane and detailed. This book seeks instead to come to grips with the underlying trends and continuities that have shaped the process and account for its most serious problems.

The way to bring these trends and continuities to light is to trace the path by which the process got to where it is. Today's acquisition process is not terribly old, having been born in the early 1950s. At that point the United States took up the challenge of accommodating a large, expensive, and risky technical and military undertaking into a political system inherently uncomfortable with what it takes to do a good job of developing technology. The emerging accommodation has been an unhappy one, despite repeated attempts at acquisition reform. Weapons acquisition has become far too much a reflection of the American political process, leaving little room for the technical process it must be if it is to function well.

DIMENSIONS OF THE PROCESS

Over the past forty years the nation has struggled to integrate three separate but equally important and legitimate dimensions of the weapons acquisition process. At the core of the process lies the technical dimension; weapons acquisition is the way the nation transforms basic science and technology into new and advanced weapons. Weapons are not ends in themselves, however. They exist to serve military and security goals. Hence the process has a military dimension; it is the way the nation transforms matériel and technology into combat power. Finally, weapons acquisition has a political dimension, too. It is the way taxpayers' money is transformed into the arms that help provide a public good called national defense. Each dimension has special requirements that are often in tension with one another and with the requirements of the other dimensions.

The Technical Dimension

For the United States, with its strategic emphasis on technological superiority, the technical dimension of the weapons acquisition process is defined by the inherent uncertainty that comes with pressing beyond the existing technological horizon. This uncertainty is most obvious at the level of basic science and innovation. Thomas J. Peters has observed that most inventions come "from the wrong industry at the wrong time for the wrong reason."[2] There is no way to plan for orderly innovation to provide better weapons. At best, military organizations can plan only to respond creatively as innovations appear.

Disruptive surprises do not disappear as new technology leaves the realm of basic science to be embodied in the advanced components of new weaponry. The process of developing weapons holds out its own surprises, leading one experienced observer to distinguish "*known-*

unknowns," whose existence "can be foreseen in advance" from "*unknown-unknowns*" that "simply cannot reasonably be foreseen."[3] Speaking of predictions made about cost and performance in military development programs, for example, Burton H. Klein, one of the early and foremost students of military research and development (R&D), noted that "errors of 30 or 40 percent can hardly be regarded as errors."[4]

Authorities like Klein found that in resolving these uncertainties analysis was no match for building something and testing it. In the 1930s, for example, both the Navy and the Air Corps ignored the jet engine because paper studies consistently asserted that the idea was infeasible. But in 1938 the British Postal Service paid an inventor to build a demonstration model that quickly proved the engine's merit.[5] On the basis of an extended study of military development projects in the 1950s, Klein concluded that "sharp improvements in [cost-performance] estimates begin to occur only after the missile, radar, or engine is in test."[6] Because surfacing good information remains the primary purpose of the weapons development process and testing remains the best way to get it, emphasis on prototype testing has been a recurrent theme in the nation's attempts to reform the acquisition process.

Yet prototypes cannot resolve many of the important uncertainties that surround weapons development. Integrating advanced components into a weapon system can toss up surprises very late in the development process. Normally the shift from prototype construction techniques to hard production tooling also introduces new design problems. Information on reliability, hence on the life-cycle cost of a new system, may not surface "until a system is being operated and maintained in the field by the actual user."[7] And operational military units will introduce another set of design problems by using new weapons in ways ignored during prototype testing.

Good information is useful only if people have the flexibility to respond to it. Because flexibility is easily threatened by growing financial and emotional commitments to a project, those who have studied research and development recommend an austere approach to technology development in which financial commitments, and especially the investment in production tooling, are minimized. And since engineers and managers working directly on a project are best positioned to respond quickly and flexibly to emerging information, students of military R&D generally recommend that responsibility for design be delegated to those closest to the ongoing project.[8]

Especially in the early development of new technologies, it may be unclear just which of several technologies holds out the greatest promise. Given the surprises technology holds in store for those pursuing it, there is a real danger that project choices will be made before the best choice is reasonably clear. This problem has given rise to the theory of parallel projects, which holds that it is entirely efficient to keep alternative projects alive until it is clear which is better, even if at that point one or more of the losers is abandoned.[9]

This notion of efficiency is odd to be sure, since canceled projects wreak of waste. The appearance of waste is unavoidable in a process so rife with uncertainty. Wrong turns will be taken, to be exposed only by testing and further development. Yet to see this occurrence as waste is to take a short-term view of a process that can only be properly evaluated over the long haul. The danger that haunts R&D, especially in early stages, is that in trying to save money early in a project developers will make bad choices based on misleading early data. Having eliminated interesting new ideas prematurely, they will wind up wasting more money later on. The conundrum of R&D, it might be said, is that unless one is willing to waste money early, one is likely to waste much more money later. Good R&D can survive only in an environment that tolerates a certain amount of messiness and error early in order to avoid it later.

These organizational precepts apply in their purest form to the nurturing of new technologies in their highly uncertain growth phase. It is difficult to imagine how the final development of a complex weapon system like the B-1B bomber or M-1 tank could be handled by an austere organization, especially when production looms just around the corner or may even be going on while final development is being completed. It is equally difficult at this stage, with the government about to buy a finished often very expensive product, to leave decisions in the hands of a small technical elite in the developing organization. Seen from this perspective, students of military R&D seem somewhat unrealistic, essentially treating R&D as an end in itself rather than as a means for arming the nation's forces.

Yet the organizational and managerial precepts just outlined are based on the need to deal efficiently with uncertainty. And because systems like the B-1B and M-1 are complex amalgamations of new and old technologies that present delicate integration problems, a good deal of uncertainty remains even late in development. The challenge raised by the technological dimension of the acquisition process is to find the right balance between the need for austerity and flexibility and the need to make the commitments necessary to field a real, working weapon.

The Military Dimension

To encourage the presentation of meaningful technical alternatives, students of military research and development offered one final managerial suggestion: requirements for new weapons should be phrased in mission, rather than technical, terms. Rather than say "we need this weapon," the military, analysts contended, should say nothing more than "we need to do this mission." In response, innovators may come forward with a variety of technological ways in which the mission could be done. With investments in the development of the most promising new ideas, military planners could be reasonably sure of picking the best from among them.

With this final managerial recommendation students of R&D recognized implicitly that military planners face as much uncertainty as technology developers. This concern is true in the broad sense of relating new technologies to military missions and also in the narrower sense of making refined design decisions about an individual technology project.

The quality-quantity debate frames this issue in extremes—simple-cheap versus complex-expensive. It is more useful to think of a continuum relating cost and performance in any given technology (figure 1-1). Leonard Sullivan has called this sharply rising parabola the B-36 curve, referring to the argument that "getting another mile in B-36 range would have required its weight [closely related to cost] to double."[10] A nation that chooses to pursue technological advantage will try to design weapons that lie near the knee of this curve, where costs begin to rise sharply. Missing the knee can have serious quality-quantity consequences. Norman R. Augustine argues, for example, that the "last 10 percent of performance sought generates one-third of the cost and two-thirds of the problems."[11] In any given technology project the precise shape and location of the cost-performance curve will be uncertain. But as the outline of this curve emerges during development, developers and military planners can find the knee and make design trade-offs accordingly.

Costs on the B-36 curve, or in the weapons business generally, may refer to many things. Normally one thinks of what it costs to purchase a new weapon, its unit cost, which may refer either to the cost of the

FIGURE I-I. *Technology Cost-Performance Curve*

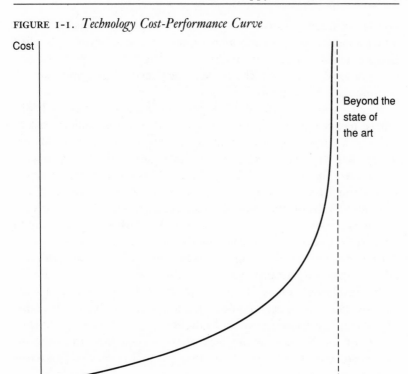

Cost

Beyond the
state of
the art

Performance

SOURCE: Based on Leonard Sullivan, Jr., "Q³: The Quality/Quantity Quandary," unpublished briefing, October 1981, p. 3.

weapon alone (drive- or fly-away cost), or may include a pro rata share of what it costs to develop the system (unit program cost). Costs may also refer to life-cycle cost, and this price too may be arrayed against performance in an equivalent of the B-36 curve just outlined. Given the time and testing required to surface data on reliability, a curve relating life-cycle cost to performance may not even be available until a new technology has been produced and fielded with line military units.

Performance, too, has many meanings. Most often it refers to a set of technical performance parameters, the performance envelope of a new fighter aircraft, for example, or the speed, agility, and armor protection of a new tank. Clearly, however, in suggesting that requirements be stated in mission terms students of military R&D meant the broader notion of mission performance, against which several different sets of technical performance parameters might be measured. This intent suggests that their notion of testing went beyond so-called developmental testing, which aims to validate technical performance, to operational testing, which assesses a new technology's usefulness in performing a military mission.

Parallel projects, offered by experts on R&D as a way to hedge against technological risk, can provide a hedge against military risk as well by leaving options open until mission usefulness is validated. There may be several promising technologies capable of satisfying mission requirements at an uncertain cost. Almost every major weapon system the services acquire is surrounded at some point, if not continuously, by debate about alternatives. Should the Army's forward air defense system carry missiles or guns? Is a turbine engine likely to be more cost-effective in a new tank than the traditional diesel? Is the Air Force's new medium-range air-to-air missile likely to be more cost-effective than shorter-range missiles like the Sidewinder that are already in the inventory? These debates implicitly refer to a series of cost-performance curves, each representing a different technology capable of performing a specific mission. In the end, the Defense Department's task is to find the best among several technologies and then aim for the most cost-effective point on that particular technology's cost-performance curve.

Thus weapons development is very much a cooperative process, including military as well as technical experts. As development proceeds, technical experts can give military experts an increasingly accurate fix on the technical performance of various technologies at different cost levels. At some point testing can begin to comprehend military utility as well as technical performance, allowing military experts to make judgments about the direction of further development. Those judgments amount to quality-quantity decisions, whether they mean moving among wholly different technologies or moving along the emerging cost-performance curve for a technology.

Although projects may start with a requirement in some general sense, in making choices on the basis of emerging information military experts redefine their requirement as development proceeds. In this sense the oft-noted distinction between setting military requirements and pursuing development obscures what is really going on. The development process is an extended process of setting and resetting requirements as information about cost and performance relationships improves in quality. The only real and unalterable requirement is the weapon, with its associated cost and performance, that finally leaves the development process and enters the military's inventory.

This implies a degree of flexibility and open-mindedness rarely associated with the military, especially in peacetime. To the contrary, there is an extensive literature on the rigidities common to large organizations, especially large military organizations.[12] As has been amply documented, they are capable of resisting innovations that might perform the same mission more effectively. And they are capable of defining what they think they need to fight the next war with a precision that neither technological nor military uncertainties can justify.

Military rigidity invites ridicule, often justifiably. But many of the sources of rigidity in military organizations are understandable and justifiable. Without standardization, so-called standing operating procedures, or SOPs, large organizations could not function. But SOPs are not standing if they are changed frequently. Military missions also impose a need for rigidity. Unique among large organizations, military forces train their members to risk their lives in combat. While dealing as they do "with life and death" should make them "ruthless in discarding the old for the new," Edward L. Katzenbach argues, "equally needed is a romanticism which, while it perhaps stultifies realistic thought, gives a man that belief in the value of the weapons system he is operating that is so necessary to his willingness to use it in battle."[13] One could also note the importance of personnel stability and unit cohesion in promoting combat effectiveness. But personnel stability requires at a minimum doctrinal stability, and this all too easily can become doctrinal rigidity.

The need for internal stability increases with organizational complexity. The more diversity and coordination required within an organization, the greater the pressure to standardize behavior and resist change. And just as weapon systems have been growing more complex over the past forty years, so have military organizations. Thus the problem of organizational rigidity has mounted steadily. Ironically, to the extent that the evolution of military technologies has increased the complexity of military organizations, it has built natural impediments to organizational change even as it has invited change.

Thus acquisition as a military enterprise is fraught with tension between the need for flexibility in pursuit of the best technical means for performing military missions and the inflexibility that stems from organizational strictures and doctrinal requirements. A perfectly flexible military organization is not likely to be very effective, while too rigid a military organization is likely to miss new and more effective technical means for carrying out its mission. There is no way to overcome this tension, any more than there is a simple way to square R&D's need for austerity with pressures to move into production. In the military dimension of the acquisition process, as well as in the technical dimension, there is a need for balance. Ideally, in clarifying the cost-effectiveness of new technologies, the technical development process can help establish that balance by exposing the costs of rigidity.

The Political Dimension

Saying that weapons acquisition is the way a nation converts public money into national defense does not begin to capture the full meaning of acquisition's political dimension. In the United States, the defense sector is a major sector of the economy. Federal contracts for weapons procurement mean jobs to voters. Large and diversified defense firms lobby the government marketplace. Whole communities often depend on defense bases, laboratories, and contractors. Weapons acquisition is political pork in the grandest sense. The politics of weapons procurement often afford the keenest insights into the essential inner workings of American politics.

At the center of the politics of procurement lies the question of access: who gets what from the federal purse. When federal "spending is on the agenda," R. Douglas Arnold has said, "so is the question of where all those dollars will be spent."[14] No simple formula describes how the federal procurement purse is allocated. Although the presence of defense contractors in political districts can affect voting patterns, acquisition issues relate to broad national goals as well as to local ones, and each member is likely to weigh these competing perspectives differently in different cases. Arnold argues, for example, that the local benefits of winning new procurement contracts "seldom create support for a program that otherwise might falter."[15] Even in the purely domestic political context, defense is likely to be only one of several issues of concern to local constituents, and within the defense component there may be several different kinds of contractors seeking federal business. Members facing this situation may engage in trade-offs in which their support for local defense contractors may not figure prominently. Finally, members with few or no defense contractors in their districts may exploit the voting freedom inherent in this situation by trading their support on defense issues for favors on issues relevant to their constituents.

Still, no one would deny that access remains a legitimate political issue. Politicians cannot be expected to leave acquisition to a small group of technical experts, however much that might yield a more effective search for new technologies or more rational industrial arrangements for developing and producing new weapons. Thus questions about what weapons are developed, where they are built, how many and how fast they are produced, which firms go out of business—in short, the kind of questions policymakers must answer continuously if they are to manage the acquisition process—are inevitably political as well as technical issues.

Only slightly less central to politics than the question of access is the question of accountability: how efficiently are tax dollars being spent in the defense sector? Historically, for example, Congress has accepted the president's program while reducing its funding, assuming that this action will produce greater efficiency. Calling for more competition, though rarely embodied in legislation, also has a long history. Finally, the effort to audit defense contractors has grown more intense over the postwar era. Cries of fraud, waste, and abuse spring directly from the politicians' pursuit of accountability.

Clearly this pursuit can conflict with the pursuit of access. The executive branch perennially seeks to close military bases and laboratories in the name of efficiency. Rarely do such moves go unchallenged on Capitol Hill. Inefficiency may also result from the presence of too many firms in one sector of the defense industry, yet here again politicians may sacrifice their interest in accountability for a more immediate and tangible concern for access. They will also be reluctant to demand efficiency if it means buying less expensive foreign components rather than something made in the United States, perhaps in their own districts. Thus public demands for greater accountability may belie a meager effort to achieve it. At the least, complex political calculations will influence how accountability is enforced.

Moving beyond immediate questions of access and accountability, politics and weapons acquisition intersect on the broad issue of how much risk society is willing to accept in seeking to protect its interests. Military officials can gauge the size of various military threats and recommend forces able to meet them. But it is up to the society that pays for such things to assess the risk that threats will actually be realized, especially simultaneously, and to determine how much of that risk it is willing to bear. The United States has never purchased the low-risk, high-confidence force recommended by its military chiefs, leading military officials to complain frequently about the so-called strategy-forces mismatch. What they are really saying, however, is that American society as a whole is less worried by the international environment, or alternatively more willing to live with risk, than its military.

To be sure, the nation as a whole does not collectively make risk assessments in some rational sense. Rather, the political system makes these calculations implicitly in the context of formulating defense budgets each year. War and crises can produce great surges in support for high levels of defense spending, as occurred during World War II, at the outbreak of the Korean War, during the Vietnam era, and after Soviet adventurism in Angola, Ethiopia, and Afghanistan left Americans disillusioned with détente. Conversely, declining defense budgets after 1969 resulted not simply from the nation's withdrawal from Vietnam but from a public disillusionment with the utility of military force and, as time went on, a sense that détente and arms control had reduced the risks of international conflict.

Such wide swings in the U.S. defense budget reflect crude risk calculations at best. Authoritarian regimes might produce more refined assessments and might also be able to evaluate technical issues on purely technical criteria. Democracies, by contrast, must square technical and military choices with the popular will by whatever institutional mechanisms exist. In the United States, public policy choices are routinely subjected to the tugging and hauling, and the pork barrel trading, that goes on continuously both in the legislature and between the legislature and the executive. These two branches, "separate institutions *sharing powers*," to borrow Richard E. Neustadt's famous phrase, tangle with each other to a degree that is largely unknown even in parliamentary democracies.[16] Meanwhile, always relatively fragmented in comparison to parliamentary systems, the U.S. political system has become even more so in recent decades, as, among other things, political parties have declined in power. This has produced a more contentious debate that yields only crude results. Yet such a process remains the only way of producing legitimate decisions for society as a whole.

THE SEARCH FOR POLITICAL ACCOMMODATION

There is tension within each of the three dimensions of the acquisition process—between the need for both austerity and commitment in the technical dimension, for example, or the contrary requirements for flexibility and rigidity in military organizations. Still more important, however, are the tensions among these dimensions, for America's military procurement muddle has resulted largely from the unsatisfactory way in which these tensions have been resolved.

In the United States, political norms and routines clash sharply with those appropriate to the development of new technologies. Technology development, for example, is essentially an authoritarian undertaking. Projects move along most efficiently when power is consolidated in the hands of a single inventor or a small and well-informed team of technical and military experts. Even the integration of a sprawling system of components like a bomber or a tank must be guided by some overarching intelligence capable of making trade-offs as troubles crop up. In the American political system, by contrast, public money is distributed in a series of pork-barrel trades marked by consensus building rather than the decisiveness needed for technical development. Political trading often links disparate substantive issues in a way that can make political decisionmaking relatively immune to technical advice. This reality is a far cry from the austere and clutter-free conditions required to design and produce new weapons.

Good R&D also requires the kind of investment pattern that can only be justified over the long haul. But the nation's founders designed a political system with an eye to emphasizing short-term calculations. Even members of Congress with seemingly safe seats tend to operate on the assumption that they are quite unsafe.[17] Nor is the short-term perspective confined to elected officials. Political appointees in the executive branch often come and go more frequently than members of Congress. Thus in both branches of the government the demands for rapid returns and near-instant accountability run strong. Pressures to take a counterproductive short-term approach to R&D investment run high. Meanwhile the political system's overall ability to stabilize the environment in which R&D is conducted is limited.

Tension is equally obvious in the relationship between the norms and strictures connected with the military and the political dimensions of the acquisition process. Sensitive to the need for standardization in their organizations and often emotionally attached to certain weapons, military officials approach weapons acquisition with great certainty. They also approach it with the strong feeling that because they risk their lives in war they should have a strong say in shaping the weapons with which wars will be fought. Yet they find their certainty and their control challenged constantly and from every angle. The challenges come not only from Pentagon agencies with an official charter to question requirements, but also from congressional staffers who may have questionable charters, questionable credentials and experience, and absolutely no responsibility for managing development projects or taking weapons into combat. The military's views on what is important can be compellingly challenged. Many truly useful military inventions have been forced upon a resisting military by civilians. But knowing that this state of affairs has been true in general is of little help in imposing change in specific cases.

The tensions among the various dimensions of the acquisition process have left their mark on the nation's approach to arms procurement from the birth of the republic. For much of the nation's history, however, the peacetime arms procurement effort was too small to warrant prolonged attention, while wartime problems were often solved with ad hoc arrangements in which politicians relaxed their traditional political norms. The real peacetime challenge came with the cold war, when the nation launched the first large and sustained peacetime arms acquisition effort in its history, an effort all the more challenging for being technically ambitious as well as large. Defense spending rose from $14.3 billion in 1950 to $45.2 billion in 1951, and to $57.2 billion in 1952.[18] Although support for defense spending waxed and waned with events in the 1960s, defense spending after 1951 never again approached the lows it had hit before or immediately after World War II. The cold war thus forced the United States to find a workable accommodation among the political, military, and technical dimensions of its new but burgeoning weapons acquisition process.

Given the sharply divergent needs of politicians, the technical development process, and the large military organizations participating in the new acquisition undertaking, no one should have expected the nation to find a perfect accommodation. The best the nation could have hoped to achieve was a working balance that would have allowed each dimension of the acquisition process enough independence and integrity to function roughly as it should. Unfortunately, the nation has instead swung from one extreme to the other. The acquisition process was born and nurtured in an era of cold war crisis. The nation's politicians handled the crisis much as they handled war, by relaxing their usual standards in the interest of "catching up to the Russians." The acquisition process was technically successful mostly because it functioned in ways America's politicians would not normally have tolerated in peacetime. Such political largesse could not go on forever, however, and beginning in the late 1950s the nation sought to bring the acquisition process under greater political control. In the process, political norms and operating routines have slowly but surely been imposed on the technical dimension of the process.

The costs of politicization have been high. Increasingly dominated by the short-term perspective of the political process, the acquisition process makes basic mistakes in the allocation of resources to R&D, where a long-term perspective is required. Increasingly dominated by the pork-barrel decision rules of American politics, the process has grown less sensitive to the needs of technology development, where flexibility and decisiveness are required. The military services have compounded these costs by organizing weapons projects to cope with the vicissitudes of American politics and also to exploit the political system to achieve their own organizational ends. In seeking to ensure their control, however, the services merely invite politicians more deeply into the acquisition process. And the outcome of the struggle for control is a process over which no one exercises much control.

Unfortunately, the other two dimensions of the acquisition process have evolved in ways that demand more control, not less. Weapons technologies have generally grown more mature over the past forty years. Today's jet engines and aircraft, for example, offer vastly higher performance than their predecessors. To achieve such dramatic improvements in performance, however, the services have pushed core technologies in these systems to extremes. Still greater performance may be possible, but it is likely to come only at much greater cost. Meanwhile weapon systems have grown steadily more complex, the interaction of their components ever more intricate. The cost of mistakes in both cases has increased, as has the demand for more refined control of the development process.

America's military forces, too, have grown more mature and complicated over the past forty years. Technology has created new capabilities. Some of these have been incorporated into weapons, but others have become the basis for new force elements. Coordinating the interaction of such elements has grown commensurately more challenging, as has the task of fitting new weapons into a complex whole. Meanwhile, starting almost from whole cloth in the 1950s, the nation has fashioned a force posture so elaborate and expensive that even Reagan-era increases in procurement spending produced no great increase in its size.[19] The point is not that money was wasted but that the managerial challenge implicit in forces of this size and sophistication is infinitely greater than what the nation faced when it first took up the cold war challenge.

Reform thus far has not produced encouraging results. Indeed the House Armed Services Committee recently concluded that "the bulk of the [acquisition] cures proposed as far back as 1948 were still being proposed in 1983 because they had never been implemented."[20] Effective reform will have to start from a more realistic view of how the acquisition process functions as well as a greater sense of the costs of leaving prevailing trends unchanged.

CHAPTER 2

The Era of Construction

AMERICANS encountered the political difficulties connected with pursuing sophisticated technologies not after World War II, when peacetime defense spending first rose greatly, but after World War I, when the military services first confronted fast-moving aircraft and engine technologies. Although defense spending returned quickly after that war to its usual peacetime low, both the Army and the Navy tried throughout the interwar era to keep up with the exceptionally rapid evolution of military aircraft. Finding their established procurement agencies too slow and stodgy to handle the task, military officials turned to commercial aircraft firms, which became the arsenals for this kind of weapon system. But neither the firms nor the services could find a satisfactory way to deal with Congress, whose insistence on long-standing political requirements for access and accountability could not be squared with the need to move quickly to field new weaponry. Try as they might, politicians and military officials were unable to find a satisfactory accommodation between the political and technical dimensions of the aircraft acquisition process.

If the nation's procurement process worked phenomenally well during World War II, it was not because the political system somehow came to terms with the technical enterprise afoot but rather because wartime urgency encouraged Congress to relax traditional concerns with access and accountability. Arguably the United States should have faced its interwar political problems again in the 1950s, when it took up peacetime weapons acquisition on an unprecedented scale. The nation did not, however, because the urgency of the early cold war produced a relaxation of traditional political norms and strictures much as occurred during World War II. That left the military services, especially the newly created and politically dominant U.S. Air Force, free to explore new and useful technologies. The 1950s became an especially creative period in the exploration of military technology.

Because the services were relying on institutional arrangements that had been inherently controversial under normal peacetime conditions, however, the acquisition process that surged into being during the 1950s was destined to be controversial once the atmosphere of crisis passed. To make matters worse, some of the more controversial features of the interwar acquisition enterprise were embellished during the 1950s, not for the sake of reaping the benefits of improved technology but to serve the political goal of protecting acquisition projects from rivals offered by other services. The nation thus emerged from the 1950s with an entrenched acquisition process characterized by politically controversial arrangements that served politically useful ends. The impetus for acquisition reform and also the basis for its failure were built into the foundations of the acquisition process.

NEW WEAPONS AND OLD BUREAUCRACIES

Nothing in the leisurely pace of technological change in the nineteenth century prepared military organizations for the dizzying speed with which aircraft technologies turned over. To be sure, the effects of the industrial revolution had crept into the realm of military affairs early in the nineteenth century. The breechloading rifle, one of the earliest fruits of that revolution, worked profound changes in the nature of land warfare.[1] The introduction of steam engines and iron armor did the same for naval warfare. Yet change came slowly. Only two truly important changes in small arms technology occurred during the century, for example—the invention of the metallic cartridge case at midcentury, and the invention of smokeless gunpowder around 1870. Metallic cartridges eased the development of reliable breechloading weapons, which multiplied in number in the second half of the century. Still, after converting to a breechloading rifle just after the Civil War, the U.S. Army did not fundamentally modernize its rifle inventory again until 1892, when it purchased the Krag-Jorgensen magazine rifle.[2]

During World War I alone, by contrast, several generations of fighter aircraft rose and fell, sometimes in months, as improvements in engines, airframes, or armament gave birth to new aircraft that outclassed others in the sky.[3] The pace of change did not slow appreciably after World War I. The interwar era saw big changes in aircraft construction and configuration—the "supersedence of the biplane by the low-wing monoplane, the change from wood to metal construction, from open to enclosed cockpits and from fixed to retractable undercarriages."[4] Motors for aircraft were changing even more rapidly than the aircraft; few engines were in production for more than a few months, Robert Schlaifer states, "before the need . . . of extensive modifications [became] . . . apparent."[5] The rapid pace of technological change encouraged Britain's Royal Air Force to write off tactical aircraft as obsolete after two years, while the U.S. Navy used three years as its measure of technological turnover.[6]

Technological advance gave rise from the start to increasing cost and complexity in military aircraft and a commensurate decline in the number that could be purchased. New communications equipment, for example, as well as more complex and higher-performance engines, propellers, and airframes produced increasing weight among certain types of aircraft. Holley notes that a "single-place, single-engine fighter weighed 1,600 pounds empty in 1918 and 2,200 pounds in 1933; by the end of the thirties the same type of aircraft ranged between 5,500 and 6,000 pounds." Prices, always correlated closely with weight, went up accordingly. From early in the 1920s the unit price of military aircraft began to overshadow prices of commercial aircraft. Given the lags between requests for appropriations and the time when money was available to spend, the air corps in both services were often able to purchase fewer aircraft than called for in original budget requests. In its fiscal 1935 budget request, the Army Air Corps asked for and was granted funds to purchase 348 new aircraft. By the time the money was available, however, sharp increases in the price of aircraft made it possible to buy only 222 aircraft.[7]

For America's military aviators, however, such a trade-off was a small price to pay for ever higher levels of performance. Unlike ground force commanders, who during the nineteenth century resisted tech-nological advance on grounds that it disrupted established organizational arrangements and undermined discipline, morale, and esprit, military air enthusiasts were impressed from the birth of their profession with the crucial importance of quality. "Aerial warfare along the front," Irving B. Holley notes of the experience of the Air Corps in World War I, "proved that an enemy with fewer but superior weapons was fully capable of containing an opposing force with an impressive numerical predominance. *Quality paid better dividends than quantity.*"[8] Thus military aviators approached aircraft acquisition with the underlying philosophy that "to ignore this advanced equipment would be to arm the nation with weapons less than the best."[9]

Yet from the start aviators had to contend with generic problems in the pursuit of the best. With the United States about to enter World War I, it was decided that copying European models was the best way to obtain large numbers of aircraft. The U.S. government sent a commission to Europe to survey the available models, apparently believing that the aircraft chosen "would be sent home, copied, and turned out in great quantities."[10] In fact, few European aircraft were turned out in great quantities. Alterations were instead introduced during production in a continuous effort to improve combat capabilities.[11] To have frozen this process, shipped the resulting design back to the United States, and waited while U.S. firms geared up for production would have guaranteed the introduction of obsolescent aircraft into the Air Corps inventory.

There was no clean and neat solution to this problem. No military organization could purchase new aircraft without testing them, yet tests could take nearly two years, during which time the aircraft might become obsolete.[12] Moreover, whatever the need for superior aircraft, an equally legitimate need existed to standardize equipment, both to reap the resultant production economies and to facilitate training and logistics. Thus it was essential to strike a balance between the military's desire for superior weaponry and other important organizational requirements.

The Bureaucratic Problem

Unfortunately, finding such a balance demanded more flexibility and dexterity than the military procurement bureaucracies could supply. The Army's Ordnance Department, for example, was notoriously slow when it came to introducing new weapons; Springfield Arsenal took seventeen years to develop, test, and finally produce the M-1 rifle.[13] But there was no need to hurry; oceans protected the nation from large-scale combat. Major combat would be preceded by considerable warning, during which, ordnance officials assumed, there would be time to mass produce the sizable arsenal required. In short, the department defined its problem as one of mass production rather than technological advance. Accordingly, over the first century of its existence the department developed an approach to technological advance that emphasized the strict separation of R&D from production, elaborate test procedures, competitive bidding for production contracts, and quality control during production.

Not surprisingly, this approach failed miserably when it came to keeping pace with aircraft technologies. Throughout the 1920s the department sought to develop its own aircraft engines. Nevertheless it became clear that those engines could not compete with ones of commercial origin. The reason: "The separation of design from manufacture, together with the restrictive rules governing Army procurement, meant that five months [were] . . . lost between the fixing of the general specifications . . . and the beginning of detailed designing; the Wright P-1 was designed, built, and put on test within approximately this same period."[14] The Navy, too, tried to develop an engine, only to come up with a design well behind what was available commercially.[15] Simply put, in the time required to perform the tests and data collection that the arsenals and bureaus ritually conducted, the technology had moved forward substantially.

Service procurement bureaucracies never did come to terms successfully with the demands of fast-moving technology, partly, perhaps, because they had become too crusty and hidebound to change. Yet part of the problem stemmed from enduring political incentives that encouraged the development of a cautious and layered bureaucracy. Military procurement officials lived always "in the shadow of a congressional investigation," most often sparked by commercial firms that, having lost in the competitive bidding for a military contract, sought redress through their local member of Congress.[16] The military bureaucracies protected themselves by developing contracting to a fine art; elaborate specifications based on endless testing, leading to carefully written fixed-price contracts, served among other things to document the military's legal case should a defense be necessary. Of course, elaborate specifications can also foreclose competition, and extensive tests can be rigged. The Ordnance Department's many critics—most of them inventors frustrated by the department's unwillingness to buy their wares—accused the department of both practices throughout its long and controversial life.[17] Military officials also learned to dilute responsibility by seeking concurrence from superiors and associates throughout their organization.[18]

The resulting stodginess imparted inflexibility as well as slowness to the military's approach to technology development. In documenting the development of aircraft engines, for example, Schlaifer noted a "failure of Army-directed development to sacrifice individual features of merit in order to hasten the success of the engine as a whole."[19] This should not have been surprising, since those individual features were the result of an elaborate bureaucratic decision process that had to be retraced with each change in design. Because the effects of a proposed design change were likely to be measured in organizational prestige and authority as well as technical merit, it often proved impossible to sacrifice design goals to expedite development.[20]

The Turn to Industry

The Army and Navy solved these bureaucratic problems by turning aircraft design and manufacture over to the nation's fledgling aircraft industry. Even during World War I the services sensed that industry could react more quickly and flexibly than they to rapid technological change. They were prodded toward this realization, no doubt, by the businessmen who were instrumental in girding the country for its war effort. One of the nation's most successful developments, the Liberty engine, was entirely a commercial effort, and a remarkably quick one at that. Civilian designers were closeted in the Willard Hotel, in Washington, D.C., late in May 1917, and in five days produced the basic design. Thirty-five days later the Packard Company delivered the first production engine. Shortly thereafter the design was altered by the addition of four more cylinders, and standing production orders were changed accordingly. The change was accepted readily, however, and mass production began only a few months after the initial design work was completed.[21]

Early aircraft entrepreneurs like Glenn Curtiss were eager to help. Indeed they lobbied aggressively on Capitol Hill for greater attention to the military uses of aircraft and greater federal funding for their industry.[22] Congress was receptive to the idea. Its members were fascinated not only with aircraft and the free-wheeling entrepreneurs who built them but with the "promise of air power," namely, the freedom "to avoid the mass slaughter of the new mass warfare, to minimize the American commitment abroad, . . . and at the same time to give the American business community a more dominating role than it could have supporting a strategy which exclusively emphasized sea or land warfare."[23] Though the standing military procurement agencies were ambivalent about the turn to industry, there was no deeply entrenched aviation "arsenal" around to offer strong opposition to the move.

Technologically, reliance on aircraft and engine firms had several advantages. Most important, it meant that technical decisions would be made close to the technologies themselves, where designers could operate flexibly in response to design problems or bright new ideas. It also allowed for the amalgamation of research, development, and production in such a way that new ideas found their way into production quickly. Indeed it would have been difficult to distinguish these activities, which took place to a great extent on or near the production line. This too had its advantages, since the experience of the Air Corps during World War I suggested strongly that "designing aircraft was difficult, if not impossible, when separated from the actual process of manufacture."[24]

In this way commercial firms became the equivalent of aeronautical arsenals. There was, to be sure, the Air Development Center at Wright Field, where after 1926 the Army Air Corps located in-house technical expertise and project offices for handling developments in the aeronautical field. But the engineering office at Wright Field was chronically understaffed.[25] That left the aircraft firms in charge of "the bulk of the technical management and integration," while "[military] project office duties included insuring the suitability and availability of government-furnished equipment while monitoring the solution of any technical problems identified during development."[26] The National Advisory Committee on Aeronautics (NACA), established in 1915, also attended to problems facing government-related aircraft (air mail as well as military). But NACA dealt principally with basic and applied research rather than the development of working aircraft, and its focus extended to commercial as well as military aeronautical problems.[27] NACA was crucial in demonstrating the usefulness of new technologies, but most aircraft and engine development work was done by the industry.

The turn to industry may have made technical and managerial sense, but it was fraught with political problems, despite the mostly favorable congressional attitude toward the aircraft industry. The political incentives that had encouraged caution and inflexibility in service procurement bureaucracies did not disappear when the bureaucracies disappeared. Instead, the turn toward industry merely transferred the focus of the political problem, bringing the industry as well as the services into conflict with long-standing political norms that had enforced bureaucratic caution in the first place. The principal bones of contention arose from two closely related and long-standing fixtures of the federal acquisition business: competition and fixed-price contracting.

Ever suspicious of their own military and the arms merchants who supplied it, members of Congress enforced discipline by insisting that military contracts be awarded competitively. The call for competition was more than a reflection of the nation's capitalist ethos, however; it was part of every legislator's kit for satisfying constituents, a way of opening the federal contracting process to constituents' businesses. No one seemed to mind that these two perspectives on competition could be incompatible. Spreading production around could sometimes be less efficient than leaving a monopoly producer alone. Rather, competition acquired more status and power because it satisfied the politicians' need for access as well as accountability.

Congress also highly favored the fixed-price contract, which described in advance the item federal procurement officials were buying and the price they intended to pay for it. In wartime, legislation permitted the executive branch to enter into open-ended, vaguely defined contracts in the interest of moving quickly. Yet rumors of wartime profiteering and the congressional investigations that inevitably followed only convinced legislators of the dangers inherent in leaving prices and products unspecified. So long as all was defined in detail in advance, so-called rapacious industrialists could be held to account.

In practice, competition and fixed-price contracts were two sides of the same coin. Fair and objective competition was impossible unless the standards by which competing firms were judged were spelled out in advance. The low prices and efficiency that competition was thought to produce would be lost if product and price were not fixed as the competition ended. To wait or to allow the product to change in some way was to risk renegotiating prices under noncompetitive (so-called sole-source) conditions. The fact that losing competitors had every incentive to claim foul play to their favorite member of Congress when these things occurred only drove the point home to federal procurement officials. Detailed contracts served important political purposes.

These traditional methods of controlling military acquisition were inapplicable to the development of aircraft and their engines. In the time required to write a detailed fixed-price contract, much less to conduct a lengthy competition against its terms, the technology described therein was likely to have become obsolete. To be sure, it was possible to hold design competitions, allowing interested firms to submit detailed design plans against the military's published performance requirements. These were thought to encourage innovation—to bring out the best American industry had to offer. In practice, however, responses to such competitions amounted to "nothing more tangible than a paper promise to perform."[28] Virtually any firm could respond, and low bids often reflected ignorance or undue optimism rather than efficiency. Contracting officers could usually distinguish reliable developers from fly-by-night outfits, but the ever-present threat of a congressional investigation encouraged them to award contracts to the lowest bidder. As it happened, even experienced contractors often bid low and then lost money as development proceeded. Design competitions thus worked against effective development and could penalize firms that were good at it.

Design competitions were also too inflexible to cope with rapidly changing technologies. Once the parameters of the competition were set—presumably in the announcement of a design competition for a specific aircraft or engine—any meddling would render the competition unfair. Hence, if between the date on which the competition was announced and the day on which a winning design was chosen a new device became available—say a more powerful engine—the service in charge of the competition could take advantage of that new device only by dissolving the competition and starting anew. Given the pace at which new devices were appearing, design competitions could go on endlessly, or alternatively they could produce inferior aircraft.

There was a clear need to see real hardware before making final decisions about a new design, both to demonstrate the developer's talent and to allow for a quick move into production should the design have merit. To buy such hardware, the services could enter into contracts for "experimental" aircraft. Firms were hired on a sole-source basis to develop the latest and best aircraft or engine against loosely defined performance parameters. The cost of the work was subject to negotiation between the firm and service project officers. In theory this meant that the government absorbed the risks of developing the aircraft. In practice, competitive pressures in the industry encouraged aircraft and engine firms to underbid on such experimental contracts. This meant that the government and the developer shared risks, although the government probably absorbed the bigger share.

If the service chose to produce the new model, however, it encountered another problem: Congress insisted that the sponsoring service buy the rights to the new aircraft's design and let it out for competitive production bids. Having underbid during the experimental phase of the project, the developing firm would seek to amortize its development losses during production. Consequently, it invariably lost the production competition to firms unencumbered by the need to recoup development costs. Not surprisingly, perhaps, aircraft and engine firms strongly resisted the government's effort to assume control of their new designs, going so far as to refuse to bid on experimental contracts that gave the government proprietary rights to the finished design.[29]

Arguably taxpayers were getting the best of both worlds; they were paying less than the full cost of developing new aircraft, then paying less for producing the new aircraft than the developer was willing to charge. Taking a longer view of the issue, however, it was clear almost from the start that this way of doing business threatened to drive developers out of business. During World War I, for example, Glenn L. Martin perfected an excellent bomber. Its design rights were purchased by the War Department in 1919. In the ensuing competition for production, Martin lost to the Curtiss Aeroplane and Motor Company, principally because in bidding for production Martin sought to amortize some of this development expense. As Holley says, "Deprived of his airplane, Martin no longer had any incentive to improve that particular design. Worse yet, deprived of a profitable production contract as a means of reimbursing his earlier investment, Martin was soon unable to finance further development work." Holley concludes, "The statutes intended to protect the public's interest, here operated to the reverse effect and retarded the pace of research and development."[30]

The military services and Congress struggled with these problems throughout the interwar period. Investigating problems with military aircraft as well as the nation's air mail service, a special House committee chaired by Florian Lampert, Republican of Wisconsin, concluded in 1924 that "technical development of aircraft was proceeding at very unsatisfactory rates," largely because of "the destructive system of competitive bidding."[31] Committee members listened with equanimity as the secretary of the Navy stated flatly that the "principle of competitive bidding is not adapted to aircraft in the present state of the art." According to Holley, the committee concluded its hearings with the "drastic and even revolutionary" suggestion that the government "recognize the manufacturer's proprietary interest in his designs and permit the purchase of air matériel without competitive bidding."[32] Yet Congress as a whole remained enamored of its traditional norms. Thus the Air Corps Act of 1926, constructed mainly by the House

Committee on Military Affairs, ignored Lampert's findings and maintained the requirement for competitive bidding.[33]

Denied flexibility by Congress, yet confronted with the need to
build better aircraft and the complaints of some of their best developers,
the services stumbled into a shaky compromise that favored the
development of technology but only by circumventing the political
process. They avoided competition with what Holley calls an "artful
evasion": the Army Air Corp found an obscure army regulation that
allowed sole-source contracting when competition was impractical.[34]
Competition thus existed, whether formally or not, during the conceptual stage of development, as contractors vied to win experimental
contracts for the development of new ideas. But competing firms knew
that successful development would yield monopoly production rights
to the finished aircraft.

This approach to the problem posed by fast-moving technologies
gave rise to an odd but effective way of funding research and
development (R&D). Given the ephemeral nature of the conceptual
product, design competitions were undisciplined; no one knew what
the final product would look like or cost. Hence underbidding became
an established way of doing business.[35] Indeed the "artful evasion"
sanctioned the practice of underbidding by guaranteeing the successful
developer a lucrative sole-source production contract. In effect, R&D
was underfunded, while production was commensurately overfunded.
Production money thus became a "hidden subsidy" for R&D.[36] The
approach encouraged successful development by rewarding it with
profits, while it penalized firms that failed to realize their designs by
leaving them to absorb the difference between their initial bid and
actual expenses. The approach had the advantage of leaving most
management decisions to private aircraft and engine firms, where
research, development, and production could be merged and managed
with flexibility unavailable to federal managers.

These technical and managerial advantages were purchased at great
political risk, however. The artful evasion left costs and profits to be
determined by negotiation between the firms and service contracting
officials. This situation raised the specter of excessive profits, fraud,
and inefficiency—the ills competition was meant to cure. Indeed, if
production profits included a hidden reimbursement for R&D expenses,
they were likely always to look at least slightly excessive, although the
truth of the matter would have required careful assessments of R&D
and real production costs.

If this liability escaped notice for some years after the artful evasion came into use, it was probably because military R&D, even for aircraft, consumed little money.[37] Congress did notice the situation in 1934, however, during a depression that sullied the reputation of private industry and when the phrase "merchants of death" was acquiring great public currency.[38] Sensing the public mood and aware of reports of profiteering in the aircraft industry, the House Committee on Military Affairs launched hearings early in 1934 that looked into military-industrial relations in the aircraft realm. The industry was characterized as "rapacious." Federal officials who had countenanced negotiated contracts were pilloried, and the strong impression was left that aircraft firms had fraudulently absconded with obscene profits at the taxpayers' expense.[39]

Out of these hearings came legislation that inserted competition everywhere in the procurement process. Having earlier tried so-called design competitions and found them wanting, the Army Air Corps and the Navy Bureau of Aeronautics now were forced to hold "sample" competitions, whereby aircraft firms were required to submit working models of their designs. Winning firms were then awarded production contracts, normally with no further competition.

Yet these practices only highlighted the dilemma the Air Corps had been facing all along.[40] Driven by competitive pressures and the constant press of technological advance, contractors sought to incorporate the latest designs into their sample aircraft, which were rarely production ready during the competition. Hence the winner's production contract differed little from a sole-source award for further development work. So-called engineering change proposals (ECPs), by which designs were altered even as production began, were ubiquitous. Meanwhile the losing contractors got nothing. The industry was now forced to absorb much greater risks than it had under the old policy—risks accentuated by the rising unit cost of aircraft. As the decade progressed many aircraft firms lost interest in military business and shifted instead to the commercial side of their operation. Ironically, interest in conducting military research fell off as the money Congress was willing to appropriate began to rise.

Industry and military representatives cast about for a solution to these dilemmas but failed to find one that was politically acceptable. The big aircraft firms favored a return to negotiated contracts; perhaps many in the services agreed.[41] But no one was going to broach the idea after the congressional investigations of 1934. In 1938 a military board proposed a compromise. The government would choose several promising submissions to a design competition, fund their development as experimental aircraft, and then hold a sample competition to determine which was best; in short, the government would fund the development of two or three finished models and then choose the best one.[42] This solution would have confronted the industry with a reasonable hierarchy of incentives; the winning firm would have enjoyed monopoly production rights to its design, losing developers would have been reimbursed for at least part of their development costs (with losses depending on how optimistic they were in their initial bid), while losers in the initial design competition would have risked little. The services would also have acquired competitive leverage over the cost of the winning aircraft so long as there were no significant changes in design between the sample competition and the start of production. But neither Congress nor the services were anxious to pay for the development of sample aircraft knowing full well that one or two of the samples under development would be cast aside during the final competition.

Underlying dilemmas were never resolved. Instead, they were bypassed, as fear of war led Congress to relax its normal peacetime procurement strictures. The transition in public policy began in 1938, when President Franklin D. Roosevelt first announced the need for a much-enlarged air force. This almost immediately raised problems in procurement, as the services found it impossible to expedite production while complying with the time-consuming requirements for sample competitions. In June of 1940, after German tanks had stormed into France, Roosevelt's sense of urgency finally overtook Congress. In three pieces of emergency legislation passed in that month Congress granted both services sweeping prerogatives to negotiate and modify contracts, as well as to award cost-plus contracts if the emergency demanded.[43]

This allowed the services to expedite production of a series of aircraft developed during the 1930s. That most of the aircraft to see action in World War II were in some stage of development before the war began might suggest that congressionally imposed requirements for competition were not as insidious as the services and industry claimed. In fact, however, many of these aircraft were the product of experimental contracts, not the sample competitions mandated by Congress in 1934.[44] The persistent problem had always been how to get these sample aircraft into production, since competition threatened developers with losses and the use of negotiated contracts incurred wrath on Capitol Hill. War solved this problem by taking military procurement outside of the nation's traditional political norms.

COLD WAR COMPROMISES

Emerging from World War II only to find itself quickly immersed in a cold war with the Soviet Union, the United States embarked on an arms acquisition effort vastly greater in size, scope, and urgency than any it had ever before sustained in peacetime. Electronic devices like radar had proved their military value during the war; the 1950s saw an aggressive push to develop computers, better radars, and more capable communications systems. During the 1950s electronic components found their way into weapons in increasing quantities, a trend first noted in manned bombers. "The B-29 and B-50 bombers included about 10,000 electronic component parts, the B-47 approximately 20,000, the B-52, 50,000, and the B-58 nearly 100,000."[45]

Rockets, too, were used during the war. By 1956 the development of long-range missiles had become the military's highest priority. Defense Department funding for guided missiles rose from a meager 0.5 percent in 1951 of funding for research, development, and production to 8.2 percent in 1956 and then sharply upward to 23.2 percent in 1959, compensating for a drop in military aircraft production after 1954.[46]

Meanwhile, aircraft technologies changed rapidly, as the emergence of the jet engine pushed aircraft designers into the supersonic age soon after the war ended. Informal letter contracts for the F-80 (Lockheed), the F-84 (Republic), and the F-86 (North American) were issued before World War II ended, and the Air Force lavished most of its meager funding for tactical aircraft on these items. All three proved useful during the Korean War, although not necessarily in the roles originally intended for them.[47] The cold war gave the exploration of the new aircraft technologies an urgency wholly absent from military R&D before World War II.

The acquisition challenge was to American society as a whole—its military, its industry, and its political system. But it fell principally to the military services, which directly managed and controlled the development of new weapons. And of the services (now three in number, since the National Security Act of 1947 created a separate U. S. Air Force) it was the Air Force that was, "by almost any standard . . . the strongest service politically during the postwar decade."[48] Air Force prominence arose partly because of the nature of the new technologies, which offered their most immediate benefits in the aircraft—or, as time went on, aerospace—business. The service also benefited from (having, of course, proselytized for) a national strategy that emphasized strategic bombardment. The Air Force garnered about 47 percent of the overall defense budget during the second half of the decade, while the Army's budget share fell from a Korean War high of nearly 40 percent to about 22 percent in the last few years of the decade, and the Navy's share held relatively constant around 29 percent.[49] When it came to weapons acquisition, in particular, the Air Force was the pace setter.

Significantly, in organizing its acquisition effort the Air Force drew on the organizational arrangements that had evolved fitfully before and during World War II. The Air Force continued to rely on private firms that amalgamated research, development, and production in an essentially monopolistic enterprise. Cost-plus contracting was common, as was sizable cost growth in weapons projects. All of these arrangements had been politically controversial in the years before World War II. In the 1950s they were far less so, largely because the nation thought itself to be still at war, albeit cold war. As it had during World War II, Congress accepted the arrangements because they were seen as the best way to field exotic new systems quickly.

The Turn toward R&D

Despite the important role science played during World War II, the United States was ill prepared to take up the cold war R&D challenge. The war had been principally a massive production effort, and as a consequence both the military services and the defense industry retained a production orientation as the cold war began. Gen. Curtis E. LeMay commanded a newly created R&D directorate on the air staff from 1945 to 1947, but at that point LeMay's agency was absorbed into the more production-oriented Office of the Deputy Chief of Staff for Matériel. Not until 1950, and then only with the help of prominent civilian scientists, was the Air Research and Development Command (ARDC) formed, also with headquarters at Wright Field, giving greater prominence to the R&D function.[50]

The defense industry, too, emerged from World War II with a production orientation. In particular, profits came from long production runs; R&D was no more profitable, relatively, than it had been before the war. The aircraft industry went into a steep slump as the war ended, of course, and questions of R&D versus production were largely academic.[51] Defense became big business again in the 1950s, and as the market for military aircraft slowed during the decade, these firms diversified into missiles and electronics to become true aerospace giants.[52] By 1959 aircraft and associated electronics firms were gobbling up over 75 percent of the Defense Department's important contracts.[53] More important, they were on the road to becoming research firms. Stekler notes, for example, "during the Korean War 90 percent of General Electric's defense work was in production, [but] by 1959 this was reduced to 50 percent, and the remainder was in research and development. . . . By the early sixties, 71 percent of North American Aviation's sales were billed from research and development-type contracts."[54]

This change only helped make the aerospace firms more dependent on the federal government. Defense work was becoming more specialized; there was no commercial market for intercontinental ballistic missiles (ICBMs). Meanwhile, commercial aviation was growing more slowly than the military market. Military sales were always important to the nation's aircraft industry, but by the late 1950s the traditional aircraft—now largely aerospace—firms depended on military sales for 67 percent (Beech Aircraft) to 99.2 percent of their business (Martin). And in the large defense electronics companies that maintained a commercial orientation as well, specialized divisions that amounted to firms within firms carried on defense work.[55]

Less and less able to turn their backs on military business, defense firms were forced to compete more fiercely for military development contracts. Competition for development contracts highlighted the Air Force's approach to acquisition. Rarely was it formal competition; often the service would award a contract on the basis of an unsolicited bid. Yet in general the several aerospace firms knew that their prospects depended on the novelty and performance of their products in comparison to products offered by other firms. And there were lots of firms in this market; counting continuing improvement to aircraft that entered development in the 1940s, some ten fighter aircraft were developed over the 1950s.[56] Besides giving the Air Force alternatives, this situation encouraged innovation, which the service increasingly wanted.

Competition also encouraged industry to make exaggerated claims for new product ideas, however. Given that the defense industry was being asked to push beyond existing technological horizons, there was no way firms could describe future products precisely, hence competition for development contracts was necessarily a "competition in dreams." These conditions imposed penalties on firms that were overly scrupulous about the likely cost or technological problems connected with a new design. Such concerns could only be worked out during development. The challenge for program managers in the military as well as private industry was to extract as much as they could from technology's promise, to do so fast enough to stay ahead of the Russians, yet to retain the flexibility to handle emerging technological problems. This was a tall order under any circumstance.

Organizing the R&D Effort

In fact, speed and flexibility became increasingly hard to find as the decade progressed. The Air Force was spawning its own bureaucracy, with all the rigidities the Army Air Corps had sought to escape in the 1920s by turning to the industry. And the need to produce weapons quickly and in large numbers added the inflexibility that goes with embedding early design decisions in production hardware. For the moment, the youth and novelty of the acquisition enterprise saved it from many of these problems; in particular, there was sufficient pressure from elsewhere in the Defense Department, as well as on Capitol Hill, to ensure that serious challenges were handled outside the formal procurement process. A look at key aspects of the formal acquisition process, however, suggests that the trend during the 1950s was not encouraging.

WEAPON SYSTEM DEVELOPMENT. Unquestionably, the biggest formal change in Air Force acquisition practice during the cold war era was the introduction in 1952 of the weapon system approach to development. First applied formally with Convair in developing the F-102, this management concept was driven by the recognition that "the increasing complexity of weapons no longer permitted the isolated and compartmented development of equipment and components which, when put together in a structural shell, formed an aircraft or missile. . . . [The new concept] integrated the design of the entire weapon system, making each component compatible with the others."[57] The increasing complexity of weapons and the need to expedite deployment began to drive the Army Air Corps toward a rudimentary form of systems development even before World War II.[58] Then and in the 1950s, the trend was to turn to industry, which had always responded far more flexibly than service bureaucracies to technological uncertainty. The firms could also amalgamate production and development in a way that would have been impossible had the service been dealing with subcomponent developers independently. Arguably, of course, having relied on the industry in the past, the Air Force lacked technical expertise to handle development.[59] Equally important, the Air Force lacked a huge and powerful procurement bureaucracy able to block the move toward industry.[60]

Increasing interdependence of components within a weapon system multiplied risk and uncertainty in an overall project. To the extent that components interacted, each could be designed only with the others in mind; the nature of the undertaking thus encouraged developers to define component interfaces in advance of development. Yet to the extent that components were equally high tech and uncertain, nothing could be defined precisely until development had progressed some distance. Meanwhile, insofar as the search for a best component might not yield the best overall system, system requirements might be posed in addition to, or even contradicting, individual component requirements. Varying directly with the risks and uncertainty of component technologies, the potential existed for projects to degenerate into endless cycles of redesign. The turn to weapon system development thus created an enormous demand for flexible management.

PRODUCTION CONCURRENCY. Unfortunately, the need to field weapons quickly drove the Air Force away from flexibility. So-called production concurrency, with its sharp overlap of development and production activities, became the accepted way of ensuring that new weapons were fielded as rapidly as possible. North American began work on the F-100 Super Sabre, for example, at the height of the Korean War. The goal was the rapid creation of a day fighter to replace the company's highly successful F-86 Sabre jet. Given the sense of urgency imparted by the Korean War, the Air Force decided to buy the F-100 "in quantity prior to flight-testing, even though this ran the risk of extensive modifications in the future." Consequently, the first flight of the production F-100A occurred only two weeks after the second prototype aircraft first flew.[61]

In practice, the risks the service knew it was running proved very real. The new aircraft demonstrated serious problems of control and stability that were not solved in the F-100A. Although the Air Force purchased more than 200 copies of that aircraft, its term in service was marked by repeated accidents and groundings. Modifications, added to the 145th production F-100C and then retrofitted to earlier C models, finally solved the aircraft's biggest stability problems, although even the F-100C had its share of accidents. The F-100D and F-100F were purchased in truly large quantities, and these models established the Super Sabre's lasting reputation as a fine aircraft.[62]

The F-100 may have been a special case, driven by wartime urgency. Yet production concurrency in some degree became an established way of doing business, representing a sharp break in the practice of building prototypes before committing to production. In a sense, concurrency had become well established before World War II; recall that the Army Air Corps had concluded even during World War I that "designing aircraft was difficult, if not impossible, when separated from the actual process of manufacture."[63] From this perspective, formal emphasis on production concurrency was merely an exaggeration of practices devised to speed the introduction of the latest technologies into the early Air Corps fleet. But before World War II, concurrency had been applied primarily to product modifications introduced to equipment already in production. During the 1950s, it was applied to new systems developed from scratch. Given the complexity and sophistication of the weapons under development, the service needed more flexibility. Production concurrency gave it less.

GROWING FORMALISM. Making design changes was becoming time consuming as well as expensive, as the Air Force procurement bureaucracy increasingly imposed strictures on the development process. This bureaucracy was young, to be sure. Although the Air Matériel Command had been around in one guise or another for some years, the Air Research and Development Command (ARDC) did not assume formal responsibilities for weapon development until 1951. And because Wright Field had been spared many of the technical management tasks that had been delegated instead to aircraft firms, ARDC faced "extremely exacting tasks of organization with little forewarning and even less experience on which to base its actions."[64] It grew substantially during the decade, however, and with growth came the doctrines and layers of review normally associated with large organizations.

The organizations at Wright Field tended to assume certainty where little existed. In formally adopting weapon system development, for example, they tended to define interfaces—indeed, whole components—in advance in some detail. The more specific the requirement, however, the more necessary it was to process design decisions as engineering change proposals that had to be processed through Wright Field's growing organizational apparatus.[65] Meanwhile the need to ensure that initial designs complied with specifications put off testing.[66] In short, Wright Field's approach to development tended to slow the rate at which projects generated information and the rate at which designers could respond to that information.

COST-PLUS CONTRACTING. If management was growing less flexible, contracting was not; aerospace development projects were usually handled by cost-reimbursement contracts. Prime contractors were reimbursed on the basis of incurred costs as established by teams of service auditors. Trends in management and contracting were related, insofar as growing bureaucratic rigidity made it more difficult to sacrifice requirements or inelegant designs to save money. But this was hardly the only reason to rely on flexible contracts. Technological risks were high, and historically these had been covered principally, though not solely, by the government. Cost-reimbursement contracting continued this long-standing practice.

As in the interwar period, production contracting was largely sole source in nature. Given the emphasis on production concurrency and weapon system development, production competition was no more viable an option during the cold war than it had been in the 1930s, at least so far as the aerospace prime contractors were concerned. There was no real line between development and production. And even if there had been, the weapon system developer would have enjoyed a great advantage over rivals because of familiarity with the project.[67] In any case, the industry was as adamant as ever about bidding for development contracts that would have led to a production competition.[68] This response should have surprised no one; having underbid to win development contracts, aerospace firms were hardly anxious to forgo monopoly profits that would help compensate for whatever losses were incurred during development. In this way, too, cold war contracting extended practices that had developed years earlier.

FORMALITIES AND REALITIES. The growing formalism at ARDC headquarters implied certainty about development prospects and outcomes. Yet little of the certainty emanating from the Wright Field complex was validated by the decade's experience with developing new technologies. Detailed initial requirements implied certainty about project goals, yet projects routinely evaded original goals. Of the Air Force's Century Series of jet aircraft, for example, Burton H. Klein noted, "Four out of the six planes ended up with different engines [from those specified in the initial requirement]; three with different electronic systems. In order to make them satisfactory flying machines, five of the airframes had to be extensively modified; three of the fighters came out of development essentially different airplanes."[69] Klein found that the same problem affected missiles, "Almost all the major subsystems now being used in the Atlas missiles are of a different kind from those initially planned." He concluded that it was "seldom indeed that the differences between the system as it was initially conceived and as it emerges from development are only of a minor sort."[70]

Significantly, the problem applied at the operational as well as at the technical level. The F-100 was originally intended to be a day fighter; it built its reputation over Vietnam as a fighter bomber.[71] Of the Century Series aircraft just referred to, Klein notes that "three ended up by having quite different operational roles from what was originally planned for them."[72] Tactical concepts were changing almost as rapidly as technology; the interaction of both sets of uncertainties made for great confusion even as new weapons were introduced to the force posture.

In embracing weapon system development, ARDC tended to define subcomponents, especially the interfaces between them, in some detail, the more so as the decade progressed. In fact, the F-102 project, the first to be managed under the weapon system doctrine, was not especially successful. In particular, the MX-1179 fire control system originally intended for the aircraft had to be dropped, a decision that Marcelle Knaack takes as "the defeat of the weapon system concept's first application."[73] Meanwhile the ICBM program office managed to field a missile quickly even though it "ignored the dicta of the 'weapon system concept' so recently enunciated and so diligently honored elsewhere."[74]

Indeed, the ICBM program, often regarded as one of the decade's most successful, was organized outside the Wright Field complex, partly in an effort by civilians in the Defense Department to "bypass the ponderous contracting procedures that were characteristic of routine development and production."[75] Serious decisions could be made in the program office itself or taken directly to the secretary of the Air Force. Almost equal freedom pertained to funding: contracts could be written, funds shifted, and more funds requested without the need for ponderous justifications and reviews.[76] Finally, a private firm—the Ramo-Wooldridge Corporation—was created virtually out of whole cloth to manage the integration of the ICBM's many components.

Given the pace of acquisition during the cold war, not to mention the enormous technological uncertainties the enterprise faced, it would have been impossible to avoid much of the messy unpredictability just described. And the fact was that the Air Force tolerated, or was forced to tolerate (for ICBMs), enormous variety and happenstance in the management of weapon development projects. Yet the trends were not encouraging: ARDC moved to absorb the independent ballistic missile division, for example, early in the 1960s.[77] And ARDC's adherence to weapon system development and production concurrency grew each year, despite genuine setbacks in applying these techniques. The stage was being set for growing technical problems unless some way was found to induce greater flexibility into how the service was coming to manage weapon acquisition.

NEW WEAPONS, NEW POLITICS, NEW PROBLEMS

Arguably the technical problems growing out of the service's approach to acquisition might have helped to induce managerial flexibility—if, that is, Air Force acquisition management practices had been designed strictly to serve technical ends. But service management practices served political as well as technical ends; they were designed to protect Air Force projects from congressional intervention and competition from other services. The ability of service practice to change rested importantly on the malleability of these political incentives. Unfortunately, these were not malleable at all.

Congress and Interservice Rivalry

The Air Force was not facing a political indictment like that which Congress lodged against Air Corps acquisition in 1934. Had Congress applied the standards of 1934 to aerospace acquisition in the 1950s, the entire enterprise would probably have ground to a halt, since evolving acquisition practice extended and sometimes exaggerated features of the acquisition process roundly condemned in 1934. Traditional attitudes reappeared briefly as ardor for the nation's Korean War effort cooled and members of Congress began again to focus on their "traditional concern with economic stability and efficiency in defense spending and administrative management."[78] As the decade progressed, however, and especially after the launching of Sputnik late in 1957, traditional concerns gave way to a desire to see weapons fielded quickly.[79] In fiscal 1957, Congress appropriated more money for strategic bomber production than President Dwight D. Eisenhower had requested. Meanwhile cost growth in the Air Force's ICBM program was funded with equanimity except in 1957. After Sputnik's launching the program's "financial crisis, force structure uncertainty, and program slackness vanished."[80] Growing concern for the nation's strategic position led Congress to push increasingly for more R&D, with little of the concern for efficiency traditionally evident in peacetime.

Because they were so concerned about the nation's military position, however, members of Congress found it more difficult to accept the interservice rivalry and duplicative developments prevalent throughout the decade. Interservice rivalry was at its most vicious around the end of World War II, when the Army Air Corps seemed to be fighting not for its independence but for a monopoly on national military strategy. "Why should we have a Navy at all?" the commanding general of the Army Air Force asked in 1945, answering that "there are no enemies for it to fight except apparently the Army Air Force."[81] Meanwhile army generals spoke of absorbing the U. S. Marine Corps, or of keeping it alive merely as a small amphibious attack force. After the National Security Act of 1953 legislated a three-division floor on the size of the Marine Corps, the continued existence of all services was ensured. But fights for mission dominance continued, leading to duplication in weapons development, as the services fought for proprietorship of a specific mission by seeking to outdo rivals in developing weapons appropriate for that mission.[82]

The nation's major interservice weapons disputes are easily recalled. The Army and Air Force competed for control of medium-range ballistic missiles, building the Jupiter and Thor, respectively.[83] These two services also clashed over surface-to-air missiles, with the Army's Nike Hercules competing for mission dominance with both the Bomarc and the land-based version of the Navy's Talos missile. And all three services built long-range ballistic missiles, each competing to help launch the nation's first manmade satellite in the months after Sputnik. Not all duplicative development was the result of interservice rivalry. Some, like that involving the Thor and Jupiter, resulted from a conscious policy choice to hedge against uncertainty, running the economists' "parallel projects" through two or three services.[84] Even then, however, service rivalry surfaced as development progressed.

Members of Congress could be ambivalent in certain cases of duplication, since many had personal ties, through prior service or reserve membership, to a service, and all were interested in protecting the interests of constituents. As the decade progressed, however, partisanship declined somewhat. After 1953 the viability of each service was ensured; at issue thereafter was the less crucial issue of who got how much. The industry was becoming more diversified. The well-being of constituents came to rest less and less on a single project and more and more on the overall size of the budget. Finally, the existence after 1947 of armed services committees that oversaw all services, in contrast to the army and naval affairs committees that had overseen individual services through most of the nation's history, reduced ties between legislators and services. "Congressmen tended to become less the partisans of a particular service," Samuel Huntington noted, "and more the partisans of defense in general against other interests and, within this general concern, the arbiters among competing service interests."[85]

As partisans of defense in general, members of Congress could easily construe uncontrolled duplication and interservice feuding as wasteful. As early as 1950, Senator W. Stuart Symington, Democrat of Missouri, expressed concern because "five different groups were working on one type of missile."[86] But concern picked up dramatically later in the decade, especially after Sputnik, when multiple projects and the Pentagon's seeming inability to choose among them seemed inexcusably wasteful of resources urgently needed to catch up with the Soviets.[87] In May of 1957, for example, the House Appropriations Committee pointed to "an apparent lack of timely, effective, and decisive action on the part of the Office of the Secretary of Defense in achieving a well-rounded, coordinated guided missile program at a minimum cost commensurate with an adequate system."[88] As the decade progressed, various of the legislature's military committees leaned toward intervening in Defense Department affairs to settle cases in which interservice rivalry seemed to be wasting time and money.

Finally, the problem of "wasteful duplication" brought new congressional actors into the acquisition arena. The Armed Services Committees in both houses of Congress had entered the 1950s with eyes focused on their traditional domain of military construction, leaving acquisition issues to powerful defense subcommittees of both Appropriations Committees. Yet Armed Services Committee members could not help but notice that the "action" in defense had moved to acquisition. Their interest was piqued in particular by the Nike-Talos dispute, because air defense meant the purchase of real estate and fell under "military construction" in the defense budget. In a complex political tangle with the executive branch over passage of the fiscal 1957 Military Construction Authorization Act, the committees forced the administration into action: late in 1956 the secretary of defense gave the Army control over surface-to-air missiles with ranges of less than one hundred miles, and by 1958 the Talos project had been canceled.[89]

Convinced that their intervention in the Nike-Talos case had spurred the administration to higher levels of efficiency, the Armed Services Committees moved to formalize their involvement in the acquisition process.[90] To the fiscal 1960 Military Construction Authorization Act they attached a rider (section 412b)—also known as the Russell amendment—that required formal, annual authorization of funding for the procurement of aircraft, missiles, and naval vessels starting with the fiscal 1961 defense budget. For these items, congressional approval now became a two-step process including authorization and then appropriation of necessary funding.

Congress also helped bring other actors into the acquisition arena, largely in the interest of eliminating duplication. Prodded by the executive branch as well as its own concerns, Congress passed the Defense Reorganization Act of 1958. Although the reorganization focused on the role of the Joint Chiefs of Staff and the creation of regional military commands to replace the services as operational agencies in deploying military forces, in two areas it moved to shape acquisition in ways hoped to be less wasteful. On the one hand, Congress largely accepted an executive branch press for increasing the defense secretary's legal power, as well as the size and power of his personal staff, the so-called Office of the Secretary of Defense (OSD). The 1958 act "permitted assistant secretaries of defense to issue orders to military departments, providing they had authorization in writing from the secretary of defense."[91] On the other hand, aware that programs once officially launched by a service were hard to cancel thereafter, Congress created within the OSD the Advanced Research Projects Agency (ARPA) to, among other things, explore new technologies "in an objective and detached manner" that precluded the services "from acquiring proprietary interests in 'their projects.' "[92] Thus the executive branch, like Congress, acquired more agencies with a charter pertaining to acquisition.

It would remain for Secretary Robert S. McNamara to exploit both the powers and the new agencies. At this point reference to the reorganization act and the Russell amendment merely highlights the nature of congressional concern with weapons acquisition. These important legislative moves had little to do with project management, competition, contracting, and so forth. Their focus instead was on defense management in a much broader sense. When applied to acquisition this meant increasing the political tools available to rationalize the nation's defense acquisition effort, especially by eliminating "wasteful duplication." In practical terms, it meant creating the tools by which programs could be canceled.

The Emergence of a Military-Industrial Strategy

Political moves to cancel projects created incentives to organize acquisition projects in ways that made cancellation difficult. And because the absence of political attention to the specifics of project management left such matters to the services, that is precisely what the Air Force, in particular, did. In the process, the service even exaggerated many of the controversial organizational patterns used in the 1930s, finding that in the 1950s these patterns helped sustain political support.

THE INDUSTRY AND PORK. Historically, the Army's arsenals, as well as the Navy's bureaus and shipyards, had established close and enduring political ties to state and local legislators. This basic pattern did not change in the 1950s, but the aerospace industry proved better positioned than the arsenals to play politics. "Army arsenals could generate support from the congressmen of their districts, but the aircraft companies could do this and also engage in all the public relations and propagandizing activities which their private status and funds permitted."[93] More important, perhaps, than their public relations activities, aerospace firms were in a position to choose subcontractors with an eye to congressional districts and votes. In this sense, the turn toward weapon system development had strong political connotations, since the dispersion of system funding to a host of contractors and subcontractors purchased a wide net of support for the new weapon among members of Congress.

Military-industrial relations were not wholly incestuous. Service program managers no doubt benefited from industrial lobbying on Capitol Hill. But in the day-to-day management of a project, the service's interest in holding costs down and the industry's interest in making profits could produce serious wrangling over contracts and costs. At the higher level of service plans and programs, too, friendly relations could break down. Firms lobbied for themselves, not the service. Firms that lost business or wanted more might take to Congress a case against service plans and recent service decisions. And to the extent that firms competed with one another for contracts, their support of one or another group within the service could exacerbate tensions within or among services. Finally, as firms picked up contracts from two or even all three services, their loyalties became blurred.[94] Thus the military-industrial relationship was, as John K. Galbraith said some years later, "a complex two-way flow of influence."[95]

Still, once the energies of a particular firm or set of firms had been enlisted in support of an ongoing project, much of this ambivalence fell away, and industrial support was ensured. Firms working on specific projects knew that their customer was not an executive branch agency but a political process fraught with risks as great as, though totally different from, those that commercial firms might encounter in the market. Just as a commercial firm would reach out to influence its market, so defense firms sought to influence the political process. Their efforts, like those of the project's uniformed manager, were directed at sustaining support for a project as it moved through the harrowing process of budget approval.

THE MILITARY-INDUSTRIAL BUY-IN. Industry, perhaps better than service program managers, could also exploit the prevailing fascination with exotic technologies. As Army Gen. James Gavin put it, "Industry can make extravagant claims for their products and convince Congress of the accuracy of these claims, even if they are not valid."[96] Often the claims were far from realistic. As had occurred during the interwar years, competition for new development projects encouraged great optimism. Firms bought in by understating risks and likely cost of achieving promised performance.

Underbidding by defense firms may have been long-established practice, but during the 1950s it was often reinforced by service program managers. "As advocates of new programs, government operating agencies have often encouraged contractors to estimate costs optimistically, recognizing that higher headquarters might be shocked out of supporting a program whose true costs were revealed at the outset."[97] In effect, program managers faced their own competition, generated by the plethora of new technologies under exploration, the sensed enormity of the nation's security needs, and, of course, their personal need to succeed. Thus if before World War II buying in was mainly an industrial strategy for winning federal contracts, during the 1950s it became a military-industrial strategy for funding diverse projects.

The extent of the optimism enforced by these competitive pressures was registered by the cost growth, 200 percent to 300 percent, according to one study, that marked 1950s weapons projects.[98] By modern standards cost growth on some of the more successful aircraft projects could be stupendous. Alan Gropman notes that the F-102 was produced "at more than four times the manufacturer's original estimate." Meanwhile the F-94 "came in at more than two and a half times its original estimate," even though "it was a derivative system with relatively few technological unknowns." Finally, the Bomarc missile "cost more than seven times as much as its first estimate."[99] No doubt some of this cost growth was the unavoidable result of the massive technological uncertainty that marked many of the decade's principal weapons projects. Yet Peck and Scherer concluded that "a substantial element in program cost overruns and schedule slippages" could only be explained "as the direct result of competitive optimism."[100]

CREATING MOMENTUM. Having bought in to get the project started, the military program manager was forced at some point to brief members of Congress (or, for that matter, higher levels of his own service staff) on the need for larger-than-planned amounts of money as the project progressed. Despite the generally positive congressional attitude toward aerospace acquisition, no program manager could look forward to doing this. To handle this problem, program managers "sought to disclose cost increases only gradually, after programs . . . [had] gained momentum and cancellation . . . [had] become difficult."[101] It was a classic "camel's nose under the tent" strategy, with momentum here defined principally as the amount and dispersion of money invested in a project.[102]

Momentum could also be generated by adroitly timing development decisions in individual cases to accord with the service's political needs, even if this meant subordinating technical issues to politics. During the B-36 controversy of 1949, for example, the Navy complained that the Air Force was using "unusual procedures" to push the bomber's development:

> Admiral Denfeld [chief of naval operations] . . . claimed that twice within the year . . . the Air Force had decided to concentrate even more of its budget upon procurement of B-36s without consulting the Defense Secretary or the Joint Chiefs.
>
> He insisted that at the time of these increments in the Air Force's commitment to the B-36, its prototypes had not been adequately tested and that no results were available from the joint studies undertaken in the fall of 1948 to evaluate all aspects of strategic air warfare.[103]

The evolving formal characteristics of the Air Force approach to weapons acquisition were neatly compatible with this political strategy.

Weapon system development, for example, tended to maximize the total value of individual projects, hence the rate at which costs were sunk. Construction of a production line concurrent with development increased sunk costs at a still faster clip. As a rule, Charles Hitch and Roland McKean noted, it was "allegedly much easier to get money from Congress for the development of impressive weapon systems with undoubted military utility if they succeed, than to get it for components with no highly specific end use in mind."[104]

Meanwhile early fielding of new weapons could be construed publicly and politically as project success, whether or not the weapons worked well. Note, for example, Robert Perry's remark about early test flights of Thor and Atlas. "The public was anxious to believe that the vehicles being tested were in all important respects equivalent to operational missiles, and with the missile gap controversy nearing its peak, test officials were willing to cooperate."[105]

The Emerging Tensions

The Thor missile was not ready for deployment when these tests took place, and it underwent significant redesign just before reaching operational units. Such a sequence highlights the obvious tension between political pressures on the acquisition process and technological demands. Much the same point could be made about the F-100A, which set a world speed record despite serious problems in handling the aircraft when it traveled in other than a straight line. The F-100 became an outstanding component of the nation's tactical Air Force. More than 2,000 were purchased between 1954 and 1972, many seeing active service over Vietnam. But early F-100s were not very functional, nor was retrofitting major design fixes to fielded aircraft an efficient way to resolve design uncertainties that should have been revealed in preproduction tests. The nation got a good aircraft, but later than it thought, and for more money than it should have paid. Unfortunately, other examples from the era were not so minor. Nor was the problem confined strictly to technical developments in individual projects.

Political pressures only compounded the inflexibility that had begun to mark the Air Force's approach to the technical problems posed by weapons development. The Air Research and Development Command's growing bureaucracy had already begun to impart rigidity where flexibility was required, partly by assuming certainty in initial requirements where little existed and partly by imposing layers of review that dulled sensitivity and responsiveness to the demands of the design process. Political incentives reinforced these trends by encouraging commitment to production well before design uncertainties had been resolved. At the least, the costs of development were much higher when carried out on production systems. Given that the systems rushed to the field were immature and less than functional, taxpayers were being asked to pay a premium for no good strategic reason.

Many other examples, besides the F-100, can be cited. The Air Force began training crews and maintenance technicians for the Thor missile before its design had even been tested. Its crews, confronting a deployed missile they had never seen in training, were forced to rely extensively on the contractor's expertise to keep the missiles operating at all.[106] Convair was on the verge of producing the F-102 when engineers finally solved high-speed flight problems by applying the area rule, first discovered in Germany before World War II, to the aircraft's fuselage design. Much of the production tooling already financed had to be recast as a result.[107]

Given the uncertainties and surprises inherent in any high-technology program, production concurrency would have been costly under any circumstances. In weapons acquisition, however, competition-induced optimism at the start of a new project almost guaranteed that designers would need flexibility as the project moved along. Political pressures, by contrast, removed flexibility by encouraging program managers to hold information to a minimum while increasing the project's commitment to production. At the least, political incentives raised the costs of searching for truly efficient designs. At worst, they risked burying the best design in a series of suboptimal retrofits. In this sense, political incentives set the acquisition process against itself. They encouraged, but did not acknowledge, the taking of risk while denying the flexibility needed to deal with it.

Despite the rigidities evident in individual weapons projects, overall the Defense Department's approach to weapons acquisition had much to recommend it. Given the great uncertainty of most of the era's military technologies, it was essential to plan alternative approaches to various missions. Although a good deal of intentional parallelism and duplication occurred in some projects (especially the ICBM program), to an important extent this duplication was supplied inadvertently by interservice rivalry. The wasteful duplication so deplored on Capitol Hill thus was not entirely wasteful. Indeed duplicative developments and the interservice rivalry that gave birth to them were seen by students of the R&D process as positive attributes of the cold war acquisition process. As Burton Klein noted in the mid-1960s, "If the military R&D programs had been entirely concentrated on those systems that were regarded as the favorite choices ten years ago we would not be in a very good strategic position today."[108] Hitch and McKean argued at about the same time that "duplication is a rational necessity when we are confronted with uncertainty." They also argued that "competition is our best protection against bureaucratic inertia." They concluded, "If inter-service rivalry did not exist, we would be forced to invent something very like it."[109]

Arguably interservice rivalry and project duplication also benefited individual projects and the aerospace industry. Recognizing that contract awards within individual projects were usually made on a sole-source basis, for example, Stekler argued that "even after contracts have been awarded, the force of competition is felt indirectly through interservice rivalry because pressure is placed on the firms holding contracts with the agency whose mission is in jeopardy. . . . Interservice rivalry thus has encouraged interproduct competition."[110] To Congress, with its persistent interest in competition, interservice rivalry provided the competitive discipline absent from individual projects. Finally, in providing information, alternatives, and a modicum of discipline to the acquisition process, interservice rivalry was, as Samuel P. Huntington said some years later, "a key aspect in the maintenance of civilian control."[111]

These positive aspects of the nation's 1950s approach to weapons acquisition depended on the political system's ability to pick and choose. But program managers sought to deny freedom of choice by building momentum into their projects. Thus at the level of the force posture as a whole, as at the level of individual weapons projects, the acquisition process worked against itself: having set up the possibility for later choices it then sought to deny the flexibility needed to make those choices.

The Thor-Jupiter controversy that Armacost studied exemplifies this phenomenon. Members of Congress called repeatedly on the secretary of defense to eliminate the wasteful duplication inherent in having these two intermediate-range ballistic missiles under development. Yet Congress also made it almost impossible to do so, as a Defense Department official later made clear. "If the Defense Department suggested cancelling the Air Force's Thor program . . . a Congressional delegation from California would be down our necks. And elimination of the Army Jupiter program would have half the

Alabama delegation plus a couple of representatives from the Detroit area fighting us."[112]

Political obstacles to choice thus made it difficult for defense planners to spend money wisely in deploying a reasonable and balanced force posture. By the end of the 1950s, for example, the nation had deployed four fighter bombers, three fighters, and two strategic bombers. Missile forces included three ICBMs (one from each service), two intermediate-range ballistic missiles (IRBMs), and various air defense missiles. Given the era's strategic uncertainties, multiple deployments might have made some military sense. But it is unlikely that deployments in these multiples served a useful military purpose.

The Thor-Jupiter controversy gives us some insight into the political utility of the Air Force's approach to acquisition. Neither Congress nor the Defense Department was confronted with an even choice between these two missiles, largely because of the Air Force's much greater emphasis on production concurrency. Consequently, Congress was confronted with "a choice between the [Army's] Jupiter, with its more limited immediate production capacity but with a more impressive test record, and the Thor, with its more impressive production facilities yet only marginal test performance."[113] In the crisis that followed the Soviet launching of Sputnik, the fact that only the Thor was ready for mass production proved to have considerable political appeal. After having pressured the secretary of defense to choose between these two missiles, Congress now authorized purchase of both—at a cost of approximately $200 million over the cost of choosing only one missile.[114] Crisis gave concurrency a status at least equal to technical merit.

To the extent that momentum precluded choice late in the development process, the only real choice open to policymakers was at the start of a project. But this meant that real choices were based on information available early in development that was clouded by uncertainty and very likely distorted by competitive pressures.

As Armacost said in his study of the Thor-Jupiter controversy, "political obstacles to clear-cut decisions emerge as the intellectual obstacles are being removed."[115] That is partly a generic problem for American democracy, since in developing new technology one has to spend money to get better information, and spending money creates political momentum that makes choice difficult. But the Air Force exacerbated the problem by delaying the arrival of better information while maximizing sunk costs as early as possible. The service thus protected its choices by effectively preempting everyone else's.

CONCLUSION

The 1950s were exceptionally creative in the annals of American military research and development. The Defense Department explored a wide range of technologies during the decade and deployed weapon systems by the decade's end whose performance was hardly understood at its beginning. In particular, of course, the nation fielded a variety of ballistic missiles. The development of whole families of jet aircraft, bombers as well as fighters and interceptors, was also successful but received less national attention. The best aircraft would, with continued improvement, serve the nation's defense for the next two decades. And within all of these systems were complex electronics components that grew more important as the decade progressed.

But success came under odd political circumstances. Strong political objections had surfaced in the years before World War II to the institutional arrangements that seemed essential to the development of fast-moving aircraft and engine technologies. There was great debate about these issues, as would have been expected in a democracy. The congressional hearings of 1926, for example, were far more sensitive to the needs of the aircraft industry than the Military Affairs Committee Hearings of 1934. Overall, however, Congress consistently tried to separate research and development from production in order to insert competition into the acquisition process, however unrealistic that goal was in light of the need to field advanced weapon systems.

During the 1950s, defense dollars spread among key congressional districts may have helped distract Congress from its more traditional concern with competition. But the atmosphere of crisis cannot be discounted. If early in the 1950s members of Congress registered their historic concern for efficiency in defense procurement, by mid-decade their anxiety had turned toward the Soviet threat. Consequently, they were concerned with results, broadly defined, rather than with how those results were achieved. Congress was also faced with the vexing questions that came with the nation's first effort to field a large force in peacetime. Which weapons should the nation buy? In what numbers? When should they be replaced or modified? Under these circumstances, interservice rivalry and its twin, duplicative development, loomed far more important on Capitol Hill than the arcane details of how projects were managed.

Under this special set of political circumstances, the Air Force elaborated an approach to weapons acquisition that worked, more or less, but that used organizational arrangements that had been politically controversial in the years before World War II. Indeed, the more controversial features of the aircraft acquisition process were embellished during the cold war, partly to generate political support for new weapons project. The amalgamation of research, development, and production, for example, figured prominently in the congressional critique of the acquisition techniques of the Army Air Corps mostly because such a combination rendered competition for production of new aircraft impossible. Cold war emphasis on production concurrency meshed research, development, and production further, making sole-source contract awards inevitable. Yet now such awards were used to help create momentum and the appearance of progress in individual projects, thus ensuring continued political support. In 1934 turning management control over to the aircraft industry was thought to leave too much discretion to rapacious defense industrialists. Yet during the 1950s those industrialists received even more managerial discretion. Their ability to lobby and place contracts at will was vital to garnering project support on Capitol Hill. Ironically, what had invited congressional scorn in 1934 was used during the 1950s to insulate weapons acquisition from the vicissitudes of congressional control.

These institutional and managerial arrangements were not the only elements of the Air Force's approach to acquisition that risked inviting congressional intervention. Precisely because the acquisition process moved projects so fast, it neglected the serious needs of the nation's force posture. Rapidly fielded weapons, for example, were often immature weapons. Moving them quickly to the field may have increased voting support on Capitol Hill, but it did not necessarily increase the nation's military power. And insofar as rapid fielding imparted unstoppable momentum to individual projects, public choice was effectively confined to the early stages of development, when information was scarce and distorted, and sound judgment was almost impossible. Under these conditions the nation's force posture was likely to be shaped less by judicious choice than by the managerial and political finesse of the services and key program managers. Finally, extensive production concurrency made changing designs either expensive or impossible, robbing the design process of needed flexibility. Thus the process risked not only fielding immature weapons but creating badly designed weapons.

Clearly the early cold war years set in place the making of a serious confrontation. Political incentives encouraged program managers and service hierarchies to institutionalize acquisition practices that were incompatible with peacetime political norms and insensitive to the demands of fielding a large and ready force. These practices flourished during the 1950s because that was an extraordinary peacetime period. But times could change, and if and when members of Congress stopped to examine the details of the acquisition process, they would doubtless find much that would not appeal to them.

CHAPTER 3

The Era of
Reform

THE SENSE of urgency that gripped politicians during the 1950s has slowly ebbed, and the more they have looked at the acquisition process the more disenchanted they have become. Yet repeated attempts at acquisition reform, starting with the Defense Reorganization Act of 1958, have largely failed to achieve their aims.

The 1958 act took a broad cut at the disorder and seeming inefficiency plaguing the acquisition enterprise since 1950. Later reforms, notably the Packard reforms of 1969 and the disparate bundle of reforms that took shape in the mid-1980s, have been more sharply focused and detailed than the 1958 act, reflecting growing familiarity with the process and growing frustration with its intractability. Each reform has sought to bring the acquisition process under greater control, for the same reason that motivated the 1958 reorganization, namely, to improve efficiency. In seeking the same goals, however, each new effort has implicitly signaled the failure of the preceding one.

Mere failure would be bad enough. Overall, however, reform has been downright counterproductive because it has led to the imposition of political values on weapons development projects. The problem originated with the 1958 reorganization. In aggressively implementing the call for more centralized control over acquisition, Robert S. McNamara demonstrated instead how difficult it is to centralize power in a political system designed to prevent the centralization of power.

And in seeking efficiency by eliminating wasteful duplication, Mc-Namara focused political attention on single projects, effectively bringing political pressures and incentives more deeply into project management.

The problem was not McNamara so much as it was reform concepts that made great sense on paper but little sense in terms of the political context in which acquisition was taking place. Because those concepts were rooted in the traditional values of the political system, however, they have been impervious to change. To the contrary, as the sense of urgency that dominated defense politics in the 1950s has ebbed, traditional political values have been imposed on acquisition all the more aggressively. Hence reforms since 1958 have been no more effective than reorganization in bringing real efficiency and control to the acquisition process.

ROBERT MCNAMARA AND THE SEARCH FOR CONTROL

Robert McNamara had his work cut out for him. More weapon systems were moving through development than could possibly be placed into production, so it fell to McNamara to decide which ones would continue, which would be canceled. But McNamara also had to move the military services away from the previous administration's strategy of massive retaliation and toward his administration's preferred strategy of flexible response, which emphasized conventional, limited war. Either effort alone would have been difficult bureaucratically and politically. Together they represented a daunting task.

McNamara welcomed the challenge. From the start he made clear his desire to use the powers granted him by the 1958 reorganization to enforce change and order on the Defense Department generally, weapons acquisition in particular. Dissatisfied with the quality of military service planning, McNamara expanded the Office of the Secretary of Defense (OSD), introduced systems analysis to help make decisions, and used the two together to attack established service programs across a broad front. In the acquisition arena, the director of defense research and engineering (DDR&E) acquired far more power than he had had in the 1950s. And during McNamara's tenure in office his systems analysts—the so-called whiz kids—carved out a growing role in judging weapons choices.[1]

Yet McNamara was charging across terrain that had already been claimed by other participants in the acquisition process. Canceling programs was a political as well as a rational military or technical act. On this front McNamara ran headlong into the Congress that had complained so mightily about wasteful duplication. Meanwhile, re-shaping weapons requirements to conform to a new strategy, not to mention the dictates of systems analysis, took McNamara onto turf formerly owned by the services. Understandably, Congress and the services responded with defensive maneuvers. In the short run, these responses did not prevent McNamara from scoring remarkable successes in reshaping the nation's defense program. In the long run, however, the counterreaction to McNamara's onslaught made the weapons acquisition process more complicated on Capitol Hill and in the Defense Department.

Shaping the Force

McNamara moved quickly to bring order to the long and heavily redundant menu of weapons projects he inherited from the Eisenhower administration, terminating a number of weapons projects with a decisiveness his predecessors had never mustered. A herculean effort was made to base these decisions principally on judgments about cost-effectiveness applied across functional military areas—the so-called program categories that, in contrast to the historic budget practice of listing programs by service, combined programs offering similar capabilities.[2] Thus the strategic forces program category allowed, in theory at least, comparison among bombers and missiles, and within missiles, between Air Force and Navy long-range ballistic missiles. And under tactical air forces were grouped wings of Air Force, Navy, and Marine Corps fighters and attack aircraft. Meanwhile, the value of the Army's ground-based continental air defense system could be compared with the value of buying more interceptors for the Air Force.

These choices were often made in the face of stiff political opposition. McNamara often incurred the wrath of particular services as well as members of Congress interested in particular projects. Cancellation of the Skybolt project, the product of an agreement between the United States and the United Kingdom, had international repercussions. And his decision to hold Minuteman deployments to 1,000 missiles rather than the much higher number the Air Force wanted meant a big battle with that service.[3] "Despite the uproar," however, "McNamara—with the able assistance of his boss, John F. Kennedy—was able to implement his entire strategic realignment package."[4]

McNamara proved adept not only at stopping projects he deemed cost-ineffective but also at shifting favored projects across service boundaries, often using interservice rivalry and duplicative projects skillfully to force a particular service to conform to his will. For example, he was able to interest the Air Force in supporting ground troops (so-called close-air support), a mission to which that service had paid little more than lip service. By allowing the Army to begin developing the Cheyenne helicopter gunship, McNamara implicitly threatened to remove the close-air support mission from the Air Force's domain, something no service could accept however little importance it attached to the mission. With this threat in place, McNamara used the Navy's A-7 project, begun in 1963 and aimed at producing a relatively cheap, slow aircraft strictly for supporting troops, as an alternative to the Air Force's desire to continue buying supersonic, multi-capable F-4s to perform the close-support mission. The effort succeeded: the Air Force bought the A-7 in what Richard Head called a case of genuine doctrinal innovation.[5]

McNamara was equally successful in forcing the Air Force to buy the Navy's F-4. In part, this effort was borne of McNamara's judgment that buying a single aircraft for more than one service was a cost-effective way of doing business. The F-4 was also better able to meet the needs of conventional close-air support than was the F-105, an aircraft "designed from radome to after-burner eyelids as a TAC [Tactical Air Command] nuclear weapons delivery airplane."[6] Again, the aircraft in question was the result of a Navy project, begun in 1952 and already in production when McNamara took office. Judging that the F-4 was compatible enough with his mission concepts and those behind the Air Force F-105, McNamara canceled the F-105 program in 1962—over strong Air Force objections—and forced the Air Force to buy the F-4.[7] That aircraft became the workhorse of both the Navy and the Air Force.

The options McNamara employed in wrestling with the services were not always the result of interservice rivalry. In forcing the Army to drop its M-14 rifle in favor of the smaller M-16—again over strong service objections—McNamara and his staff picked a hardware option developed in the 1950s at the behest of Army infantrymen unhappy with the ongoing M-14 rifle project. Interservice rivalry helped, namely, in the form of strong support for the M-16 at crucial moments from Air Force Chief of Staff Curtis LeMay. But rivalry within the Army was even more important. McNamara showed he could exploit organizational competition within as well as among services so long as he had hardware options on which to base his case.[8]

The Political Response

Congress welcomed McNamara initially. Members of Congress had approached the 1958 reorganization with some ambivalence, to be sure. They agreed to increase the size and power of the OSD, but they also stipulated that the service chiefs had a right to address members of Congress so long as they first informed the secretary of defense of their desire to do so. Still, they could not help but be impressed with McNamara's mastery of a broad range of defense topics and his obvious enthusiasm in tackling every issue.[9] Nor did the representatives have long to wait before McNamara began to eliminate the duplication that they had criticized so vocally in the late 1950s. At that point, however, they had to ask themselves whether the disease was worth this particular cure.

Tension emerged soon after McNamara took office, when he canceled the Air Force's cherished B-70 bomber project. The House Armed Services Committee immediately directed the Defense Department to spend money on the bomber despite McNamara's cancellation order. McNamara impounded the funds, raising constitutional issues that abated only when Congress relented.[10] Although McNamara succeeded in canceling the B-70, the pattern was set: the decisiveness Congress had wanted in 1958 generated a countervailing response on Capitol Hill.

That countervailing response was most visible in the continuing entry of the Armed Services Committees into acquisition project oversight. This action began in 1959 with the Russell amendment, which created an authorization process for procurement of missiles, aircraft, and ships, a step taken largely because the defense secretary did not seem to be exercising enough control over acquisition.[11] In the 1960s the reverse situation produced more of the same: McNamara was all too ready to exert control over defense acquisition, but for that reason the Armed Services Committees extended the annual authorization process to the purchase of other kinds of weapons. In 1965 they moved to authorize the production of tracked combat vehicles, for example, and in 1969 they took up the same authority for other weapons and torpedoes.[12]

In 1962–63 the committees began to authorize research and development as well as procurement, a move that surprised many on the Hill, since initially the Armed Services Committees saw no way for their small staffs to oversee research and development as well as procurement.[13] Yet the meshing of research, development, and production in the acquisition process inevitably drew the committees' interest back to the origins of new systems. So did competition with the Appropriations Committees, which the Armed Services Committees saw as usurping functions formally reserved for the authorizing committees. The driving event was, again, the B-70 controversy:

> In 1961 the Senate Appropriations Committee removed the B-70 program from the procurement account, funding it instead under research, development, test, and evaluation (RDT&E). The effect was to deprive the Armed Services Committees of their control through annual authorization. The Armed Services Committees retaliated a year later by subjecting RDT&E for aircraft, missiles, and naval vessels to annual authorization.[14]

Thus competition within the legislature, as well as between it and the executive, tended to drag Congress deeper and deeper into weapons acquisition.

The service chiefs also helped bring Congress more deeply into defense politics generally, as well as acquisition in particular. McNamara's tenure in the Pentagon was marked by the "sharp decline in number of formal disagreements among the Chiefs beginning in 1966." The chiefs had by this time learned a simple lesson: the more they disagreed, the more McNamara was "inclined to exercise his own judgment."[15] Over the same period, Enthoven and Smith noted "a pronounced tendency on the part of the Congress, particularly some members of the Armed Services Committees, to rely solely on appeal to authority—to insist that the military leaders must be followed on matters of military strategy and need because they are the experts."[16] The pattern was clear and foreshadowed in the debate over the 1958 reorganization. The more McNamara asserted his authority, the more the military chiefs exercised the right, preserved in the 1958 act, to speak their minds on Capitol Hill. The service chiefs and members of Congress thus colluded in limiting McNamara's authority.

Debates about weapons acquisition were not the only ones prompting greater congressional involvement in defense politics. McNamara's effort to achieve economies and raise force effectiveness by merging the Army Reserve and the National Guard, for example, provoked a strong reaction on Capitol Hill.[17] In a broader sense, the analytical effort embodied in McNamara's "planning, programming, and budgeting system (PPBS)" tended to clash with the political requirements and pork-barrel trading that were needed to justify and pass each year's defense budget. "In a political situation," as Aaron Wildavsky has put it, "not simply the economic, but the *political* costs and benefits [of choices] turn out to be crucial."[18] Insofar as McNamara tried to base policies on a wide range of defense issues on economic criteria, he helped to consolidate a congressional reaction.

But weapons choices meant large blocks of defense dollars, and hence a big concern about constituents' satisfaction so far as it was tied to the defense budget. Canceling projects like the B-70 and the F-105 and focusing acquisition on fewer projects may have made economic or even military sense, but it had to extract a toll in political support. To some extent that toll was levied on McNamara; his reception on Capitol Hill in the final years of his tenure was decidedly cooler than it had been in 1961.[19] More important, however, the toll was levied on the acquisition process, in the form of increasing congressional oversight and involvement.

Politics and Program Management

Unfortunately, McNamara's efforts to assert control over weapons acquisition made project management a more political undertaking. This time the dynamic evolved less in response to project cancellation— getting the services to stop doing something was relatively easy—than in response to McNamara's attempts to get the services to do something.[20] That aim had posed no problem to Eisenhower, mostly because both he and Congress left the services to themselves when it came to defining weapons requirements—the performance parameters and technical specifications that guided developers—and managing projects. By contrast, McNamara wanted to impose a shift in strategic emphasis, and a shift in method, away from allowing weapons projects to proliferate and toward fewer but more important and strategically appropriate development programs. To do so, McNamara and his staff were inevitably drawn into the process of writing requirements for new weapons. The intrusion could provoke pitched battles, as civilians and military officers wrestled to control the capabilities of future weapons.

POLITICS AND MILITARY REQUIREMENTS. The perverse effects of McNamara's action on development have been studied at length for the F-111, or TFX, fighter-bomber project. On entering office McNamara confronted a well-advanced Air Force requirement for a follow-on to the F-105, and a less well-developed Navy requirement for a new fleet interceptor. Arguing that "the cost of two new aircraft . . . was not justified by the performance improvements over existing aircraft" and "that the essential operational requirements of the two Services could be met with one plane and that a great deal of money could be saved in that way," McNamara moved to combine the two requirements in a single development project.[21] The resulting requirement represented the Air Force's performance goals, with added constraints on size and weight to make the aircraft compatible with carrier operations.

But service requirements were remarkably inflexible. Each "represented years of effort by the service and hundreds of agreements among interested parties within each service." In short, "each had behind it a whole array of organizational resources, sufficient to overwhelm the consideration of imagined alternatives lacking organizational sponsorship."[22] Forces like these tended to impart rigidity even to single-service weapons projects undertaken during the 1960s. As a rule, military requirements were sacrosanct.[23] For the multiservice F-111 project, setting requirements meant little more than shuffling separate Air Force and Navy requirements into an aircraft that was all things to all comers.[24]

Since optimism traditionally prevailed in the early stages of development, before contractors had to engage in the discipline of building something, defining the F-111 on paper was easy. In fact, the original Air Force requirement alone strained the limits of feasibility by calling for an aircraft capable of flying unrefueled across the Atlantic, landing at unprepared airfields, and dashing supersonically at low altitudes to deliver ordnance. The Air Force, working with the National Aeronautics and Space Administration, found that a variable-sweep wing promised to meet all of these requirements except one—the low-altitude, supersonic dash capability. Yet the Air Force's final requirement included the supersonic (rather than subsonic) dash capability, raising questions about technical feasibility even before McNamara constrained the aircraft's size and weight.[25]

In adding the Navy's requirements, McNamara helped produce specifications that could not be met.[26] Seeking to hold requirements constant, however, the developer sacrificed them haphazardly, yielding an aircraft of much utility as a long-range strike aircraft but hardly the one McNamara had in mind when he launched the TFX project. "Even though the designers did not achieve a supersonic-dash capability over a meaningful range, they pursued this goal with sufficient determination to impose severe losses in other dimensions. . . . In attempting to reduce drag for the sake of the supersonic dash, a design was adopted that caused highly dangerous engine stalls under demanding flight conditions."[27]

For the F-111, and as a rule, McNamara tried hard to force the services to define their needs and the technological approaches likely to meet them in detail before development began.[28] This so-called project definition phase of development seemed sensible, especially when strategic and operational concepts were the focus of heated debate. Yet the F-111 experience highlighted serious flaws inherent in demanding an early, rigid definition of the project. First, some of the aircraft's more serious technical problems could not be predicted on paper; many felt that the F-111 would be heavier than expected, for example, but few foresaw the engine-inlet problem that produced stalling. In short, there were serious limits to the value of analysis in advance of actual development work. Second, more time for the F-111 did not signify more thought. The services knew what they wanted, and their demands changed very little during the elaborate definition phase that preceded development. If anything, lines hardened as each service sought to ensure that it would get what it wanted from the project, whatever McNamara's wishes. What the F-111 project needed was flexibility as development proceeded, not more elaboration at the start.

CONTRACTS AND CONTROL. The project definition phase of the project was intended, in part, to lock the F-111 design into a detailed contract at an early stage and then turn the project over to industry for development. For this strategy to work, however, the contract had to be accurate from the start; the strategy would fall apart if someone found an excuse to change the contract, by writing engineering change proposals (ECPs), for example, once development began. Given the project's technological risk, writing such an accurate contract would have required more perspicacity than anyone possessed. It would also have required more realistic cost estimates than either defense firms or service program managers had ever submitted. McNamara and his staff were arguably insensitive to the unpredictability of technology. But they were well aware of the problems created by approving a project on the basis of contractors' initial cost estimates (the buy-in).

McNamara blamed the buy-in on the cost-plus contracts used so extensively during the 1950s; by virtually guaranteeing that the government, not the contracting firm, would cover all costs, these encouraged optimism. McNamara's corrective was the incentive contract. Firms agreed to both "target" and "ceiling" costs at the start of development, normally under competitive circumstances. If the firm's costs fell below the ceiling cost, it received some share of the difference; if it overran the ceiling cost, it carried the expense itself. The contractor thus faced the prospect of having to "pay for his own optimism," but also the promise of a reward for being more realistic about development costs at the start of development.[29] The use of cost-plus contracts declined sharply soon after McNamara took office, while the use of incentive-type contracts rose commensurately.[30]

The F-111 was one among many programs to face the new contracting regime; it also vividly illustrated the problems inherent in incentive-type contracts. The aerospace industry emerged from the 1950s with excess capacity. Its business base was declining, and McNamara's attack on wasteful duplication only exacerbated the problem. This placed pressure on profits and also created enormous incentives to win business, even if it took a buy-in to do so.[31] The winning developer could still hope to recover cost overruns through contract changes prompted by ECPs submitted as development proceeded, or in the monopolistic production phase of the program. Thus incentive contracts did not eliminate optimism; in competing for the F-111 development contract, both Boeing and General Dynamics produced cost estimates well below what was predicted by estimating models available at the time and lower still than what General Dynamics experienced in developing the aircraft.[32]

It was simple enough to reimburse optimism in the 1950s; under cost-plus arrangements, the industry solved unexpected technical problems and billed the government accordingly. With an incentive contract, especially one embodying the optimism on which General Dynamics launched the F-111 program, the costs fell mainly on the contractor—unless the contractor could present a legal case for having met contractual obligations, induce contract changes by submitting ECPs, or find some way to blame the government for cost increases.[33] General Dynamics exercised all three options as the F-111 program evolved. But such actions shrouded a complicated and risky technical undertaking in complex legal battles that took time, imparted more rigidity to the program, and created animosity between General Dynamics and the government. Design decisions became legal as well as technical issues, not to mention the objects of interservice dispute, thus forcing high-level officials in the Pentagon bureaucracy to make technical decisions.[34] The resulting environment hardly favored the development of sophisticated weaponry.

To make matters worse, McNamara did nothing to reduce the extensive production concurrency that marked 1950s projects. In the F-111 project the Air Force issued a production contract before it had seen the results of any prototype flight tests. Coulam contends that concurrency was used in this case because the practice had become so deeply entrenched during the 1950s.[35] Schedule compression may also have stemmed from a desire to use the new aircraft in Vietnam as soon as possible. Whatever the reason, concurrency ensured that the sizable technical problems inherent in the F-111's design did not surface until well after the aircraft had entered production. Even then, the production rate was increased. Not surprisingly, it proved prohibitively expensive to retrofit design solutions for serious problems. Hence "the first 141 F-111s were never modified as required."[36]

These problems strongly suggest that the contractual approach McNamara advocated was insensitive to both technical uncertainty and the incentives confronting defense contractors. Yet by the time the F-111's technical problems surfaced, McNamara had added another layer to his contracting scheme. Late in his tenure as defense secretary, McNamara introduced "total package procurement." System prime contractors were asked to bid on an entire system package—research, development, production, and even some operating costs—at the start of development. The goal was principally to prevent firms that bought in from getting well (recovering additional costs) during production, which presumably would discourage them from buying in in the first place. The approach also promised to carry the benefits of early competition into the monopolistic production phase of a program.[37]

McNamara's goals were laudable, but his incentives were far less powerful than those already in place. As in the F-111 project, optimism hardly disappeared. All of the development inflexibilities evident in the F-111 can be found in the most notorious total package project, the C-5A. Worse, the effort to force Lockheed, the C-5A's developer, to absorb the costs of its optimism and unforeseen technical problems in the aircraft's development drove the firm to the edge of bankruptcy. As it happened, "unknown to the Secretary of Defense,"[38] the contract for the second lot of C-5As contained an inordinately complex pricing formula that would have allowed Lockheed to recover earlier losses— in short, to "get well."[39] But by the time Lockheed would have invoked the formula, the C-5A project was mired in political controversy. The aircraft's price and Lockheed's future had become the subject of much higher-level political bargaining. Even putting aside the political controversy, however, total package procurement failed; it was out of touch with the realities of both technology development and the defense industrial base.

EXTENDING THE SYSTEM. The F-111 project was only the most notorious and studied of McNamara's many controversial acquisition projects. McNamara and his staff quickly became involved in the planning of all three services. Flexible response gave each of the three its own missions; ground forces in particular found a place in the nation's defense after a decade of serious neglect. Meanwhile, it was part of McNamara's managerial scheme to standardize the process of acquisition across the services, even though there were limits to how far he could go. Each service was composed of different acquisition organizations, often dealing with wholly different technologies. Within these limits, however, McNamara brought order and standardization to acquisition management.

The most glaring change affected the U.S. Army. McNamara was incredulous to discover, early in his tenure, that the Army's Ordnance Department treated various parts of the service's weapons systems as separate development items. For example, the Army developed rifles and their ammunition in separate arsenals commanded by separate elements of the Ordnance Department. In one of his earliest confrontations with the department, he forced it to appoint a general officer as the system project manager for the M-14 rifle. The next year, he reorganized Army acquisition by creating the Army Matériel Command, passing over the chief of ordnance to appoint a transportation officer to head the new command.[40] On paper, at least, the Army was now organized for weapons acquisition much like the U.S. Air Force, with its Air Force Systems Command.

Finding the Army's arsenals too cautious in their approach to technology, McNamara closed some of them, while he encouraged the service to turn to industry, just as the Air Corps had in the years after World War I. McNamara bypassed the Ordnance Department's laboriously planned tank modernization scheme in favor of the MBT-70 main battle tank project, run jointly with West Germany. Its principal developer was General Motors, not the Tank-Automotive Command.[41]

McNamara turned the development of the technically ambitious Cheyenne helicopter gunship over to Lockheed. Meanwhile, other projects languished in the predevelopment project definition phase, as the OSD and the Army assessed and reassessed the merits of various designs or struggled to control the requirement for new systems.[42]

Overall McNamara reshaped Army acquisition along lines already established by the Air Force.

The Costs of Control

In contrast to its beginning, McNamara's tenure as secretary of defense ended on a series of sour notes. The loudest and sourest was of course the Vietnam War. But clearly the notes that accompanied the weapons acquisition process were only slightly less cacophonous. McNamara and his staff were embroiled in innumerable wrangles with all three services over requirements for everything from rifles to ships and aircraft. Many projects in which McNamara invested energy and prestige suffered ugly technical problems. Early F-111s crashed with alarming regularity when sent to Vietnam, for example, while the M-16 rifles that McNamara forced the U. S. Army to buy began in 1966 to suffer dangerous jamming problems. Congress and the service chiefs grew accustomed to allying in opposition to McNamara. And there were many members of Congress in a position to erect roadblocks to the defense secretary's initiatives.

All of this made Robert McNamara enduringly controversial. Still, no secretary of defense could have escaped controversy at this juncture in the nation's postwar experience. Almost any defense secretary facing the panoply of weapons and conflicting strategies emerging from the Eisenhower administration would have had to act aggressively to gain control; Congress recognized this fact in passing the reorganization act of 1958. And gaining control would have required canceling weapons emerging from development projects organized to make cancellation politically difficult. There might have been a more politically astute approach to some of these issues, but the effort to tread more softly might easily have failed. Given the attitudes that produced the reorganization, failure, too, would have been controversial.

Moreover, politicians were growing less tolerant of the vicissitudes of development. Neither the C-5A nor the F-111 project was markedly more troubled in development than earlier projects greeted with enthusiasm on Capitol Hill. Cost growth in the C-5A project, Alain Enthoven later opined, was only 60 percent, much lower than the 1950s norm.[43] And problems with early F-111s were no more extensive than those suffered by early F-100s. The urgency attached to key 1950s weapons projects was slowly but surely waning, taking with it political tolerance of the messiness and uncertainty of technology development. McNamara's aggressive approach to his job no doubt prodded the change along, but much of it was engendered by the growing unpopularity of the Vietnam War. And the trend may have started even earlier, when it became clear that the missile gap in fact favored the United States rather than the Soviet Union. It is reasonable to question whether the nation could have sustained post-Sputnik levels of urgency much longer than it did, regardless of who ran the Defense Department.

Finally, almost any secretary of defense taking office in 1961 would have had to consolidate weapons requirements in some fashion, since wasteful duplication had been a hot political issue in the late 1950s. McNamara's economic calculations carried him further in this direction than the political system had expected. He faced no strong political pressure, for example, to fold Navy and Air Force requirements into a single project, as he did with the TFX. At worst, McNamara could be accused of taking his mandate to extremes.

In doing so, McNamara highlighted serious underlying problems in the overall direction that acquisition reform had taken with the 1958 reorganization. That reform had sought to consolidate power over acquisition in the interest of eliminating duplicative weapon projects. In the face of McNamara's aggressive centralization, however, members of Congress discovered that, for constitutional as well as personal political reasons, they could not possibly cede that much power to the executive. Having passed the 1958 reorganization, Congress sought to undo its effects. Over time, the effort brought more political actors into the acquisition process. Acquisition management emerged from the interaction that much more complicated and difficult.

Meanwhile the effort to eliminate wasteful duplication had perverse effects. It drove politics more deeply into the technical dimension of the acquisition process. McNamara was right to call for more analysis of defense and weapon issues, but analysis applied to weapons at the start of development could not help but be misinformed, since the information needed could only be produced by real development work. More important, in the absence of hard empirical data the project definition phase could easily become a highly politicized battle for control that could extend into the development process. In projects like the F-111, the struggle to shape requirements added risks to the initial requirement and inflexibility to the ensuing development. By contrast, allowing the service to develop weapons and then seeking to impose choice among alternatives left the technical development process fairly free of political interference.

More broadly, eliminating wasteful duplication worked against the goal of consolidating political power over acquisition. The manipulation of duplicative projects and interservice rivalry focused the defense debate on real weapons, real costs, and real performance capabilities. By contrast, the elaborate project definition phase of new projects yielded only the illusion of certainty. The existence of hardware alternatives also helped alleviate the problem of political momentum. Although it was never easy to cancel a project, it was easier to do so when the alternative was another aircraft—an F-4 or an A-7—rather than a return to the drawing boards. In the absence of duplicative development projects, the only real choice was the decision to start a project, which was likely to be woefully ill informed.

DAVID PACKARD AND THE SEARCH FOR COMPROMISE

Changing political attitudes and serious technical and cost problems in some of the weapons McNamara set into development left the acquisition process as controversial when McNamara left office as it had been when he entered it. But the focus of controversy had changed. In the late 1950s Congress was less concerned with the specifics of projects than with interservice rivalry and duplication. McNamara, too, was concerned about duplication, and tried with some success to eliminate it—at the cost of building problems into the development of individual weapons. In doing so, McNamara merely directed attention to the management of individual projects—to "problems of poor performance and late delivery as well as cost overruns."[44] The F-111, and even more so the C-5A, became lightning rods for strong congressional and public criticism of acquisition management.

Public concern prompted newly elected President Richard M. Nixon to appoint a blue ribbon commission to study the acquisition process, this one dubbed the Fitzhugh Commission after its chairman, Gilbert W. Fitzhugh of Metropolitan Life Insurance Company. While given a broad charter to examine defense management, Fitzhugh and his associates were explicitly asked to comment on "defense procurement policies and practices, particularly as they relate to costs, time and quality."[45]

Congress and the Fitzhugh Commission developed, among other things, a thorough indictment of McNamara's total package approach to procurement. "There is only one approach [to weapons acquisition] that the Panel thought should be generally rejected, as being inconsistent with sound acquisition principles. That is the concept of total package procurement. . . . It is difficult to imagine total package procurement of a large weapon system which would be either in the Government's interest or the contractor's interest."[46] More important, many students and practitioners of military R&D were allowed to place into the record many of the basic "lessons learned" of good R&D. These provided the basis for the second big wave of acquisition reform in the postwar era.

The Packard Initiatives

The effort to put these lessons into practice in the Defense Department fell principally to David Packard, the Nixon administration's first deputy secretary of defense and an industrialist (Hewlett-Packard) with considerable defense experience. The Packard Initiatives were published in May 1970, establishing a basic approach to weapons acquisition that, with minor modification, remains in place to the present.[47]

The ten Packard Initiatives were aimed at four principal goals:

—Improve the quality of information available from development. Packard called for more hardware testing, not only by developers but by military forces as well. To improve the objectivity of operational test agencies, he established operational test and evaluation agencies (OTEAs) separate from developing commands. He also established a Cost Analysis Improvement Group (CAIG) within the OSD to improve the quality of cost estimates during development.

—Enhance program flexibility. Packard was anxious to make cost as important to program managers as mainstream performance goals like speed, altitude, and maneuverability. He assigned "design-to-cost" goals to programs, whereby program managers would presumably be forced to sacrifice performance in order to hold their projects below a target cost. Normally this was the cost of a single unit—aircraft, tank, or whatever—although in his initiatives Packard also stressed that operations and support costs (so-called life-cycle costs) should be kept in mind during development. To encourage program managers and to protect them, Packard tried to strengthen their independence and lengthen their tenures. Finally, Packard wanted to reduce production concurrency. Combined with the call for more testing of hardware prototypes, this directive became the basis for the "fly before you buy" dictum that soon became linked with Packard and his initiatives.

—Restore competition to weapons acquisition. Packard wanted "to reduce risk and stimulate contractor efforts" during development. But he also wanted to discipline contractors as they approached production, going so far as to call for "prime-contractor competition through full-scale development to avoid developer monopoly at the time the initial production contract is negotiated."[48]

—Regulate the OSD's involvement in acquisition. Packard established the Defense Systems Acquisition Review Council, or DSARC. This committee, which includes high-level service and OSD representatives, meets to approve the start of development (DSARC I); meets again to decide whether the project deserves to go on to full-scale development (DSARC II); and meets a third time to approve the move from full-scale development into production (DSARC III).[49] More recent reforms have abolished the DSARC in name, at least, but retain the basic milestone and review structure Packard set in place.

These initiatives reflect a well-developed understanding of the requirements of managing technology development. Moreover, by introducing key decision points (so-called Milestones corresponding to the DSARCs) during development, Packard tried to reduce tension between the services and the OSD without sacrificing control over the process. Indeed the OSD's control would be enhanced, since decisions would be made on the basis of more valid information. Packard's initiatives seemed to find a reasonable middle ground between the demand for control and accountability, on the one hand, and the demand for sensitivity to technology, on the other.

The Changing Political and Organizational Environment

As was true under McNamara, however, what sounded sensible on paper suffered in implementation. Project management had always been responsive to political incentives as well as management directives. If anything, however, political incentives were becoming more powerful and more perverse in their effect. Implementation of management directives also had to be filtered through a complex and entrenched organizational structure among the military services, which was operating more powerfully as the years went by. Packard's initiatives made sense, but those who managed acquisition projects had little desire to conform to them and plenty of incentives to avoid doing so.

The trend toward increasing congressional oversight of acquisition that began in 1959 leaped to higher levels in the 1970s as the post-Vietnam Congress sought lower defense budgets and greater efficiency in acquisition. Representatives were now more likely to see the defense industry as a wasteland rather than the arsenal of democracy. More important, Congress was fast becoming more democratic, as a series of acts passed in 1974 undermined party discipline and made it easier for individual members to get involved in overseeing weapons projects. The decline in party discipline was not alone in making members of Congress more responsive to constituents' concerns rather than to issues of national importance. For example, although better information usually makes for better decisions, the widespread use of computers and automated information systems raised the importance of local politics as representatives and constituents became informed "of the incidence of local benefits under every imaginable formula."[50] Finally, congressional staffs continued to grow in size. In 1959 one observer questioned whether the Armed Services Committees had the staff to oversee acquisition. Today both the committee and individual members maintain staffs that do little else.

In short, the incentives for members of Congress to interfere in acquisition and the institutional means to do so rose sharply in the early 1970s and continued to rise thereafter. These trends had two consequences for weapons acquisition. On the one hand, project managers and high-level service staff officials were spending more and more time briefing members of Congress or responding to their inquiries. "Between 1970 and 1985," Secretary of Defense Caspar W. Weinberger later noted, "there was a 1,172 percent increase in reports and studies requested by Congress." By 1983 Defense Department witnesses "trudged to Capitol Hill 1,306 times to appear before 96 committees for 2,160 hours of testimony." Congress made 830 detailed program adjustments to service budgets in 1970. In 1985 it made 3,163.[51] This represents more than a drain on a project manager's time. It dilutes his control over the shape of weapons destined to enter the service's inventory.

On the other hand, increasing fragmentation in Congress has tended to increase the virulence with which members attack weapon projects. There may well be good reason to criticize a project or how acquisition is managed, but intramural competition on Capitol Hill encourages exaggeration. In stridently criticizing the Air Force's B-1B bomber, for example, Chairman of the House Armed Services Committee Les Aspin has been driven not only by strong feelings about the aircraft's technical problems but also by the need to outflank Representative John Dingell, who has used his position on the House Energy and Commerce Committee to criticize acquisition. This "war of the watchdogs" has produced a level of rhetoric only partly related to the bomber's flaws.[52] To the services, Congress has grown less rather than more capable of dealing objectively with the complexities of weapons development.

Meanwhile, technological advances have increased the organizational complexity of the military services, enhancing the sources of institutional rigidity. The trend is most visible in the Army. The infantry division of 1945 was composed principally of infantry with its rifles and machine guns backed up by artillery. By 1955 the infantry division had acquired a small armor component, reflecting the rise of the combined arms team, as well as armored vehicles, rocket launchers, and more artillery.[53] By the end of the Vietnam War, the helicopter had achieved prominence, and almost all Army divisions acquired a large aviation component. Similar trends affected tank divisions. Growing organizational complexity increased the press toward more detailed specifications for new weapons able to fit into this fine organizational mesh. And it also produced more complicated standard operating procedures, contributing to organizational rigidity. On the military as well as the political front, the institutional environment was becoming less and less hospitable to the needs of technical development.

Packard in Practice

If Packard was seeking to bring simplicity and order to the acquisition process, the broader determinants of acquisition behavior were clearly moving in the other direction. Packard's initiatives were implemented in the fine technical detail of regulations and directives. Projects showed the outward markings of the new approach—DSARCs were held, competition was imparted to early development, and so forth. Yet in broader terms the services managed acquisition much as they had from the start, except when Packard personally intervened.

In particular, the services were less than anxious to take Packard's "fly before you buy" dictum to heart. Rather, production concurrency retained popularity despite Packard's attempt to emphasize more developmental and operational testing. There was some progress. A Rand Corporation study of procurement during the 1970s showed an increase in developmental testing of new weapons before the decision to go into production. But it also said, "It is not clear that there is a corresponding increase in the demonstration of *operational suitability* before, or even soon after, production go-ahead."[54]

On some important projects, however, even this assessment was optimistic. Note, for example, Robert Coulam's comment about comparative test schedules for the F-111 and the F-15. The F-15 was developed when the services were supposed to comply with fly-before-you-buy directives:

> The initial production commitment for the showcase program of the Laird- Packard [fly-before-you-buy] reforms, the F-15, occurred four months after the plane's first flight, precisely the same time lapse between first flight and production commitment as occurred on the F-111 program. First production deliveries of the F-15 to the operational command occurred 28 months after the plane's first flight, a five-month *shorter* testing period . . . than was scheduled on the F-111A program.[55]

In a recent General Accounting Office study on U.S. Army weapons projects, analysts found that this practice continues to this day. "The Sergeant York [DIVAD], the Patriot, and the Abrams tank systems moved from development to production before major problems revealed by the tests were resolved. . . . Some . . . tests were incomplete, and others were deferred or waived before key decision points. Also, tests were generally conducted in unrealistically favorable environments."[56] To this criticism could be added what members of the House Armed Services Committee called the Air Force's "buy before fly" approach to fielding the B-1B bomber.[57] From Packard's day to the present, production concurrency has been an integral part of the weapons acquisition process.

And it continues to play a role in deterring outside intervention in service projects. Russell Murray, a former assistant secretary of defense for program analysis and evaluation, argues that by the time initial test data begin to surface unflattering information about a new system's performance, contracts have been let, production workers have been hired, and the costs of slowing down to redesign components is prohibitively high, especially if one accepts the services' arguments that they already know how to fix the design. Murray comments, "Sometimes those arguments are valid. More often, however, they are blatant attempts to frustrate the operational testing process."[58] He might have added that the arguments are true because the services organize their projects to ensure that the costs of intervention in an ongoing project will be high. In the process, they raise the cost of responding to new information, just the opposite of what is required from a technical point of view.

Packard's effort to improve cost estimating procedures was only slightly more successful than his attempt to reduce concurrency. Cost growth no longer approaches 1950s levels, to be sure. Rand's study of acquisition policy in the 1970s charted real cost growth (subtracting the effects of inflation) at 3 percent to 6 percent a year after DSARC II (the start of full-scale engineering development) as a rough norm.[59] That should not be surprising, however. Cost estimating has grown more scientific over time. Moreover, many of the expensive technologies at the core of today's force posture are more mature than they were in the 1950s, reducing technological uncertainty and giving cost estimators more empirical data on which to base their cost projections.

Yet the evidence suggests that optimism permitted by early uncertainty and enforced by political and organizational pressures continues to produce initial weapons requirements that are technically unrealistic and almost always underpriced. Packard created the Cost Analysis Improvement Group (CAIG) to correct for this optimism, and CAIG routinely produces higher initial estimates than either the services or industry.[60] With technical discipline weak, however, even after early development CAIG's estimates have been easily ignored. Rand analysts found that "unexpected development difficulties" were a major source of cost growth after DSARC II in 60 percent of the 1970s programs they studied.[61]

Cost growth has been especially high in ambitious projects exploring new and still uncertain electronics technologies. Cost growth in the advanced medium-range air-to-air missile (AMRAAM) program is 120 percent and climbing, while that in the Air Force's Low Altitude Navigation and Targeting Infra-Red for Night (LANTIRN) project is over 100 percent and climbing.[62] And the Air Force admits that the estimated cost of its B-2 Stealth bomber, now almost ready for production, grew 20 percent over 1988 alone.[63]

Moreover, the Rand study evaluated cost growth from a narrow technical perspective of questionable relevance to the Defense Department's overall planning problem. At Milestone II, the department formally commits itself to producing the finished product. But few projects are canceled once they start, and planning documents are crammed full of new projects based on Milestone I cost estimates. Thus Pentagon planners must contend with cost uncertainty from the start of a project, not just after Milestone II. Cost growth before Milestone II tends to be fairly high, since this is the period when technological uncertainties are highest.

Packard hoped to generate real alternatives by developing competing technologies between Milestones I and II. But the services had learned from McNamara the threat posed by developed hardware alternatives, and this, combined with their natural tendency to "start the acquisition process with a fairly firm notion of what they want" made them more reluctant to cooperate.[64] But while Packard sought to open options, the services wanted to eliminate them at Milestone I by presenting the OSD with a well-defined, single alternative.[65] In practice the tendency to confine prototyping to the so-called demonstration and validation phase of an acquisition project, which lies between Milestones I and II, emerged and is general practice today. Yet as a rule the intricately detailed formal requirements hammered out before Milestone I greatly constrain the exploration of alternatives in the prototyping phase. This means basic technology choices are still made before Milestone I and are based, as they were in the McNamara era, on analysis rather than extensive development work.[66]

With attention focused on a single weapon rather than real alternatives, the formulation of requirements for new systems continued to exhibit the consensus building that marked the F-111 project, and for many of the same reasons. Service requirements remained the product of "years of effort by the service and hundreds of agreements among interested parties within each service."[67] And early optimism continued to weaken technical discipline, making it fairly easy to combine contradictory requirements on paper, much as McNamara did with the F-111. To make matters worse, the growth in the OSD and in the size of congressional staffs worked to spread the consensus-building process over a wider array of participants. Indeed, the increasing intrusion of Congress into oversight of new projects reinforced the need to sell the project in the Pentagon, since Pentagon bureaucrats unhappy with the direction a new project was taking could always "back channel" their complaints to congressional allies able to influence the project's funding.

As an example of the disparate forces that can shape the goals and structure of a new project, consider the requirements process for the Army's M-1 tank project. Responsibility for formulating the tank's requirement was lodged formally with the Main Battle Tank Task Force, which convened in January 1972. But the tank's overall requirement was an amalgamation of requirements enforced by agencies and actors around the government.[68]

—The target for the tank's unit cost was set, roughly, by members of Congress, especially members of the House Armed Services Committee, who worked hard in 1971 to have the Army's XM-803 (derived from the ill-starred MBT-70) canceled, partly because its $600,000 price tag was too high. The task force arrived at the formal target of $508,000 per tank by subtracting what was calculated to be a politically acceptable amount from the XM-803's cost.

—Task force members could see no justification for using competition in the tank's development, since there was "no sound basis for determining the cost savings to production resulting from competitive development."[69] Still, competitive prototyping was an important part of the Packard Initiatives, and the House Appropriations Committee also wanted "a prototype program to build a limited number of tanks of two different designs for test and evaluation."[70] Finally, using a figure "pulled out of the hat," the task force calculated the production savings that would result from competitive development and organized a prototype competition.[71]

—The tank's six-year development schedule was set by Army Chief of Staff William Westmoreland, who was responding to public criticism of the length of time required to develop new systems. The decision was extremely controversial within the task force, one of whose members referred to it as "radical surgery by executive fiat."[72]

—Originally, the task force and associated staff agencies settled on a weight goal for the tank of roughly fifty-two tons, a compromise between one group in the armor community that favored forty-eight-ton tanks to maximize mobility and reliability (inversely proportional to weight) while minimizing cost, and a group favoring a fifty-eight-ton tank to maximize armor protection. In the major Army staff meeting on the M-1 requirement, however, Gen. Creighton Abrams, about to replace Westmoreland as chief of staff, raised the weight limit to fifty-eight tons to take full advantage of new armor technology. Although the fifty-two-ton goal had been produced by the Army's armor community, to members of the task force "Abrams *was* the armor community, and the decision was 58 tons."[73]

—The engine power requirement evolved directly from Abrams's weight decision, which forced the service to drop plans to develop a low-risk 750-horsepower engine in favor of one delivering 1500 horsepower, despite the fact that this high-risk item "might fail in development."[74] These fears were misplaced. Although, in the end, the M-1 was equipped with a new gas turbine engine, with a unique set of technical and operational risks, the XM-1's 1500 HP diesel engine progressed smoothly in development. Success may have occurred because the XM-1's predecessor, the MBT-70, also required a 1500 HP engine, and for the same reason: integrating West German and U.S. tank requirements drove up tank weight and hence engine power requirements. Problems in the development of that engine contributed to the MBT-70 program's cancellation. Nonetheless, engine work in the 1960s may have reduced the risks of developing a similar engine in the 1970s.[75]

Few would argue that service chiefs have no right to set development schedules, or that a man of Abrams's experience had no right to raise the weight target that the tank task force had produced. Nor can it be said that any of these requirements was outlandish by itself. Tanks weighing more than sixty tons already existed, for example, while the Air Force had by that time almost completed developing the F-15 fighter in less than six years. Yet taken together the tank's requirements process placed the M-1 project in a mild squeeze between increasing weight and engine risk, and cost and schedule goals that were set largely without regard to risk. And that squeeze resulted because, despite its charter, the Army's tank task force was largely unable to integrate requirements, that is, to make trade-offs in a sensible way.

It might have been easier for the Main Battle Tank Task Force to enforce discipline had risks and costs been more easily verified—had the task force been able to assert with confidence that the tank would weigh well over sixty tons, raising serious questions about deployability aboard the nation's transport aircraft and its ability to use small bridges in West Germany, its principal area of deployment. Initial optimism during the project definition phase makes this a difficult tack to take, however. But for that reason, the conditions for future problems are set. As development progresses, the political danger connected with breaking an established consensus encourages program managers to accept cost growth rather than sacrifice performance.

Consensus building continues during the development of a weapon. A principal source of cost growth in 1970s weapons projects was the tendency to enhance requirements as development continued, mostly in an upward direction.[76] Secretary of Defense Donald Rumsfeld modified the M-1 tank's requirement in 1976, for example. In response to calls for a two-way street within the NATO alliance, he insisted that the service replace the M-1's 105mm gun with a 120mm tank gun developed by West Germany.[77]

Far from opening the development process for judicious review, as Packard had hoped, the DSARC instead opened the ongoing project to consensus building. During that process, the wrangling that generated the initial requirement may be reenacted, perhaps with new actors, or even new agencies. Meanwhile new technologies may have arisen since the previous DSARC, each proffered with great optimism about cost and performance, and some of these no doubt will find their way into the "new" requirement. Although ongoing development work will have resolved some developmental uncertainties, new ones can still be introduced at each important decision point.

The seeming rationality of the decision structure Packard imposed—and that is still imposed—on the weapons acquisition process masks a reality shaped by powerful underlying political and organizational forces. Decisionmaking about technology has come to have a distinctly American political flavor. Unfortunately, over time legislative modes of behavior have been transferred to the technical decisionmaking process, where they have encouraged behaviors that run counter to those likely to produce successful development.

Anomalous Success

If Packard remains among the most successful acquisition managers the Pentagon has seen, his success had less to do with his initiatives than with his excursions outside the established acquisition bureaucracies. The best known of these was the lightweight fighter competition. The opportunity to develop such an aircraft arose partly because of growing frustration with the rising cost of each new generation of fighters. It stemmed as well from rising frustration with the Air Force's pronounced tendency to rely on radars and air-to-air missiles in air combat, despite evidence from Korea and Vietnam suggesting that maneuverability—the ability to dogfight—might be much more important to success. In the mid-1960s, Lt. Col. John Boyd developed his innovative energy-maneuverability theory to help explain this phenomenon, and he and several colleagues tried to influence the requirement then taking shape for the next Air Force fighter, which would become the F-15. They were only partially successful, however. They managed to reduce the F-15's size, weight, and cost, but "the F-15 was a smaller departure from precedent than had been hoped."[78] In the early 1970s, advocates for lightweight fighters allied with David Packard to see their desires embodied in hardware. They were aided by Packard's emphasis on prototyping and the popularity prototyping enjoyed in Congress, as well as rising concern on Capitol Hill about the cost of the F-15 and the Navy's new F-14 fighter.[79] The political and organizational stage was set for developing a real alternative to the ongoing F-15 project. Thus the so-called Lightweight Fighter (LWF) program was born.

The program was staged in a way that minimized service resistance while maximizing political support. Although it was carried out under U. S. Air Force auspices (the program manager worked out of the Air Force Systems Command, for example), the program was funded initially by the OSD rather than by the service. It was presented either as a "technology demonstration" project, or as a potential complement to the F-15—hence the "hi-lo mix" concept, developed at the time, which envisioned a force posture of sophisticated and expensive weapons backed by larger numbers of simpler and less expensive systems.[80] Meanwhile it was sold on Capitol Hill as an experiment in austere competitive development, involving the "fly-before-you-buy" principle then popular with Congress.[81]

The LWF development ran from January 1972, when Northrop and General Dynamics were selected as competing contractors, through January 1975, when General Dynamics was awarded the contract for full-scale development of what would become the F-16. Mostly because it was run outside formally established acquisition bureaucracies, design and development work was relatively free of bureaucratic encrustation. The LWF requirement document was remarkably short, twenty-five pages, and to a great extent performance oriented. At the height of the test program, the service program office was held to a fairly austere fifty to sixty people.[82] Generally, the competing contractors were left to themselves to design and initially test their prototypes. Planners envisioned an extensive, year-long test phase, though this period was cut short when Defense Secretary James Schlesinger chose to enter the winning prototype in the competition for a fighter for several European countries. This decision made it necessary to choose a winning contractor by January 1975, before Northrop had completed its year of testing. The General Dynamics prototype, however, was submitted to far more extensive testing than usual.

Significantly, the development of an alternative to the F-15 also opened the possibility for choice similar to choices McNamara had made in the early 1960s. With the F-16 now available, Defense Secretary Schlesinger confronted the Air Force with the choice of buying a limited number of F-15s or enlarging its force posture by substituting the less expensive F-16. Given that the force posture implications of the F-15's cost were troubling even the Tactical Air Command, the decision was easy.[83] Clearly this was not the sharp choice McNamara often successfully enforced in the early 1960s; the Air Force got not one but two aircraft. Still, in the years since, the F-16 buy has been expanded much more than the F-15 buy, suggesting that the F-16's availability ameliorated what would have been a continuing financial crisis for the nation's tactical air force.

Having chosen the aircraft as a competitor in Europe's fighter competition as well as an alternative to the F-15 domestically, Schlesinger now turned the "technology demonstration" project over to the Air Force Systems Command for full-scale development. There it was submitted to much the same managerial practices that were applied to other mainstream systems. The program office quickly grew in size, and a new, more detailed, and more demanding set of requirements was leveled at the project. The F-16A was rushed into production with roughly the same concurrency that marked the F-15 and F-111 programs. Still, of the F-16 (and the A-10 prototype, another Packard project), Lynn and Smith argue that "the number of changes was relatively small and the planes emerged as the recognizable progeny of their prototypes."[84]

THE THIRD WAVE

David Packard was called back to Washington in 1985, this time to head President Ronald Reagan's Blue Ribbon Commission on Defense Management. So far as weapons acquisition was concerned, Packard said at his first press conference, things were no better in the 1980s than when he took office as deputy secretary of defense in 1969.[85] Evidently, even he realized that the Packard Initiatives had produced only marginal changes in acquisition.

This time Packard had plenty of help. Congress criticized the acquisition process in the late 1960s, but for the most part left reform to the executive branch. During the 1980s, by contrast, the legislature approached the problem more actively. In 1982 Congress mandated the creation of an assistant secretaryship in the Pentagon for operational test and evaluation. In 1984 it passed the Competition in Contracting Act, setting targets for increasing the use of competition in military procurement. And in 1986, as part of a broad congressional effort to reorganize the nation's defense policymaking apparatus, the Defense Acquisition Improvement Act introduced a host of reforms, many of them echoing suggestions made in the 1986 Packard Commission report.[86]

Thus, ironically, the most sweeping defense and acquisition reforms since 1958 emerged during the largest peacetime defense spending boom in the nation's postwar history. The irony is easily explained.

President Ronald Reagan succeeded in making it politically unpopular to be against defense or in favor of a tax increase. The only politically feasible action left for those concerned about burgeoning federal deficits was to call for greater efficiency. And there certainly seemed to be a need for that, with the Pentagon paying $340 for hammers, $640 for toilet seats, and seemingly excessive profits to contractors. Meanwhile, if doubling the money spent on weapons procurement solved some defense problems, it had little effect on the acquisition process. Production concurrency remained as evident and controversial as it had in the past, for example, while service project managers seemed to have less control than ever over the projects. If anything, rapidly increasing procurement spending only made things worse. There was a limit to the speed with which acquisition managers could spend money wisely.

The Prospects for Packard II

If the final test of acquisition reform is the emergence of better weapons from the acquisition process, it is far too early to judge the success of the reforms Packard's Commission and Congress jointly imposed on acquisition management. Insofar as the Packard Commission's report echoed much of the technical and managerial wisdom embodied in the Packard Initiatives, however, there are strong grounds for questioning why such reforms would succeed today when they failed before. The Packard Initiatives failed largely because they were overpowered by broader political and institutional forces. If anything, those forces operated more powerfully in the 1980s. Congress in particular brought to bear the ambivalence that its members have always brought to acquisition, producing conflicting directives and pressures sure to drive Packard II to the same end as Packard I.

The urge to centralize, evident in 1947 and 1958, reappeared in 1986 in response to continuing problems with interservice rivalry and the growing sense that the authority of project managers was "vastly diluted."[87] Thus Packard and Congress sought to streamline and centralize acquisition management by calling for an under secretary of defense for acquisition who would have "full-time responsibility for managing the defense acquisition system." And "acquisition executive" positions were established in each service, creating a straight chain of command from the undersecretary to service project managers.[88]

Arguably the effort to centralize power will engender the same countervailing political pressures that engulfed Robert McNamara.

Members of Congress want centralized control of acquisition until they get it. Then they rediscover that weapons issues are at once political as well as technical. As it happens, other legislation had already made the point. In 1982 the Pentagon finally filled the Inspector General position mandated by the Inspector General Act of 1978, thereby creating another level of oversight so that Congress, as well as the defense secretary, could evaluate projects. Nor does the appointment of an assistant secretary for operational test and evaluation, a position mandated by Congress, streamline the acquisition process. More recently, Congress has taken steps to protect Pentagon whistle blowers whose traditional outlet has been Capitol Hill. As was clear during McNamara's tenure, members of Congress understand the need for a simplified approach to acquisition but legislate in ways that complicate rather than simplify.

The story has not been any more encouraging within the Defense Department. Packard II created an acquisition executive chain of command for program managers without eliminating the existing chain that linked service technical agencies and higher-level staffs. It is doubtful that project managers will be free to ignore their own service hierarchies. Hence their reporting burden is likely to increase rather than decrease. Meanwhile, the creation of an undersecretary for acquisition position only complicates overall acquisition management, since this official is likely to compete for influence with the deputy secretary of defense, who has handled acquisition in the past. The resignation of Richard Godwin, the first undersecretary, occurred partly because of competition with Deputy Secretary of Defense William Taft.

The rush to produce systems like the B-1B, the Army's Sergeant York (DIVAD) air defense gun, or the Air Force's advanced medium-range air-to-air missile (AMRAAM), repeatedly raised questions about the wisdom of rushing new weapons into production without adequate testing. Eventually, DIVAD was canceled, while production funding for AMRAAM was withheld pending further tests and cost studies. And the Air Force's request for several hundred million dollars to solve the B-1B's problems prompted serious controversy on Capitol Hill.[89] This concern led Congress in 1982 to create the assistant secretaryship for test and evaluation.[90] Meanwhile the Packard reforms favored the use of prototypes, calling on the Defense Advanced Research Projects Agency (DARPA), to stimulate "a greater emphasis on prototyping in defense systems."[91]

Yet the assistant secretary for operational testing confronts political and technical pressures that encourage production concurrency. If the Packard Commission report called for more testing, elsewhere it indicted the Pentagon's "unreasonably long acquisition cycle—ten to fifteen years for our major weapon systems."[92] Thus, despite complaints about production concurrency, Godwin asserted just before he resigned that the "Pentagon will be relying more on concurrent development and production to shorten the time it takes to field major weapons systems."[93] It is not clear why, under these conditions, a new assistant secretary for testing will have better luck here than Packard had with his showcase F-15 program. Meanwhile, although the services have assigned a few projects to DARPA for rapid prototyping, at this writing DARPA has been granted no budget funding to begin work.[94]

The Packard reforms emphasized flexibility in development, something Packard had tried to do in 1969 by raising the importance of cost, strengthening program managers, and limiting production concurrency. Packard II replaced the DSARC, at least at Milestone II, with the Joint Requirements and Management Board (JRMB), and charged this body with doing what the DSARC had manifestly failed to do— assess the wisdom of proceeding into full-scale development while balancing cost with performance in the ongoing project. It is not clear why changing the name of an organization and calling for more flexibility in development will produce something that has been missing from acquisition for decades. Why should the JRMB have better luck on this score than the DSARC, which the Packard Commission regarded as "not the proper forum for effecting this [cost-performance] balance"?[95] It seems doubtful that the program manager's life will be any simpler, or the prospects for flexibility in development any greater, under the new arrangements.

Finally, Packard and Congress agreed on the need for budget stability, hence on the wisdom of trying to achieve a two-year cycle for the defense budget, as if two years of stability were meaningful for weapons projects lasting ten or more years. The 1986 Department of Defense Authorization Act ordered the Defense Department to prepare a two-year budget for fiscal years 1988 and 1989. At the same time, however, the Armed Services Committees agreed to observe such a cycle only if the Appropriations Committees did so, which they did not. Thus the same intramural competition that helped bring more committees into the acquisition process now works to keep them there. In any case, the need to cut the defense budget between fiscal 1988 and 1989 led the Defense Department to submit an amended budget in fiscal 1989, raising questions about whether the two-year cycle had been observed even by the agency most anxious to have it.[96]

The Attack on Industry

Although reform advanced on a broad front in the 1980s, the defense industry has taken the brunt of the attack. Reports of overpriced tools and spare parts and excessive, occasionally fraudulent overhead claims brought new meaning to the phrase "fraud, waste, and abuse." The public and Congress also found it disturbing that defense firms made much higher profits in the early part of the decade than the average manufacturing firm. Early in the 1980s a concerted effort emerged to discipline the defense industry.

The effort has moved along three separate paths. First, overhead claims have been subjected to increasing inspection, despite calls for streamlining the acquisition process, and indictments have been leveled at firms and individuals suspected of making fraudulent claims.

Second, in the Defense Appropriations Act of 1987 and also in a series of changes to the *Federal Acquisition Regulations,* the government reduced allowable profit levels, the rate of progress payments, and certain overhead claims, forcing the industry to absorb marginally greater costs. Certain actions and the motives behind them were complex, but the overall effect was to lower the industry's profits.

Third, since the early 1980s Congress has insisted on more competition in military procurement. When Frank Carlucci, the Reagan administration's first deputy secretary of defense, took his thirty-one Carlucci Initiatives for managing the Defense Department to Capitol Hill for approval in 1981, for example, members of Congress insisted that he add a thirty-second—demanding the extensive use of competition. Evidently unimpressed with Carlucci's efforts in this area, and increasingly displeased with spare parts horror stories, Congress passed the Competition in Contracting Act in 1984, ordering the military services to use competition in contracting in increasing amounts each year. The act also mandated the creation of "competition advocates" within each service, to ferret out sole-source purchases that could be submitted to competition.[97]

With these actions the political system returned to the perspectives of 1934. In place of the rhetoric of that era about rapacious industrialists, the 1980s reference is to fraud, waste, and abuse. But the call for more competition has been the same in both cases, though today it is more likely to affect subcontractors than defense prime contractors. Unfortunately, it is no more clear now than in 1934 that politically popular reforms respond adequately or accurately to the deeply institutionalized realities of today's government-industry relationship.

The profit issue is an example. Many scholars question whether profits in the defense sector can even be measured. Data are scarce and subject to widely differing interpretations.[98] Among those willing to do the measurement, debate continues about which measure—return on sales, return on investment, and so forth—is the most appropriate.[99]

Political debate came to rest on the fairly simple premise that defense firms made much higher profits in the early 1980s than comparable nondefense firms. This conclusion was reached, however, after the Reagan administration's defense spending boom had ended. By the middle of the decade defense industry stocks were greatly discounted on the stock market, suggesting that investors saw their financial prospects more skeptically than politicians; falling defense budgets would take a toll from the industry's profits. That, of course, was precisely when the new profit policy was introduced, ensuring that profits would be lower still.

Meanwhile the place of competition in weapons acquisition is at least as ambiguous and potentially counterproductive now as it was in 1934. Historically, the congressional demand for competition encouraged the traditional service procurement bureaucracies to move slowly and cautiously in awarding procurement contracts. In his study of the Competition in Contracting Act, Andrew Mayer suggests that now, as then, more competition means that "the procurement process may become somewhat slower."[100] Consequently, it is not clear how members of Congress can pass the CICA while at the same time lamenting the ever-lengthening time it takes to develop and field new systems.

Moreover, historic trends toward the purchase of more expensive aircraft in smaller numbers have long since passed the point at which competitive production of key aerospace systems is likely to pay for itself, let alone save money. The drive for more competition has focused on subsystems that enjoy longer production runs. Yet components for these systems were often already purchased competitively by prime contractors. Whether or not the contractors passed the savings on to the Defense Department is a separate issue, which continues to be a problem. During hearings on the F-16C fighter, for example, the Air Force claimed that only 25 percent of the money appropriated annually to that project went directly to General Dynamics for "airframe fabrication and putting it [the aircraft] together." The rest of the money went to subcontractors, many of which competed for the business. According to the Air Force, over 60 percent of the F-16 appropriation was spent on the basis of competitive bidding.[101]

Hammers costing $430 each, and toilet seats for $640 each, suggest waste in purchasing smaller items, but part of the excessive cost of these items reflects prime contractors' markups and overhead loadings that will be transferred to other components rather than eliminated by enforcing more competition for the purchase of tools and spare parts. Meanwhile the effort to break such items out of prime contractor operations and submit them to competition has added a sizable bureaucracy to the Pentagon, with costs that raise questions about the wisdom of the move.[102]

Questions about markups and prime contractor profits raise the central issue, which the Competition in Contracting Act does not really address. Today, as in 1934, no one has solved the problems that make competition for production anathema to the acquisition process. Research, development, and production continue to be merged, not only in large defense prime contractors but among subcontractors as well. For better or for worse, rightly or wrongly, firms encouraged to buy in retain the need to get well during production. Under these conditions, profits, to an extent that varies from case to case, represent an unrecognized subsidy for facing the risks of research and development. In threatening that subsidy, competition for production reduces incentives to take risks.

In the past, the call for more production competition encouraged aircraft manufacturers to turn away from the government and toward the commercial aircraft market. Most aerospace firms no longer have this option, and in this sense the government has far more leverage over prime contractors today than it did in 1934. Yet one wonders if a nation that stakes its security on technological advantage wants to rely on firms that are in the defense business only because they have nowhere else to turn.

CONCLUSION

During the past three decades, complaints about the acquisition process have echoed complaints about the aircraft acquisition process in the years before World War II. Then as now, Congress wanted more competition in defense contracting. Then as now, the public seemed innately suspicious of defense firms. Then as now, financing the pursuit of fast-moving technologies was done in ways that defy an ordering that is politically satisfactory. These events should not surprise anyone. The peacetime political norms and strictures applied to aircraft acquisition before World War II were deeply rooted in American culture and political institutions. They have reemerged in the years since World War II, only to be applied to an acquisition process that employs many of the same institutional arrangements abhorred in the 1920s and 1930s. The political anomaly was World War II and the 1950s, when the acquisition process enjoyed strong political support, mostly because the political system was gripped by crisis.

Today, however, the politics of weapons procurement encompasses a much broader range of activities than it did before World War II. Then the struggle for political support was confined to broad features of the acquisition process, in particular, to types of contracts and the role of competition. Today, project managers must struggle to obtain and maintain political support for individual projects. And they must do so in an elaborate bureaucratic and political structure absent before World War II. The Pentagon's bureaucracy interacts at almost every level with Congress and its expanding staff, bringing the pork-barrel machinations of American politics into project management. The arcanely complicated process of designing and developing weapons has been drawn out of the industry and into a political system that operates in ways decidedly unsympathetic to the demands of sophisticated technology development.

Arguably this state of affairs was inevitable. Weapons acquisition is a public function that lacks simple governing mechanisms like the market. The sheer age of the acquisition enterprise would have brought bureaucratic encrustation, while the unprecedented size of the enterprise invited greater political attention, with the consequent attempt to manage the process from the political level. The Army and Navy turned to private industry for aircraft in the years after World War I mostly to escape the oppressive bureaucratic and political tangle that had affected the service arsenals and bureaus. Yet in many ways, over the postwar era the nation has witnessed the "arsenalizing" of the defense industry.[103]

Still, it is worth noting that reform has not only failed to prevent arsenalizing but may well have contributed to it. In giving the defense secretary more power and a larger staff, for example, the Defense Reorganization Act of 1958 produced a big increase in the number of institutional actors with some claim to a formal role in weapons acquisition. American politics offers those actors opportunities to ensure that their claim is honored, especially if, as has been the case, Congress proves reluctant to let the defense secretary exercise the power granted by the 1958 act. The problem is not a specific reform, however, or a specific defense secretary; rather the problem is rooted in a political system designed to check centralization and effective indeed in achieving that end. Centralizing reforms continue to become law. Given the constitutional framework in which they occur, they also produce more layers of bureaucracy. And more layers of bureaucracy make it more, rather than less, difficult for defense officials to centralize power.

The effort to eliminate duplication has also had perverse effects, despite the undoubted wastefulness of some of the duplication extant during the 1950s. If the procurement process focuses from the start on a single option, then the development of that option will be raised to a preeminence in the Defense Department and on Capitol Hill that invites political intervention. Indeed, the struggle to control the initial requirement merely draws the political process back into the origins of new systems, where it registers as bureaucratic and political bargaining for support on such issues as cost, schedule, and basic performance characteristics. To the extent that lasting bargains are struck at this point in development, however, they are likely to be based on the mushy information then available.

It remains to be seen whether some reforms might succeed where the kind chosen so far have failed. Clearly, however, far more radical reorganization is in order, a reorganization that basically alters the relationship between the political system and the acquisition process. As troubled as politicians may be by features of the acquisition process, the political system as a whole has so far been unwilling to contemplate change this great. Reluctance is not surprising; a political system accustomed to muddling through will probably engage in radical reform only in response to massive failure. And the fact is, the failures of the acquisition process tend to appear on the margins. If the costs of this way of doing business are marginal, however, they are nonetheless high.

CHAPTER 4

Mismanaging Modernization

RUSHING weapons out of the laboratory, through development, and into production has been the most persistent feature of the weapons acquisition process. The practice is supported by seemingly unassailable strategic logic. A nation that stakes its security on technological advantage has every reason to field the newest and best technologies as quickly as possible. As the Packard Commission noted in 1986, "We forfeit our five-year technological lead by the time it takes us to get our technology from the laboratory into the field."[1] The high levels of production concurrency that speed entails seem efficient. "For multibillion dollar weapon systems, stretchouts in acquisition are big money."[2] Behind these arguments is a powerful political logic. Rushing creates and sustains political momentum. Investing in production early increases sunk costs and makes cancellation politically more difficult. Rushing also ensures that data from preproduction testing, which may surface lingering problems that belie earlier optimism, do not surface until after a new system is safely into production. With so much to recommend it, rushing's persistence should not be surprising.

Because it restricts the range of technical choice, however, rushing can also be costly. It is always cheaper in the short run to move a new project quickly into production. Yet this economy is false if it forces designers to solve remaining technical problems later, when doing so is more expensive. And speed promotes a false sense of security if it places inappropriate, unfinished, or unready weapons in the field.

Cases like the F-100 and F-111 aircraft suggest that the nation has already incurred such costs, although such examples tend to be written off as the unavoidable and seemingly marginal by-products of the race to stay ahead of the Russians.

The costs of rushing are growing. It was possible to rush ballistic missile developments because so many components were under development simultaneously that design errors could be corrected as development progressed. But as the nation has come to rely on analysis rather than duplication to hedge against error, the chances for fielding the wrong technology have multiplied. Meanwhile, as weapons and forces have grown more mature and complicated, so have the design challenges that appear at the end, rather than the beginning, of the development process. Rushing to production thus makes even less sense now than it did in the 1950s.

Ironically, the nation need not rush to stay ahead of the Soviets, nor is rushing the best way to place operationally useful weapons in the field. There are straightforward acquisition strategies for accomplishing both aims. Yet alternatives require more coherence and stability than American politics provides. Thus the services have perfected an approach to acquisition that bends requirements for sensible modernization to suit their political environment. The services rush less to stay ahead of the Russians than to stay ahead of the American political system.

THE DILEMMAS OF MODERNIZATION

If technology were stable, the services would face the straightforward task of replacing old weapons only when they wore out. But technology has long since ceased being stable, and today most important military technologies are moving rapidly. Military organizations now modernize rather than replace, and in modernizing they must balance the need to move quickly in order to capture a new technology's full benefits with the need to move slowly in order to make wise decisions. Modernization decisions thus pose dilemmas that are as complex and uncertain as the technologies with which they deal.

A useful metaphor for considering the dilemmas of modernization is the S-curve, which charts "the relationship between the effort put into improving a product or process and the results one gets back for that investment."[3] The curve highlights an early growth phase when change comes quickly and return on investment is high, followed by

FIGURE 4-1. *The Technology Growth S-Curve*

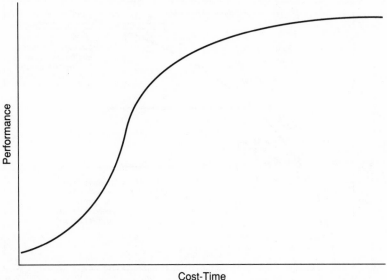

a mature phase when improvements are much more difficult and expensive (figure 4-1). The S-curve may apply to specific technologies. The development of computers, for example, has relied on the successive exploration of vacuum tubes, transistors, integrated circuits, microcircuits, and today very high-speed integrated circuits.[4] Or it may be applied to systems. Analysts at the Rand Corporation, for example, have produced something akin to an S-curve in measuring the pace of technological change in basic airframe and engine performance in U.S. jet fighter aircraft (figure 4-2). As these analysts noted, "It has become increasingly difficult to sustain the rates of technological improvement that we have grown accustomed to in the past," suggesting the jet engine and airframe system is entering its mature phase.[5] Tank armor and engine technologies are also relatively mature. Performance improvements are still possible, but they come slowly and at great expense.

Mature technologies have much to recommend them militarily and technically, precisely because most of the big uncertainties surrounding their performance have been resolved. Most have been in military inventories for years. Their military role is well understood, probably as a result of real combat experience. Logistics and training support

FIGURE 4-2. *Technology Advance in Jet Aircraft over Time*

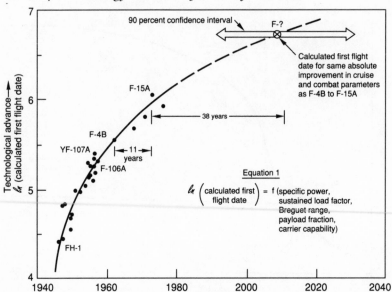

SOURCE: William L. Stanley and Michael D. Miller, *Measuring Technological Change in Jet Fighter Aircraft*, R-2249-AF (Santa Monica, Calif.: Rand Corporation, 1979), p. 46, fig. 11. Equation 1 uses "parameters such as specific power, sustained load factor, Breguet range, and payload fraction to measure technology. The equation form describes the rate at which technology has advanced from the 1940s to the present." For information about equation 1, see p. v.

have probably been in place for some time. Organizations that use the technologies have become familiar with them. Further development, if slow and expensive, is nonetheless predictable.

Yet clearly the continued pursuit of mature technologies, to the relative exclusion of all else, is a sure ticket to technological parity with one's adversaries. Sooner or later the Soviet Union, too, will emerge on the flat of the S-curve, at which point neither sizable investments in R&D nor a frantic effort to rush new inventions from laboratory to field units is likely to buy much of a technological advantage. For the leader—in this case the United States—leading too long by investing heavily in mature technologies can be a senseless waste of money.

The nation that wishes to preserve its technological advantage must move constantly onward to new growth technologies. These can stand alone or be integrated into a larger system otherwise composed of mature technologies. For example, electronics and laser technologies have been added to the tank. If the problem with mature technologies is knowing when to stop, the problem with growth technologies is knowing which one to choose. Given the enormous uncertainties that surround potential cost and performance of a new and untried technology, it is easy to mistake rapid early progress in a particular technology for evidence of great potential. In reality, the potential may belong to another technology that is off to a slower start. This is why early students of R&D called for parallel development projects.

Identifying the right technology is only part of the problem of growth technologies. The second problem is knowing when to buy. The costs of modernization can be great and not just financial in nature. Of course that may not always be the case. For example, a new digital fuel pump for a jet engine may be cheap (at least compared with the cost of the engine), barely noticeable in the logistics system, and undemanding on training or maintenance routines, since the device is merely replaced when it fails. At the other extreme, however, are important systems or components whose purchase may easily cost billions or tens of billions of dollars, and whose introduction to the force sets in motion a series of ripples as operators, maintenance crews, and logistics pipelines accommodate something new and different. Then modernization takes a temporary, but potentially great, toll on unit readiness and effectiveness, as well as on procurement budgets.

When that happens, modernizing once in a particular sector of the force posture is likely to be good grounds for not modernizing again, at least soon. Thus it is usually unwise to purchase a new technology while it is still in its early stages of growth, since the device or system thus purchased might very likely be obsolete when fielded yet too expensive and widely deployed to replace immediately. At best, the nation would be stuck with an obsolete piece of equipment. It may also have fielded a flashy new device that lacks reliability or military usefulness. At worst, however, buying too soon—even if the basic technological choice is correct—will leave the nation's adversary with the perfect opportunity to move ahead technologically by jumping to a higher point on the S-curve. To add insult to injury, the adversary may even capitalize on development work done in the United States in making its modernization choice. Such is the advantage enjoyed by those who are second in the technology race. The leader in the technology race would be wise to wait until the technology has developed to the upper knee of the S-curve where most of its potential can be realized in the deployed system, and where at best the leader's adversary can achieve parity, not superiority, in the technology race.

Much depends, of course, on the slope of the S-curve. The maturation of the engine and airframe combination illustrated by Stanley and Miller, for example, was sufficiently slow that waiting to reach the knee of the S-curve would have left U.S. forces decidedly behind the Soviets. In these cases, it makes sense to buy at intervals along the S-curve, hoping always to make the last serious purchase at the knee of the curve. Conversely, for truly fast-moving technologies, it makes sense to prototype and test devices until it is reasonably clear where the knee of the curve is located. Then modernization can commence. Obviously, there is always a basic need to generate enough information to have a reasonable sense of the shape of the S-curve before deciding to modernize.

These examples cast a different light on the modernization problem than that captured in the notion that the nation does best by moving faster. A nation that possesses the best technology and the best scientists need not for those reasons alone field the most advanced or effective weapons. Moreover, the key issue is not how speedily the nation rushes new devices to the field, but rather the validity of choices about which technologies to push and at what rate. And because rushing restricts the information on which valid choices are based, the nation that rushes risks frittering away its technology lead in an uninformed dash to preserve it. Case studies suggest that, on the margins, that is precisely what the United States has done.

The Pursuit of Immaturity

The established pattern of weapons development—early closure on a single option followed by a rush through development to production before much technical and virtually any operational testing has been completed—practically guarantees an occasional bad choice. The prevalence of optimism early in the development cycle only raises the chances of its happening.

These kinds of errors are especially evident in electronics, where innovative new technologies have multiplied during the past two decades. On the one hand, the microelectronics revolution has opened a promising new realm of precision-guided weaponry. Pressure to move these devices quickly to the field can be intense. On the other hand, technological and operational uncertainties run high, making it essential to test thoroughly before production, not simply to fly before you buy, but to try—operationally—before you buy. Failure to do so can produce expensive but largely useless hardware.

TV-MAVERICK. The initial Maverick missile, the so-called electro-optical (EO), or TV-Maverick, illustrates the point. Developed between 1966 and 1970, this antitank missile, designed to be delivered from a relatively fast-flying jet aircraft, mounts a TV camera in its nose, which feeds pictures to a small television screen in the aircraft's cockpit. Once the pilot pinpoints a target, the missile locks on to that particular picture and homes in on the target with no further commands from the pilot. In theory, EO-Maverick should make an enormous contribution to the ground battle in Europe, where massive numbers of Soviet tanks pose the principal ground threat. Precisely for this reason there was an interest in fielding the new missile as quickly as possible.

Nothing in the missile's development cautioned against rapid deployment. Technical development was completed on time, and there was development money left over with which the program manager ran additional technical tests. Production began on schedule, and production rates quickly rose to an economically acceptable level. Maverick became one of the few success stories to come out of Robert S. McNamara's "total package procurement" era.[6]

The same cannot be said for the missile's operational history, however. EO-Maverick can spot dark spots against light backgrounds but has trouble separating camouflaged tanks from surrounding trees and jungle. Put into operational service during the 1972 Easter Offensive in Vietnam, the missile performed rather poorly.[7] Equally important, the missile demands an enormous amount of the pilot's attention and forces him to fly dangerously close to his intended target. Such attention may be possible in set-piece tests but probably not in the heat of battle. Indeed, if the battle is unfolding in Europe and involves large Soviet tank formations, rolling antiaircraft systems like the ZSU-23/4 radar-directed gun system are likely to discourage U.S. pilots from using Maverick at all.

Systems analysts and some pilots have called Maverick a waste. Even an under secretary of defense for research and engineering has admitted publicly that for the EO-Maverick, at least, "R&D has failed."[8] And the Air Force implied as much when it stopped production of EO-Maverick in 1976 and moved on to the newer version, the imaging infra-red (I²R) Maverick. By that time, however, the service had purchased some 20,000 EO-Mavericks at a cost of more than $1 billion (1985 dollars).

Interviewed in 1985, former Director of Defense Research and Engineering Richard DeLauer noted in passing that "the Maverick air-to-ground missile is coming along pretty well."[9] In some sense he was right. The newer versions of the Maverick, both laser-guided and I²R models, may have more operational utility than EO-Maverick, although I²R Maverick too has its critics.[10] Arguably the Air Force learned something from developing EO-Maverick. Yet it seems clear that learning is all the service should have done. EO-Maverick should have remained a data point in the ongoing effort to determine the growth potential and military utility of new and apparently promising technologies. In buying too soon the Air Force made this learning process very expensive.

BUILT-IN TEST EQUIPMENT. Given the services' preferences for haste in fielding new technologies, it should not be surprising that Maverick is not an isolated case. A case with more far-reaching implications concerns the extensive use of built-in test equipment or BITE in a whole series of operational aircraft starting in the early 1970s. Here again, technology's promise was hard to resist. Here was the chance to deploy sophisticated electronic equipment that would diagnose its own problems. Operators and line maintenance crews would have no need for degrees in electronics. Instead they would pull and replace components, normally designed as easily removable black boxes, as the on-board BITE dictated. Using intermediate-level test sets, maintenance crews would then isolate the errant circuit board in the malfunctioning black box, replacing it with a new one from inventory and shipping the flawed board back to higher maintenance levels for repair by skilled experts. BITE thus promised to eliminate the maintenance burden posed by the proliferation of increasingly sophisticated electronics gear to the line units.

The rise of BITE paralleled the rise of sophisticated electronics in aircraft, starting with the F-111's Mark II avionics suite in the mid-1960s. The rise in BITE's effectiveness, however, has come much more slowly. As recently as 1981 the Defense Science Board Summer Study Panel concluded that, so far as BITE was concerned, "What has been achieved so far has been grossly inadequate. The [intermediate level] systems designed to detect faults and help the maintainer to isolate and replace the failed unit have become very complicated . . . and, therefore, represent a large acquisition, maintenance and operational burden."[11]

In fact, the Defense Science Board was referring to only part of the BITE problem.[12] Given the difficulties inherent in predicting how new equipment will be used, it has been difficult to make BITE work well initially. At the least BITE must be reprogrammed in light of operational experience with the new system of which it is a part. As Gen. William E. DePuy relates, however, "faults arrive in pesky combinations which defeat the diagnostic algorithms [imbedded in BITE]." DePuy also noted that, when BITE failed, "trouble shooting by the repairman is required." But this necessity means that field maintenance technicians must be trained in the theory of the components they must repair—precisely what BITE was meant to obviate. DePuy says, "A return to 'theory based' maintenance training would be shockingly expensive and probably would move the AFQT [personnel quality] prerequisites up another 10 to 15 points."[13]

Whether it is effective or not, reprogramming cannot solve two of BITE's seemingly generic problems. On the one hand, it has proved inordinately difficult to build in test equipment sensitive enough to pick up equipment failures, but not so sensitive as to pick up spurious signals as evidence of failure and hence provide operators and maintenance technicians with repeated false alarms. So-called no-fault removal rates have remained high in operational units, as maintenance crews spend part of their time pulling black boxes that do not, on further testing, show evidence of flaws or damage.[14]

On the other hand, BITE can analyze components but not interfaces—the plugs and sockets that hook together the innumerable components of an aircraft avionics suite (there are forty-five black boxes in each F-15). Indeed BITE components are hooked together in this fashion, leading to what one engineer called a catch-22 situation. "The more comprehensive, accurate and sophisticated he [the avionics designer] makes BIT[E], the more he reduces reliability, and hence availability, due to the sheer number of added components."[15]

The unreliability of BITE and the signals it sends to operators and maintenance crews exacerbate the problems with BITE's intermediate-level computer diagnostic equipment. This equipment is extremely complex, breaks down frequently, and requires highly skilled operators.[16] Rather than solve a maintenance problem, BITE seems to have compounded it.

Solving these problems is expensive. To compensate for the unexpectedly long repair times and time wasted on false alarms, the services must buy more spare parts. If parts are unaffordable, they may be forced to adopt a high-risk spare parts stockage program that may leave units unready and ineffective should war come. Units supported in this way are likely to cannibalize some weapons to keep others operating, a practice "which can in turn increase the failure rate, as the black boxes that are still working fly more sorties and experience a correspondingly greater breakdown rate."[17] Finally, lacking sufficient spare parts at the front line, units may be forced to depend on depots that may not be available in the early days of combat.

Optimistic reports of BITE's performance in the F-18, first fielded in the early 1980s, suggest that problems with BITE may be abating. If true, BITE may be maturing to the point at which it will deliver on its promise. But this possibility hardly excuses choices made starting nearly two decades ago that implanted a very immature technology in a broad and critical swath of the nation's force posture. Those choices have had far-reaching negative effects on readiness, training, the cost of maintenance, and even the inherent resilience of the overall maintenance system. In buying too soon, the services have been forced to rely on a technology whose field performance has been "nothing short of a disaster."[18]

The Pursuit of Parity

As technologies mature, performance improvements come more slowly and at higher cost. Thus the decision to modernize comes less frequently. For technologies fully onto the upper flat of the S-curve, modernization decisions will look more like replacement decisions. Clearly, the acquisition process has to distinguish mature from newer technologies and handle the mature ones in a much more judicious manner.

At first glance, this would not seem difficult. Mature technologies have probably been in service inventories for some time, leaving them fairly well understood. Rand analysts can document an evolving S-curve for them, whereas the lack of data prevents them from doing so for newer technologies. Equally important, because improvements are likely to be less momentous in mature areas, the sense of urgency is likely to be less pronounced. Hence the need to rush blindly forward should be relatively absent from the development of mature technologies.

Yet various pressures make the U.S. acquisition process less sensitive than it should be to the needs of mature technologies. In part, pressure arises from the well-documented tendency among military organizations to seek progressive improvements in areas of performance traditionally held important.[19] Such pressure is likely to fall especially hard on mature technologies, precisely because they have been in military inventories for some time. By itself such pressure can push the demand for more performance to or beyond technological feasibility. The avowed preference of the U.S. military for development of weapon systems sustains this tendency, since it encourages the services to treat all technologies in a particular system alike. Finally, early optimism about cost and risks encourages the services to assume that the flat of the S-curve lies farther away than it really does. All three sources of pressure encourage the services to lead too long, with consequences ranging from opportunity costs to operational problems in systems pushed beyond reasonable design limits.

The Air Force's F-100 jet engine, developed between 1970 and 1973 as part of the F-15 (or F-X, as it was initially called) project, is an example. As the Rand Corporation's William L. Stanley and Michael D. Miller suggest (see figure 4-2), jet airframe-engine performance is approaching the flat of its performance curve. The F-15A lies above the performance-time curve, suggesting that this engine-airframe combination was slightly ahead of its time. The F-X project's ambitiousness lay almost entirely with the F-100 engine. Indeed, after its unhappy experience with the F-111's variable-sweep-wing configuration, the service reduced airframe development risks by sticking with a fixed-wing configuration. With the engine, by contrast, the Air Force sought an engine thrust-to-weight ratio of eight to one, when engines with ratios of four to one were "the best that could be built."[20] In practical terms, the service was looking for an engine "rugged enough to generate 3,000 pounds more thrust than its predecessor while at the same time cutting the weight of the engine by 1,000 pounds."[21]

Those formulating the F-X requirement knew that the engine was the most ambitious and risky part of the project. Developmental risks were muted, however, by the optimism of the moment. The Development Concept Paper (DCP) on which the F-15 program was started deemed the engine development risk acceptable, partly because the riskier engine technologies had been "proved in principle by demonstrator engines developed under . . . [other Air Force] programs."[22]

When the engine failed its first military qualification test (MQT) early in 1973, it became clear that the required engine performance might surpass what was then feasible. But by that time the rest of the F-15 project was moving smoothly toward a November 1974 production deadline, creating enormous pressure to hold the engine's producer, Pratt and Whitney, to its contractual production obligations. The Air Force program office did so, but partly by derating a key part of the engine's MQT.[23] Testing problems continued to surface, but by October 1973 the F-100 finally passed its MQT and was certified as ready for production.

The engine's problems did not suddenly disappear with production, however. Rather, durability problems plagued the F-100 throughout the rest of the decade. To some extent, they stemmed from unforeseen rigors through which pilots put the F-15. But the engine's problems were also related to the fact that the Air Force " *misestimated* the state of the art and [was] . . . forced to continue to struggle for a level of performance not yet well within the realm of practicality."[24]

The engine's development thus continued in the form of a major component improvement program, or CIP. The Air Force poured nearly $700 million into the program between 1974 and 1985.[25] CIPs are not unusual. As J. R. Nelson asserted on the basis of his study of the life-cycle costs of jet engines, "the development of engines beyond the MQT . . . is often more costly than the entire development program up to the MQT."[26] Normally, however, the purpose of continued development is, as improvement implies, to improve the engine beyond original requirements. For the F-100, by contrast, the CIP sought merely to bring the engine up to standards specified in the original development contract.

Meanwhile the Tactical Air Force was forced to contend with unexpected and serious reliability and performance problems in fielded F-15s. Pilots were impressed with the F-100's exceptional power and responsiveness. But as the engine endured more operational use, it became more famous for its tendency to stall, especially when its afterburner was in use. While Pratt and Whitney struggled to find a design solution to this problem, the Air Force had to restrict the F-15's use to reduce the chance of a stall. As Robert W. Drewes said, "Inadequate technology was forcing pilots to fly the engine rather than the aircraft."[27] Some problems were mitigated because the F-15 was a two-engine aircraft. By the same token, however, fear for the F-100's performance heightened as the decade progressed and the Air Force began to accept the F-16, powered by only one F-100, into its inventory.

Temperatures in the engine ran exceptionally high, especially during stalls, when the flow of cooling air through the engine diminished sharply. Perhaps more important, temperatures fluctuated sharply, as pilots put their aircraft through maneuvers not even possible in previous aircraft. Thus the F-100 experienced an unexpectedly high rate of component failure, especially turbine failure, which is often "a euphemism for engine blowup."[28] The maintenance burden on line units was much higher than predicted, and operating costs rose accordingly.

Most of these performance and reliability problems were solved by the mid-1980s, which Air Force officials attributed to their service's successful effort to induce competition into the high-performance fighter engine business by bringing General Electric's F-110 into competition with Pratt's F-100 in the "great engine war." But it is difficult to distinguish the effects of competition from those produced by the F-100 CIP. Arguably the original F-X engine requirement placed the F-100 several years ahead of its time. The derated MQT requirement imposed in 1973 may have been closer to performance that was technologically feasible at that time. By 1985 the engine's technology maturation curve had in this sense caught up with it—but only after a painful, expensive, and often dangerous decade.

The F-100 is only a single case. Yet it is the product of patterns of behavior common across the breadth of the acquisition process. Moreover, most of the rapidly changing technologies the services explored so aggressively in the 1950s are today like the jet engine—still at the core of the nation's force posture but more mature. If the services continue to demand even higher levels of performance from such technologies while rushing new designs to the field, the Air Force's experience with the F-100 is likely to be replicated across the force posture.

Modernization and the Soviet Threat

All of us are consumers of sophisticated devices—stereo components, home computers, and the like. All of us make modernization decisions, and most of us probably take the considerations just outlined into account, implicitly if not explicitly, when we do so. We recognize that those who rushed to buy the first hand-held calculators saw technological advances quickly push prices and size down, while performance improved. Many interested in buying a personal computer have been engaged in a seemingly endless waiting game, as prices fall while performance increases. As private consumers, we are probably more guilty of waiting too long than of buying too soon.

Yet the nation countenances the opposite behavior from the Pentagon, presumably because the threat demands nothing but the best, and the quicker the better. Yet for defense technologies no less than for commercial devices, getting something fast and getting the best (that is, the most cost-effective) are not the same things. The real question is whether the United States can afford to wait. The answer depends on how likely war is.

If the United States were convinced that war with the Soviet Union were certain to occur in, say, a year, the nation might forgo any further modernization, freeze units in their current configurations, train the force to its highest quality, and stockpile spare parts and munitions as quickly as possible. If war were certain to occur in, say, five years, the United States would probably find the best of the new technologies, deploy them to the force over the next three years, then spend the next two years training the force on the new equipment while, again, the nation purchased munitions and spare parts to operate the force in combat. Finally, if the United States were certain that war would occur in ten or fifteen years, it would make sense to forgo modernization while the R&D community probed the technological horizon for several years. At some point the best of the available new technologies would be imparted to the force in time to allow for training and the purchase of spare parts and munitions. In short, when war is likely to occur has a direct effect on our approach to modernization.

No one can predict the future, however. Instead, the government holds that war with the Soviet Union is always possible (and could come with little warning) but rarely imminent. There are pressures in this situation to rush new systems into production as if war were "just over the horizon"—that is, likely to occur just after the particular purchase at issue is completed. Fear of tactical surprise understandably compounds these pressures. But uncertainty at the strategic level makes it not only wise but essential to modernize systematically and judiciously, neither hurrying the process nor passing up the chance to modernize when information confirms the wisdom of so doing. In particular, buying too soon on the premise that the threat demands it is likely to be costly and hence counterproductive to the long-term defense effort.

THE COSTS OF CONCURRENCY

Rushing through development and into production is encouraged by the assumption that most design uncertainties are resolved early in development. As valid as that assumption may be in general, it is striking how much serious and costly design work remains to be done in the full-scale engineering phase of development, where "unexpected development difficulties" accounted for 60 percent of cost growth during the 1970s.[29] Part of the problem stems from changes in requirements that impose new design uncertainties late in development. Nonetheless, designers and project managers cannot predict the concerns that may be raised as technology evolves.

The problem is more pronounced than ever in software, fast becoming "the pacing technology of advanced fighters."[30] The Defense Department's software costs totaled $4 billion in 1980, roughly $10 billion in 1986, and are expected to reach $30 billion by the early 1990s.[31] Software defects often surface only under operational conditions. Software test and validation thus almost always take longer than expected. The original test program for the F-16C's APG-68 radar system, for example, called for 144 test flights over twelve months, beginning in June 1983. As of April 1986, over 500 sorties had been flown in support of the radar's development, yet only 35 percent of its formal requirements had been tested.[32] Despite such experiences, the services often start software projects after the associated hardware project has already begun. The inevitable rush to finish development has helped produce a crisis in an area that is of growing importance to national security. Resolving this crisis will require a more judicious approach to production, not just slowing the move to production but slowing production until the software has matured.[33]

The usefulness of this approach is not confined to software, because the problem extends well beyond the reluctance with which individual technologies yield information. Important parts of virtually any design process unfold late in development, even after production begins. Some of these have to do with technology and design, but some stem from the demands operators place on new weapons. Equally important, emasculating the test process at the end of development misshapes the incentives designers face, hence the designs they produce, at its beginning. In both senses the costs of production concurrency are higher than defense officials admit.

Short-Circuiting System Integration

Responding to public criticism of the B-1Bs electronic countermeasures (ECM) suite, the commander of the Aeronautical Systems Division of the Air Force Systems Command admitted that "some of the problems with the ECM system occurred because its components (. . . 118 black boxes) had been tested in isolation, but not together as a system before delivery of the first B-1Bs to Dyess AFB [air force base], TX, in the summer of 1985."[34] Yet the assumption that components tested in isolation would not interact in new and unpredictable ways belies a wealth of historical evidence to the contrary. Indeed, on the basis of case studies of weapons developed principally in the 1950s, the Rand Corporation's Robert Perry argued that, in effect, the latter phases of the design process may be the most challenging:

> It is not the laboratory-scale demonstration of some technical capability that proves difficult, but the eventual transition to operational utility. Science is not the obstacle, it is engineering. *All* of the devices [that caused problems in the projects he had studied] . . . demonstrated nominal feasibility; every major feature of Navaho and Snark worked modestly well—in isolation.[35]

One of the best examples of this phenomenon is the engine-inlet compatibility problem that haunted early production models of the F-111. To function, a jet engine needs high-quality air—air of predictable pressure, relatively free of distortion and turbulence.[36] The quality of air running through the engine depends on what happens before it enters and as it is leaving. This flow depends on the shape of the fuselage, inlet, and exhaust nozzles, and of course the aircraft's flight profile. Bad blending of these components can produce performance failures in an engine that otherwise performs exceptionally well in tests. Such was true of the F-111—the first 141 models suffered from stall problems at certain angles of attack.

Electronic components have a different kind of problem. As with any electronic device, each component gives off electromagnetic emissions. Placed in close proximity, electronic components often interfere with one another. Interference problems are more common as the services demand smaller but more powerful electronic components. For the B-1B, "interference between the ECM system's transmitters and receivers" has caused the Air Force to request more than $400 million in additional development funding for fiscal 1988 and 1989. The decision to produce the system seems to have come before development was nearly completed.[37]

Integration problems are not confined solely to the latest and most complex systems. The M-16 rifle surely lies at the opposite end of the scale from the F-111 or the B-1B's ECM suite in system complexity, yet, in overall performance, this rifle experienced system integration problems almost as serious. What were seen as inconsequential changes in the powder used in the rifle's .22 caliber cartridge changed the pressure distribution in the rifle's barrel as the bullet accelerated toward the muzzle. Because the M-16, like all semiautomatic and automatic rifles, taps some of this pressure to energize its reloading mechanism, the rate at which the rifle reloaded—the cyclic rate—changed with the powder. This produced a series of small but nontrivial malfunctions that contributed to the rifle's serious jamming problems when it was first introduced in Vietnam. Simple design changes eventually solved the problem, but not before soldiers died when their newly delivered weapons failed them.[38]

When the U.S. Army approved the ill-fated Sergeant York division air defense gun (DIVAD) in 1977, to cite another example, it was widely seen as a uniquely low-risk venture. It meant the integration of reasonably well-understood components—a chassis from the old M-48 tank, one of two gun systems already in production in Europe, and, for guidance, a derivative of the APG-66 then being installed in early production F-16 fighter aircraft. Early development work by General Dynamics and Ford Aerospace, which were competing for production, seemed to confirm this risk assessment. In September 1980, the director of defense research and engineering told members of the House Armed Services Committee that there were no technical reasons for slowing DIVAD's progress. Maj. Gen. James P. Maloney of the Army's R&D staff told the same group that the gun "has done very well in testing, and is moving with great speed through the development cycle."[39] A shoot-off was completed in November of that year, and in May 1981 the service awarded Ford Aerospace a preproduction contract for further development, with check-tests to be held late that year. Pending the results of those tests, the Army hoped to award a production contract by mid-1982.

Program realities were less encouraging than progress toward program milestones suggested, however. The shoot-off was delayed for two months "because the prototypes which arrived at the Fort Bliss testing range were too technically immature."[40] Interviews with a member of the Army's DIVAD program office suggest that the delay should probably have been longer given the developmental needs of both prototypes.[41] The check-tests, run from November 1981 through January 1982, surfaced little improvement in the Ford Aerospace design. And so-called RAM-D (reliability, availability, maintainability, and durability) tests had to be delayed from February 1982 to May of that year to allow the firm more time to perfect its design. The central, though by no means the only, design problem seems to have stemmed from durability and operational difficulties connected with placing an aircraft radar in a ground vehicle.

By mid-1982 DIVAD stood amid a gathering storm that in the end saw the project canceled. The DIVAD debate was affected partly by the argument that missiles are more appropriate than guns for air defense. But behind this conceptual debate lay continuing technical problems in the DIVAD prototypes. Nevertheless, the Army secured a production decision on grounds that most design deficiencies were on the verge of correction.[42] So confident was the service of this assessment, apparently, that it signed a fixed-price contract forcing Ford Aerospace to absorb the costs of correcting design flaws—so long as the project remained on schedule. The contract thus raised the cost of dealing with design problems, or, conversely, created disincentives to slowing the program.[43] But the service soon found that "workmanship and quality control problems" prevented it from accepting any production DIVADs.[44]

The storm now widened, as congressional resistance to further funding helped precipitate the creation of a DIVAD review panel in the Defense Department. The review panel insisted on more testing, which surfaced operational flaws that the Army attributed to the short notice given it before running the tests. There was some truth to the Army's concerns. At this point DIVAD was under attack, fairly and perhaps not so fairly, from a number of quarters, and as much by missile advocates as by those unhappy with the system's design maturity.[45] Yet the Army could not escape its test data. When the Army Matériel Systems Analysis Activity evaluated the DIVAD's initial production tests, run from December 1984 through May 1985, it found that the vehicle failed 22 of 163 contract specifications, with 7 of the 22 serious failures in the gun's overall operational effectiveness. Later that year the service's Operational Testing and Evaluation Agency concluded that the gun could perform its mission but could not meet reliability and maintainability requirements. Among other things, the gun's availability during tests was 33 percent, against a required 90 percent.[46] Meanwhile the OSD's operational test agency found that DIVAD required too much maintenance to be operationally suitable. Principally on the basis of these tests, the secretary of defense canceled DIVAD on August 27, 1985.

It remains uncertain whether DIVAD could have been made to work, whether missiles are more appropriate than guns for division air defense, or whether a division's air space can be defended without the sophisticated technology military reformers criticize so frequently. The only issue in question here is the maturity of a design that was hurried along partly because DIVAD's components had been developed elsewhere and risks seemed low. Perhaps in relation to a fighter aircraft's development, DIVAD's risks were low. Evidently even fairly simple designs are not easily integrated.

Forgetting about Force Integration

At the end of the design process another kind of integration process unfolds that affects weapons design, this one involving the new weapon and the organizations that will use it. Design is guided by assumptions about how a new system will be used. These assumptions are normally made on the basis of experience with similar systems already in the field, even though new systems and the organizations that receive them have a disturbing habit of confounding the best planners by combining in new and unpredictable ways. This occurrence is probably less true for systems that are marginal improvements over older systems, since these are likely to be used in only marginally different, and hence fairly predictable, ways. But to the extent that the acquisition process moves truly important technological advances to the field—and that is its mission—there will be uncertainties about a new system's use as well as its design, and as its use is clarified, its design may have to be modified. The more the acquisition process fulfills its mission, the more likely there is to be an interesting, perhaps exciting, but largely unpredictable adaptation between the new weapon and the force it joins.

Two examples illustrate the problem. Despite its new laminated armor and turbine engine, the U.S. Army's M-1 tank, produced beginning in 1981, might be considered a marginal improvement over successors that have filled the Army's inventory for decades. The new tank's smooth ride and turret stabilization system, however, opened up new operational possibilities that led to unexpected problems with reliability and spare parts demand. As an Army witness explained in 1982 to a Senate Armed Services Committee upset with reports of the tank's lack of reliability,

> The gunners found they could even gage the target before the [M-1] vehicle came to a stop, so the driver would shift into reverse with the engine revved up and the vehicle still moving forward, possibly 5 or 6 miles an hour. This we hadn't done with other tanks because we hadn't the capability. . . . We found the transmissions couldn't stand the stress caused by shifting while moving.[47]

The Army solved the problem by fitting the tank with a device that prevented drivers from shifting at speeds above three miles an hour. Meanwhile, the service continued to seek improvements in the M-1's otherwise troubled power train. The costs of maintaining the new tank, and by inference the vehicle's spare parts requirements, proved much higher than predicted—in part, but only in part, because no one could predict how it would be used.

Much more serious consequences stemmed from Pratt and Whitney's F-100 engine. While this engine's reliability problems stemmed from multiple sources, one, ironically, was the impressive nimbleness of the F-100 when it worked. Propelled for the first time by an engine that responded rapidly to wide shifts in throttle, pilots spent "little time . . . at full power or very high Mach number. Much more often, speed stayed below Mach 1.5 with power settings changed often and abruptly as pilots trained to outmaneuver the foe." So-called thermal cycles—throttle movement from idle to maximum power and back down again—"accumulated at far more rapid rates than planned," placing stresses on the engine unanticipated by Pratt designers or Air Force planners.[48] Indeed the original requirement for the engine had little to say about thermal cycles, and the engine's qualification tests involved no cycling.

Although the Air Force had successfully locked Pratt and Whitney into a contract that obligated the firm to correct design flaws in its engine, the unpredicted uses to which the engine was put allowed Pratt to escape contractual discipline. "Pratt lawyers contended [that] Pratt had no contractual obligation to eliminate stall stagnations without receiving more money since the F-100 had been designed and qualified to the Air Force specifications. After all, the Air Force had accepted the design for production. If the Air Force later wanted to add requirements to change the performance, that change was an additional tasking, not a part of the original contract, and subject therefore to additional charge."[49] The component improvement program, which amounted to federal funding for further engine work, was in effect the answer to this complaint.

As is always true of new weapons technologies, both the M-1 tank and the F-100 engine invoked changes in the tactical and support doctrine of their respective services. Although such disruptions may eventually produce more effective fighting forces, in the short term they usually lower force readiness. This problem, partly a result of the complexity of the established force, has grown more complicated as technological advance has produced more complex military organizations. Rushing a new tactical aircraft to the field may have made sense in the 1950s, since the forces were little more than the aircraft, and support elements and doctrine were as often as not defined around the aircraft's capabilities. By contrast, today's doctrine is well established and calls for an interactive approach to air warfare, including tactical aircraft, airborne and ground warning systems, air-to-air missiles, and an elaborate support structure. The force integration problem is commensurately more difficult and demands more time, care, and patience than ever before.

The challenge posed by force integration is much like the software challenge. Both problems highlight the limits of what can be discovered in the laboratory, hence the importance of getting new weapons to the field for operational use. Yet rushing a new weapon into high-rate production not only forecloses design options but unnecessarily disrupts established operating routines. In short, it is important to get some weapons to the field but not many. Better operational testing in advance of high-rate production is the best way to meet this challenge.

The Rush to Reduced Effectiveness

Prevailing service practice amounts to fielding new systems early and then allowing the design process to catch up by the use of ECPs and retrofits. Unquestionably this approach can produce impressive results. For the M-1 tank, for example, the Defense Science Board noted that after early tests surfaced poor reliability, a concentrated reliability improvements program led to great success, with the M-1 demonstrating 278 to 326 mean miles between failures.[50] The F-100 engine also achieved acceptable reliability, though over a much longer period. Here, however, the engine's problems stemmed not simply from a lack of design maturity at the time production began but also from the ambitiousness of the Air Force requirement driving the engine's basic design. As a rule, retrofits can produce surprising improvements in reliability, although this practice often amounts to introducing new technology to simplify designs while holding performance constant.[51]

The same Defense Science Board panel that lauded reliability improvements in the M-1 tank also noted, however, that "experiencing technical failures in deployed systems is quite clearly a poor way to learn that they exist."[52] Panel members also said "the single most serious cause of unsatisfactory operational availability is the inability or failure to provide adequately for the support of deployed systems."[53] Clearly, so long as weapons are fielded prematurely the services lack the information needed to design and organize, let alone purchase, the necessary support system. It is an approach that risks yielding less, rather than more, military power.

In the face of a ready adversary, this approach makes little sense. If Soviet forces are as ready as defense officials say they are—if their forces in Eastern Europe, for example, are sufficiently well-manned and supplied to attack by surprise—then clearly the United States cannot afford to sacrifice readiness when it modernizes its forces. If, on the other hand, Soviet forces are not as ready as is often suggested, then there is no need to rush new weapons to the field. When the services urge greater production concurrency and a more rapid move into production on grounds that there is an urgent need to meet the threat, they contradict themselves.

They also forgo design improvements that could improve the long-term effectiveness of their forces. A Rand Corporation study noted recently that "we rarely know support-related performance levels (and therefore shortfalls) until well after *high-rate* production begins (by which time major design changes are essentially foreclosed)."[54] To the extent that this observation is true, important design changes may never be imparted to early models of a new system. Hence the fielded fleet is probably less effective, on average, than would otherwise have been true.

Serious performance problems in early models of the F-111, for example, led to important design changes, in particular, the reconfiguration of engine inlets to prevent stalling. The need for change was discovered so late that the appropriate changes were considered too expensive to impart to the first 141 F-111s. Nevertheless, the Air Force rushed F-111s to Vietnam, thinking their capabilities were sorely needed there. The service lost 3 of the first 6 F-111s deployed to Vietnam in the first month's action and quickly withdrew the aircraft. It did not redeploy F-111As to the Republic of Vietnam until 1972.[55] Thus in a misguided effort to obtain combat advantage in the short run, the Air Force accepted a fleet of F-111s less effective over the long run than the fleet it could have had if it had slowed production, tested more extensively, and solved the aircraft's problems before the first 141 F-111As entered the inventory.

The F-15 experienced far fewer problems in development than the F-111, despite a fairly high degree of production concurrency. Nonetheless, in modeling the program at a slower pace, Allen D. Lee found the following evidence of potential savings and long-run performance improvements. "Costs decreased about $7 million; Air Force retrofit labor decreased by 180,000 man-hours; and overall (fleet) effectiveness increased modestly (because more F-15s were outfitted with larger fuel capacity and newer electronics technology)."[56]

For the F-15, a general fear of the threat, specifically, the MiG-25 Foxbat, seems to have prodded the service into a high degree of production concurrency. Yet when F-15 production began in 1973 the United States was backing away from an aggressive military policy while it sought to engage the Soviet Union in arms control and détente. Although the quality of Soviet aircraft continued to improve, the threat of war was, if anything, lower than in the years before or since. Moreover, the Air Force had emerged from Vietnam with a very ready force that included large inventories of munitions and spare parts and a plethora of trained and experienced crews. There seems to have been no need to rush the F-15 to the field, especially when doing so sacrificed the overall capabilities of the service's F-15 fleet.

In three case studies, Allen D. Lee shows that a more judicious approach to production including "minimized concurrency, extended low-rate production, and intensified testing and use of test information" could have produced "increased design maturity, substantially reduced modification costs, and significantly increased system effectiveness."[57] In short, in habitually rushing systems into production, the services accept long- as well as short-term effectiveness problems. The extent of such problems, and of the benefits of what Lee calls a phased acquisition strategy, varies from project to project. But the rush to production varies very little. It seems to be a constant in all but a handful of programs. The result, whether one takes a short- or a long-term perspective, does not produce the kind of force the nation should want to fend off the kind of threat that is invoked to justify the rush to production.

Discouraging the Pursuit of Reliability

Extensive production concurrency can also affect weapons design in its earlier phases by relieving designers and engineers of concern for reliability and maintainability. The problem occurs because mainstream performance parameters such as speed, power, accuracy, and maneuverability are normally demonstrable in early developmental testing, but reliability cannot be demonstrated until much later, often during early phases of operational deployment. The final exam for reliability usually occurs after a new system is safely into production, hence the real final exam is the developmental test of mainstream performance. Production concurrency thus confronts designers and military project managers with powerful incentives to trade away reliability in pursuit of performance.

Reliability's second-class status does not stem from concurrency alone. Inflexibility in the requirements process, as well as the military's understandable desire for performance, is also at work. But the early visibility of performance rather than reliability achievements makes it difficult indeed for project managers to combat pressures favoring performance.

Initial optimism about cost and performance results in funding and schedule constraints as well as performance shortfalls as development proceeds. So-called management reserve funds that might be used for reliability testing and enhancement are drained away in the pursuit of performance.[58] In asking Congress to fund cost growth, program managers and service staffs imply that such contingency funds have already been spent—in an environment that encourages the pursuit of performance.

Arguably reliability can be designed back into a completed system later on, in an elaborate test-redesign-retest process that can produce impressive reliability growth in fielded systems. Such was the Army's defense of DIVAD. But reliability limits—so-called inherent reliability—are set by choices made very early in the design process.[59] Once a design is finalized, its inherent reliability is to a great extent set and with it are set supportability and life-cycle costs.[60] Unless developers worry about reliability early in the design process, they run the risk of fielding systems of inherently low reliability potential.

To make matters worse, reliability tends to vary inversely with the press for performance, especially as performance demands probe the limits of technical feasibility. Thus the effort to use "technological advances . . . to increase performance, obtain greater precision, and add functions" often comes at "substantial cost in dollars and reliability. . . ."[61] For this reason, the increasing reliability of individual electronic components has not produced a commensurate increase in the reliability of electronic systems. Note, for example, the conclusion of a U.S. Navy study of technology and reliability trends in the avionic systems of naval aircraft. "Although new technology has improved component reliability (failures per part per flight hour), it has also permitted an increase in density of functions and capabilities (numbers of parts per subsystem). This has resulted in overall decreases in system reliability and increases in maintenance manpower requirements."[62]

Reliability tends to be inversely related to design complexity.[63] Not surprisingly, those interested in fielding more reliable military equipment often speak of "simple system design as a leading principle," even if this priority means making "some sacrifice in the quantitative measure of 'efficiency' and [accepting] some restrictions in the number of functions that a new weapon . . . is supposed to perform."[64] Insofar as a "major portion of system failures occurring in operational use is due to parts failures," reliability advocates stress the need to derate parts by "reducing the electrical, mechanical, or environmental operating stresses below the maximum levels the part is capable of sustaining."[65] Such emphasis means designing below maximum levels of performance.

Evidence from programs that emphasize reliability from the beginning suggests that impressive results can be obtained without any gross sacrifice of performance. Consider the U.S. Army's Blackhawk utility transport helicopter, developed between 1972 and 1979. Burdened by the low availability and high repair cost of its large fleet of UH-1 Huey helicopters, the Army's workhorse during the Vietnam years, the Army's Aviation R&D Command designed a development program that emphasized reliability and maintainability in both items. The initial request for proposal for what was then called the Utility Tactical Transport Aircraft System, or UTTAS, listed reliability and maintainability goals hammered out on the basis of earlier tests and discussion with potential developers. More important, the program was organized to include a long series of developmental and operational tests before competitive development ended. The tests were meant to expose operational reliability and to allow competing contractors time to redesign failed components. Two years elapsed between first flight of the UTTAS prototypes and source selection, when 1,400 hours of flight tests, 255 of these operational testing on the prototypes of each contractor, were completed.[66] As a result, the UH-60 has attained "the highest readiness rates that we [the Army] have ever experienced with a helicopter in peacetime, and importantly, the supply and maintenance down-times are much lower than we have ever experienced."[67]

Two radars built by General Electric for the F-4 and F-111 aircraft, the APQ-120 and APQ-113/114, also illustrate the balance of reliability with performance. Both radars cost about the same to develop at about the same point in the 1960s. Unit costs were roughly equal. But the APQ-113/114 series was thirty-five times more reliable than the APQ-120, and different models in the series cost from 60 percent to 80 percent less to operate. The APQ-113/114's demonstrably better reliability can be attributed equally to more rigorous quality control among components, early redesign of these radars that lowered their parts count by some 40 percent (by using higher-technology integrated circuits), and an extensive reliability test program that surfaced reliability problems early and permitted their solution before production began in earnest.[68]

That General Electric developed radars of roughly equal performance but markedly different reliabilities raises questions about the relationship between these two system attributes. It may be that the relationship between reliability and performance is tightly inverse only at peak levels of performance. In substituting new technology (microcircuits) to improve the APQ-113/114's reliability, after all, General Electric technicians held performance constant while technology advanced, in effect trading potential performance for reliability and detuning components. Arguably the Blackhawk, too, was not pushing the limits of obtainable performance. The Army's RFP specified performance bands within which developers could sacrifice performance to achieve better reliability and maintainability.

Yet if these systems were not at the cutting edge of technology, neither were they far from it. The Blackhawk's T-700 engine, for example, offered twice the thrust-to-weight ratio of the older Huey engine, roughly the multiple that separated Pratt and Whitney's F-100 from its predecessors.[69] And the APQ-113 was "a new design contracted as part of the initial F-111 procurement," suggesting that it, like the rest of that aircraft, was a high-performance device.[70] Both cases suggest that balancing reliability and performance in development need not mean a drastic sacrifice of performance. Yet these cases are rare anomalies in an acquisition process that normally refuses to trade performance for anything and that uses new technology not to improve reliability but to push for more performance.

MODERNIZING FOR MILITARY EFFECTIVENESS

The force integration problem highlights the difficulties of predicting how new weapons will be asked to perform even by friendly forces in peacetime. But weapons must work in combat, and the addition of an enemy and specific operational conditions multiplies the chances for bad predictions enormously. Military history is littered with examples of such errors, which should make military officials cautious about asserting that a certain weapon is precisely what they need to meet the threat, especially if the weapon in question is just emerging from development and has yet to undergo operational tests. Useful weapons rarely come straight from the drawing board. More often they emerge from an extended adaptation process that draws on combat experience as well as operational testing. Consequently, despite the enthusiastic rush to produce new systems, some of the nation's most effective weapons are quite old.

The Potential of Product Improvements

The Sidewinder, or AIM-9, heat-seeking air-to-air missile is an example. Sidewinder is today the darling of nearly all parties to the acquisition debate. Military reformers point to it as a prime example of "brilliantly simplifying" technology—cheap, reliable, and effective. No doubt reformers also like Sidewinder because its development was resisted by the established service procurement bureaucracies. Meanwhile Air Force officials speak of Sidewinder's capabilities as "revolutionary."[71] The missile's record is impressive. Of the approximately 335 Arab aircraft downed by Israeli fighters in the 1973 Arab-Israeli war, nearly 200 (60 percent) fell to Sidewinders or the Shafrir, Israel's heat-seeking air-to-air missile, with both missiles achieving a success rate of roughly 56 percent. In the skies over Lebanon in 1982, most of the 85 Syrian aircraft downed by Israeli pilots were hit, again, by Sidewinder or Shafrir. And British pilots used Sidewinders to hit 24 of the 32 Argentine aircraft downed during the Falklands/Malvinas Islands conflict of 1982.[72]

Less noticed amidst the praise Sidewinder justifiably garners is how long it took the missile to reach its position of dominance among air-to-air missiles. The combat successes just noted occurred in the 1970s and 1980s, yet the Sidewinder was initially conceived in 1949, early designs were available for testing in 1952, and production models were deployed on Navy fighters in 1956. Early Sidewinders were effective. Chinese Nationalist pilots used the initial production Sidewinder to down four Communist Chinese MiGs during the Formosa crisis of 1958, giving the missile a success on its first introduction to combat.[73] But the missile was never as effective as the services expected, and in 1965 its initial performance against North Vietnamese MiGs was rather disappointing.

In part, the disappointment sprang from technical limitations in the missile's design. The first operational Sidewinder (the Sidewinder IA, redesignated the AIM-9B after 1962) was equipped with a seeker that, "uncooled and operating at relatively short wavelengths, was sensitive to sunlight, cloud edges, and the horizon" and thus had great difficulty separating all but the hottest targets from background clutter. Its motor burned a mere two seconds, giving the missile a range of about 2.6 nautical miles at high altitude. The motor also smoked a great deal, signaling its approach to enemy pilots.[74] Finally, the missile's airframe was capable of a limited turn radius. These limitations made early Sidewinders useful only in a stern chase of a nonmaneuvering aircraft.

Early Sidewinders failed to live up to expectations for doctrinal as well as technical reasons. Neither the Air Force nor the Navy had dogfighting air-to-air combat in mind in the early 1950s. Rather, doctrine focused on strategic bombing and defense against it. At the tactical level, the central problems were seen to be interdiction (using nuclear weapons) and interception. Thus if early Sidewinders lacked sensitivity and maneuverability, it was partly because no one thought that these capabilities were required. Rather, Sidewinder was designed "for high-altitude attack against nonmaneuvering bombers." Indeed "tests against maneuvering targets were not even undertaken until 1964."[75]

This lapse may help account for why the original Sidewinder design, procured in prodigious numbers (more that 81,000 were manufactured) remained unchanged in service inventories through the mid-1960s. The Vietnam War put an end to such complacency, however. Both the Air Force and the Navy took the original AIM-9B with them to Vietnam in 1965, where they found that North Vietnam's "extremely maneuverable" Soviet-made fighter aircraft "easily 'outflew' the missile."[76] Given the service's doctrinal preferences, moreover, this problem was hardly confined to the Sidewinder missile. Rather, it extended throughout the nation's tactical air inventory. "Even the F-4C lacked either a gun or an optical sight capable of computing a firing solution against a maneuvering target, since prevailing wisdom held that air-to-air missiles had consigned 'traditional' air combat to the past."[77] Ironically, the Navy's F-8 Crusader, a second-line aircraft, turned out to be its best fighter in terms of kills per engagement. It was armed with guns as well as missiles and was relatively maneuverable. Moreover, its pilots, dubbing themselves "the last of the gunfighters," seem to have been better trained for maneuvering air combat than pilots flying top of the line tactical aircraft like the F-4.[78]

Both services now began to adapt, more or less quickly, to combat realities. Both instituted dogfighting training for their experienced pilots. The Navy began its Top Gun school for fighter pilots in 1968, while the Air Force followed suit with its Top Off program in August 1972. The Air Force incorporated an internally mounted 20mm cannon into the F-4E, introduced in 1972. Although the Navy seems rarely to have used its cannon pod for the F-4, it ensured that the requirement for its next fleet air defender, the F-14, included an internally mounted cannon. The F-15 requirement, formulated in 1966–68, also included a gun. And although there were pressures to make the F-15 into "a very large plane relying on air-to-air missiles for air superiority," those individuals who successfully pushed to make it a more maneuverable aircraft received some assistance from the service's Vietnam experience.[79]

Finally, both services sought to turn the AIM-9 Sidewinder into a dogfighting air-to-air missile. The Vietnam experience seems to have goaded both services into a rapid series of product improvements in parallel tracks using different technologies to correct Sidewinder's evident operational shortcomings. The Navy's AIM-9D was rushed to Vietnam in 1966. With a cryogenically cooled and hence more sensitive seeker, a larger warhead, an airframe altered to produce greater maneuverability, and a motor that burned a full sixty seconds and produced less smoke, the D was an instant success with pilots. Still, only 1,000 Ds were produced, since this version was quickly overtaken by the AIM-9G, with a still more sensitive seeker. This missile in turn was replaced quickly by the AIM-9H, with which the Navy finally acquired a fully solid-state seeker (replacing the vacuum tubes in the D and G models), highly cooled and still more maneuverable air-to-air missile. The AIM-9H went to Southeast Asia for the Linebacker campaigns of 1972–73, where it was used successfully but sparingly, owing to lack of supplies.[80]

The Air Force Sidewinder family tree extends from the original, joint service B model through the E to the J. The Air Force sought the same goals as the Navy but with different technologies. While the Navy's D seeker was cooled with liquid nitrogen, the Air Force used a piezo-electric cooling system for its E Sidewinder, which entered the Vietnam conflict in 1966. Like the Navy's newer-version Sidewinders, the Air Force product improvements were more maneuverable, sported higher-impulse, longer and cleaner burning engines, and, increasingly, solid-state components. The AIM-9J was rushed to Vietnam in 1972. Between September of that year and January of 1973, it scored the highest kill-per-attempt ratio of any air-to-air missile then in use.[81]

Work on the Sidewinder continued even as the Vietnam conflict wound down in the early 1970s. As impressive as the H and J Sidewinders were, pilots remained limited mostly to shots from the rear of the enemy aircraft.[82] This rather fundamental limitation was rectified only in the 1970s, with the development, starting in 1971, of the AIM-9L. With a unique fuse and supercooled seeker, this missile could pick up the heat from aircraft from almost any approach angle. Production of the AIM-9L began in 1976.[83] The Israelis used this model Sidewinder with great success over Lebanon in 1982, and the British used it in the Falklands that same year. It was this Sidewinder variant that Air Force officials referred to when they told Congress of the missile's revolutionary implications in 1977. Incidentally, the AIM-9L is also used by both the Air Force and the Navy, as was the original AIM-9B.

Work on Sidewinder continues. Currently, the Naval Weapons Center at China Lake, where the original Sidewinder was invented, is preparing an even more effective AIM-9R for full-scale development.[84] But change is coming more slowly now, perhaps because "the AIM-9 has reached a peak of development largely through the lack of possibilities for improving its manoeuverability [sic]."[85] Attention is now fixed principally on the advanced medium-range air-to-air missile, called AMRAAM, which entered development in 1977. AMRAAM's great range will allow pilots to engage in so-called beyond visual range (BVR) air combat. Unlike Sparrow, which relies for guidance on the radar of the aircraft that fires it, AMRAAM has built into it a powerful radar that at some point in the missile's flight takes over its control, leaving the pilot free to look for other targets. AMRAAM is thus meant to be the truly revolutionary fire-and-forget missile that the U.S. Air Force, in particular, has been seeking for some time.

The Air Force's approach to developing AMRAAM ignores the Sidewinder's history. From its inception in 1977, AMRAAM has been a rush project. Full-scale development began in 1981 on the basis of a contract that included production options as well as penalties to the Air Force should those options not be exercised on time.[86] Production was due to start in 1984, rising quickly to a thousand missiles a year. Apparently that number is required to field "a critical weapon system" needed "to meet a threat all participants agree cannot be met fully with any other missile."[87]

AMRAAM's development was a most ambitious and risky undertaking. The missile's size and weight were dictated by the F-16, much smaller than the F-15 and powered by only one engine. Hence developers faced the challenge of packing a powerful guidance radar as well as a rocket engine into a six-inch diameter metal tube, with the finished result to weigh no more than 350 pounds. Early cost estimates of $40,000 to $50,000 a missile (in 1978 dollars) were based on the promise that new microelectronic circuitry could fulfill precisely these requirements. Hence early program managers dubbed the program risk "moderate" and plunged ahead.

The promise of microelectric circuitry did not pan out, however. After developing a solid-state prototype in the early phase of the project, the winning contractor, Hughes Missile Division, returned to the older traveling wave tube (TWT) radar technology on grounds that it lacked confidence in its ability to manufacture the microcircuitry radar reliably. Given the space the TWT occupies in the missile's airframe, however, its adoption exacerbated interference problems among AMRAAM's various components. Not surprisingly, as the missile neared the contractually specified production deadline, development problems began to surface, the schedule began to slip, and estimates of final cost began to rise sharply.[88]

If AMRAAM's technology was uncertain, so was its operational usefulness. No one denies that, if BVR missiles are to be deployed, fire-and-forget models like AMRAAM are preferable to semiactive radar-guided missile's like Sparrow. In operational tests, pilots using Sparrow found themselves vulnerable as they held enemy aircraft in their radars while Sparrow flew to its target. But critics question the whole concept of BVR air combat. There is no tried-and-true way of distinguishing friendly from enemy aircraft. It was largely to protect U.S. aircraft from their comrades that visual identification rules were imposed on U.S. pilots during the Vietnam war. Even putting aside the so-called identification friend-or-foe, or IFF problem, the high-powered radars needed to cue BVR missiles onto their targets act like beacons to enemy pilots, eliminating the crucial element of surprise from the air battle. AMRAAM's defenders counter that the elimination of surprise is a small price to pay for knowing the enemy's movements well in advance of contact. And Benjamin Lambeth poses a more sophisticated argument. "The side possessing a capability to fire head-on prior to establishing visual contact with the target can make the enemy predictable, if the latter knows this and lacks a comparable weapon, by forcing him to react before the engagement is joined. This is a tremendous tactical advantage."[89]

Little test data support this side of the debate. In early briefings on AMRAAM, Air Force officials claimed that the need for the new missile had been highlighted by a series of mock air battles, involving both Air Force and Navy fighter pilots and aircraft, fought over Nellis Air Force Base in 1977.[90] However, the missile evaluation part of those tests was designed to assess the capabilities of the new all-aspect

Sidewinder. Beyond visual range testing was "legislated out of the test from the start."[91] The tests showed only that pilots firing Sparrow were exceptionally vulnerable as the missile flew to its target, hence the need for fire-and-forget capabilities in AMRAAM. Operational tests in 1981 suggested the "multiple shots and long-range shots" like those for which AMRAAM is being designed "were seldom taken" by pilots armed with a simulated AMRAAM. Arguing that "these results were dictated more by the way the simulation was structured than by actual missile capability," however, the Air Force has retained its attachment to AMRAAM.[92]

The ill-preparedness of the U.S. air forces when they stumbled into maneuvering air combat over Vietnam in 1965 suggests that Air Force officials have no monopoly on wisdom when it comes to aerial combat. The Air Force approach to the product exudes unwarranted operational as well as technical confidence. The program's structure reflects an abiding fear among program managers and Air Force officials that "any hitches in future tests may prove fatal to the [AMRAAM] program."[93] Nothing in the Sidewinder story suggests that the AIM-9 will be the only revolutionary missile to enter service inventories. Combat is full of surprises, and AMRAAM may one day be surprisingly successful. But much in the Sidewinder's history suggests that the revolutionary AMRAAM, if it emerges at all, will do so only after a long process in which the missile's technology not only comes of age, but adapts, along with service doctrine, to the realities of combat. There was no operational or technical sense in rushing AMRAAM's development. Quite the contrary. This project's development and initial fielding should have gone forward with the utmost caution and a great deal of operational testing.

Mismanaging Modifications

Clearly the most sensible way to preserve the nation's technological advantage is to separate mature from growth technologies. When appropriate, advances gained from new technologies can be integrated into the mature technology, resulting in an improved weapon. Such an acquisition strategy is often attributed to the Soviets.[94] If the Soviets are overtaking the United States in technology, and if, as the Defense Department states, the Soviets take as long as the U.S. military to develop new systems, it must be because the Soviets do a better job of imparting product improvements to their force posture.[95]

To some extent the U.S. military services take this approach, too.

In tactical aircraft, for example, the U.S. Air Force spent the 1950s pouring R&D dollars into a fairly wide and varied array of aircraft and engine combinations, reflecting the sizable uncertainties that marked both principal aircraft components at that time. In the 1960s electronic components began to consume a larger share of the unit and R&D cost of tactical aircraft, to the point at which electronics accounts for roughly 30 percent of the unit cost of both the F-15 and F-16, today's premier tactical aircraft. At the same time, the Air Force has moved to develop sophisticated air-to-air and air-to-surface missiles as armament for such aircraft, meaning that the cost of the armed aircraft system is tilted even more sharply toward electronics. The number of new aircraft "systems" under development has dropped off, but newer subsystems keep them up to date.[96]

Army tank developments have evinced a similar pattern. The M-60, which formed the core of the Army's tank force from 1960 to the early 1980s, drew on a chassis and armor combination that was derived from tanks developed during World War II. In the 1950s the most important changes to Army tanks came in engines (with a belated switch from gasoline to diesel power) and armaments (main gun size grew from 90mm to 105mm). In the 1960s, by contrast, the service sought, though too aggressively, to impart sophisticated electronics to the basic M-60, making the ill-starred M-60A2.[97] Although this effort failed and the service purchased few M-60A2s, the principal advances imparted to the M-60A3 lay in electronics. Meanwhile here too munitions technologies have taken off, not only in precision-guided weaponry but more impressively with the development of hypervelocity, hyperdense kinetic energy rounds. Army practice, like that of the Air Force, has distinguished slow- from fast-moving technologies.

Broad R&D investment trends may be encouraging, but the reality beneath these trends is not. What counts is the timeliness with which important product improvements find their way into the nation's force posture. Because product improvements mean marginal changes to existing systems, however, estimates of their cost and performance are almost always more realistic than estimates for the cost and performance of wholly new systems. Inevitably decisionmaking is biased in favor of starting new projects, even though in retrospect product improvements could have provided a more cost-effective product.

The Army's Bradley fighting vehicle is an example. When it finally entered production in 1981, the Bradley gave the Army an infantry carrier with firing ports to allow soldiers to engage the enemy while on the move. The infantry had opted for such a vehicle to replace its portless M-113 in 1964, however, and had been forced to make do with modestly improved versions of the M-113 in the intervening years. In 1968 the Bradley's developer, FMC, Inc., even offered the Army an improved M-113, dubbed the XM-765, which featured a new and more powerful engine, better armor, a turret-mounted 20mm cannon, and gunports. But the Army rejected the XM-765 as "inferior in mobility, carrying capacity, ballistic protection and cost" when compared with the estimated cost and performance of the wholly new fighting vehicle then under study with the aid of computerized cost-effectiveness models.[98] Unfortunately, the new vehicle's development did not begin for some years, and when it did the optimism built into the Army's computer model slowly but surely became apparent. Thus sharply biased comparisons withheld a needed conceptual innovation from U.S. forces for roughly a decade.

The bias against timely product improvement is exacerbated by the need to sustain political support for new projects. There is nothing more dangerous to a development program entering the difficult transition to production than the appearance of an interesting product improvement to an older system. For example, briefings on the M-60A2, a promising upgrade to the Army's standard M-60 tank, helped crystalize opposition in Congress to the Army's XM-803, a derivative of the MBT-70 tank that most legislators thought too costly and complex.[99] Cases like this merely confirm to the services the wisdom of suppressing product improvements until their revolutionary new systems are safely into production, at which point the product improvement may remain a cost-effective buy but will reach the force much later than necessary.

Lawrence J. Korb, former assistant secretary of defense, relates, for example, that in 1985 Air Force officials told his company, Raytheon, "Do not under any circumstances mention tail-control Sparrow to Congress," since the product-improved Sparrow might have threatened the service's ongoing AMRAAM project just as AMRAAM's technical problems were becoming controversial on Capitol Hill. "Had the Air Force improved the Sparrow," Korb said, "we probably could have 'kept up with the Russians' and saved some money in the bargain."[100]

Another example is the Army's impressive T-700 engine, which today powers its Apache and Blackhawk helicopters. The T-700 was available in 1974 and by 1976 had undergone maturity testing that demonstrated its impressive reliability. There is no longer any doubt that the T-700 can be mated to the airframe of the Army's older Cobra helicopter, since the U.S. Marine Corps began accepting AH-1W

SuperCobras, mounting two T-700s, early in 1986.[101] Yet the Cobra did not see this improvement until long after the engine was available and also after the Apache and Blackhawk helicopters had entered production. Interviews with officers connected with the Apache program suggest that the timing was no coincidence. A conscious effort was made to delay Army and Marine Corps improvements to the Cobra until the Apache was safely into production.

Few of these stories are published. Decisions to suppress alternatives are usually made quietly and at a point in the acquisition process when high-level attention is absent. Yet interviews with service personnel suggest that the practice is widespread. Evidently it is not an unreasonably long acquisition cycle that deprives the nation's forces of the benefits of new technology but rather an ingrained and extensively used mechanism for preserving political support for new weapon systems.[102]

CONCLUSION

It is impossible to write about the rush to production without engaging in conspiratorial talk about service strategies to undermine the nation's political processes. Such talk is fair enough. The services often schedule testing and other project events to influence the political process. And military officers who invariably give pessimistic assessments of the threat will as project managers shift to the other extreme, often giving rosier assessments of their project's status than even the most optimistic outside observer would give. Meanwhile alternatives are often ruthlessly suppressed to prevent their undermining projects preferred by the services.

But then congressional staffers conspire to throw a harsh light on programs they oppose, even if that means distorting complex test or financial data. Industry conspires to influence the vote of individual legislators. And officials in the Office of the Secretary of Defense conspire to beat the services at their own game or to reinforce service conspiracies when their goals are compatible. Political appointees who refuse to play the game are likely to be ineffective. The politics of procurement, perhaps American politics generally, can be seen as a series of conspiracies and counterconspiracies in which individuals and groups seek to manipulate a fragmented political process to their advantage.

Acquisition is especially dependent on conspiracy. Development projects evolve over long periods of time, incredibly long compared with the year-length perspective that dominates the political process. While the inherent uncertainties of technology development leave plenty of room in which to slant information to achieve service goals, they also open those goals and the technical process aimed to meet them to endless debate. Finally, the riskiness of the undertaking makes it almost inevitable that even good projects will at some point toss up unflattering information. These characteristics open acquisition projects again and again to the threat of political interference, even cancellation. It may well be that the only way to get weapons out of the American political process is to conspire against it.

Whether justified or not, however, the conspiracy is enormously costly and growing more so. The acquisition process systematically cheats the latter phases of development even as they grow more important. It just as systematically confuses a set of technical specifications with military effectiveness, a luxury only available in peacetime. Meanwhile product improvements that might allow important development projects to be managed more judiciously are delayed. The services and the nation as a whole lose both ways. They get useful product improvements late, if at all, while they get important projects far too soon. And to make matters worse, the hardware that military units get may be inappropriate or at least unready.

CHAPTER 5

Perverse Priorities

PROJECT managers, service staffs, and even service secretaries complain mightily about the time they spend reporting to Congress on the minute details of ongoing weapons projects. Members of Congress respond by calling attention to the frequency with which the Pentagon's bloated bureaucracy intervenes in project management. Some even deplore their own immersion in project minutiae. No one likes things this way. All agree that project managers should have authority commensurate with the enormous responsibility they shoulder, while Pentagon policymakers and members of Congress should focus on grander strategic issues. Yet repeated reforms aimed at streamlining the acquisition process have failed. Members of Congress and senior defense officials find it impossible to rise above the elaborate review of each year's budget submission and the arcane detail of projects therein.

The origins of this conundrum are simple. Budgets can be used for planning and control only if those shaping the budget know what they are buying—only, that is, if budget choices can be made on the basis of good information. Yet by the time defense officials and members of Congress know what they are buying, cancellation requires enormous political will. It is easier to stop and start projects in their early stages, but of course such choices are made on the basis of cost and performance information that is almost always wrong. Thus real choices are based on bad information, while good information is available only when freedom to choose has all but disappeared. The acquisition process is not organized in a way that allows members of Congress and defense officials to make the kind of strategy and force structure decisions they want to and should make.

Instead the acquisition process is organized in a way that sucks politicians and policymakers ever deeper into the details of project management. If the only real choice policymakers have is the one that launches new development projects, and if the validity of that choice erodes as costs rise and requirements are altered, then those charged with holding the Defense Department accountable have no choice but to review the situation as it unfolds. And because requirements enhancements over the course of development may direct a project away from goals originally envisaged for it, those concerned with matching weapons with strategy have a similar need for review. Providing for the common defense becomes a matter of tinkering with minute changes in each year's procurement budget.

Weapons acquisition is legitimately a political undertaking, but under these circumstances the politics of procurement are played out over the course of development. In the process, the issue of what weapons the nation buys—the stuff of national strategy—becomes inextricably mixed up with how the nation buys weapons—the arcane technical issues that would be better left to technical experts. The results are perverse whether one looks at weapons, force planning and strategy, or at the broad question of who, if anyone, actually controls the structure and organization of the nation's forces.

THE REQUIREMENTS MORASS

The problem starts at the bottom of the acquisition process, in an elaborate requirements process that establishes cost and performance goals, as well as detailed technical specifications, for new projects. These then form the basis for the requests for proposals (RFPs) that become the basis for competitive bidding on the project by interested firms. The requirements process often unfolds almost invisibly within Defense Department bureaucracies. Yet political forces nonetheless operate powerfully here, at the very start of a new development project. Combined with the optimism that normally prevails at this point, political pressures encourage consensus building that imparts too much risk and restrictive detail to early requirements and makes it difficult to back away from that risk later on.

The Unit-Veto Rule

In the political and organizational milieu in which requirements for new weapons and components are formulated, political forces create a powerful unit-veto system. As the manager of the Defense Department's stockpile program said in 1985, "It is almost impossible to make effective program decisions without some support from *every* [governmental] actor."[1] Sometimes the threat of veto comes directly from Capitol Hill, where it can be driven by constituent contractors or the personal interest of key legislators. Support can be purchased, perhaps, by ensuring that contracts are let to key districts or by understating likely costs.

More often, the threat of veto comes from individuals and agencies in the Defense Department who attach important goals to a new project, especially an expensive or operationally important one. In chapter 3, the brief recounting of the requirements process behind the M-1 tank offers an example. Schedule length came from the service chief of staff, the tank's weight goal came from the chief of staff-designate, while members of Congress placed a ceiling on unit costs and the Office of the Secretary of Defense (OSD) forced the service to lower development cost estimates partly to satisfy Congress. Members of the Main Battle Tank Task Force were unhappy with several of these requirements but were in no position to object.

Consensus-building pressures have grown over time. Weapon systems are now more complex, increasing the number of capabilities under consideration in any given project. The defense bureaucracy has steadily acquired new agencies, many relevant to acquisition, raising the number of agencies seeking a voice in the requirements process. And because the number of new systems under development has generally declined, those agencies must focus their attention on a more limited range of new projects. As the Fitzhugh Commission noted long ago, "The tendency to concentrate development efforts on a few very large systems . . . encourages the services to include in a basic new weapon all the improvements in various components that have been developed since the last system."[2]

Sometimes project managers are able to avoid consensus-building pressures. But doing so can be costly, since an "important dissent may seriously delay a program considered by others to be urgent."[3] Political pressures loom in the background, since failure to achieve harmony at the start of a new project may cause serious problems later on. "Government operates principally by consensus," former Under Secretary of the Army Norman R. Augustine once stated. Thus government "has little discipline in preventing dissenting views from becoming disruptive after a decision has been made."[4] Insofar as it offers an obvious forum for dissenting views, Congress can critically shape the requirements process even when legislators do not intervene directly in it by providing a way for dissenters to circumvent the formal Pentagon hierarchy. This confronts program managers and service staffs with political risks that must be weighed against purely technical risks as requirements for a new system are formulated.

The fate of DIVAD, discussed in chapter 4, is a good example. Pressed by Congress to get DIVAD's development under way, the Army overrode the concerns of those in the Defense Department who strongly favored missiles rather than guns for this mission. When the project later encountered problems unrelated to the gun-missile debate, missile advocates threw their weight behind DIVAD's critics, thereby helping to end the project. Missile advocates would argue that the project would have survived had the correct initial choice been made. They forget that there is also a gun constituency in the service. The lesson for program managers is clear. Given that cost, reliability, and maturational problems are likely to haunt any project as it moves into production, it is best to buy off other opponents as early as possible. Not surprisingly, DIVAD's replacement sports both missiles and guns.

Such buy-offs are easy in the permissive environment that prevails as projects start. Costs and performance are presented optimistically at this point, making all things possible. Personnel rotation policies compound the problem. Most project managers are not likely to be participants in the project later on, when the tough technical choices embedded in the original requirement must finally be faced. The same can be said for service staffs. Almost every feature of the project managers' environment encourages them to add to the evolving requirement whatever is necessary to achieve organizational harmony.

If consensus building is encouraged partly by optimism at the start of development, then the emergence of more realistic data over the course of development should undermine the established consensus, forcing trade-offs to the surface. But consensus-building pressures do not disappear during development. To the contrary, the continuing pressure for consensus results in additional weapons requirements rather than trade-offs that would stabilize or keep a lid on the cost of weapons. Military requirements proposed early in the development process are held no less dearly by their proponents as development nears its end. And the political risks of violating an established consensus are likely to be as high late as they were early. Insofar as real costs and real design problems tend to surface late in development, project managers may be even less anxious to break the consensus as production approaches.

Meanwhile at this point in the development process members of Congress tend to look askance at any sacrifice of performance. Having been promised certain capabilities, members of Congress are predisposed to regard the sacrifice of some of those capabilities as evidence of the dishonesty of service project managers. Alternatively, because performance is by this time written into detailed contracts, members will blame the industry for fraud, waste, and abuse. Although members of Congress may press for lower costs, they are usually referring to the achievement of greater efficiency in producing the performance objectives that were initially formulated.[5]

The Costs of Consensus Building

The drive for consensus contributes to the length and elaborate detail that so often marks initial requirements and RFPs. As the Packard Commission noted, RFPs are often "thousands of pages in length," not counting the "generic specifications [so called milspecs] included by reference."[6] Such detail makes no sense. It implies that the Defense Department knows exactly what it needs and what technology will give. Yet the record of the last forty years is replete with weapons that only vaguely resembled their initial requirement, while weapons that have met technical requirements reasonably well have been used in operational roles quite different from those originally envisioned for them.

Nor can it be argued that forty years' experience leaves the Defense Department better equipped to predict technical and operational requirements in advance. The Defense Science Board recently expressed its belief about the requirements problems posed by software, which is among the newest and most challenging of growth technologies. "Users *cannot*, with any amount of effort and wisdom, accurately describe the operational requirements for a substantial software system without testing by real operators in an operational environment, and iteration on the specification."[7] Meanwhile chapter 4 made clear that even in more mature systems the services repeatedly confront technical and operational surprises.

Those who insist on detail in requirements, however, are not trying to make sense, at least at the level of the overall project. Rather, they are trying to protect the specific capabilities or technologies that matter to them. The more they can embed their own project goals in detailed specifications, the surer they are that those goals cannot be traded away during development.

The Packard Commission inadvertently suggested that this strategy succeeds when it lamented that requirements detail "forecloses . . . trade-offs between performance and cost."[8] For those individuals wishing to shape the new weapon, that restriction is a virtue. Weapons with many capabilities look good analytically because analysts use the rosy cost and performance estimates proffered when new projects get under way. Pressures to avoid trade-offs as these rosy estimates give way to reality, however, can produce systems that are flashy but not cost-effective and systems that perform so many functions that they perform none well. Overall, pressures for consensus create a systematic tendency toward so-called gold plate.

For the Air Force's F-15 fighter aircraft, for example, consensus building during the requirements process added questionable capabilities and costs to an aircraft that most observers legitimately regard as an outstanding fighter aircraft, perhaps the world's best. Nonetheless the aircraft's top speed of Mach 2.5 (two-and-one-half times the speed of sound) is disturbing. As Benjamin S. Lambeth has pointed out, "Speeds much above Mach 1.4 are virtually useless in maneuvering air combat."[9] Meanwhile high speed is expensive. It creates the need for variable air inlets, for example, that add weight and complexity to airframe design. High speed, in short, is not cost-effective.

The Rand Corporation's airframe cost model suggests that lowering the F-15's top speed from Mach 2.5 to Mach 1.5 would have lowered airframe cost by 26.5 percent. Given an average F-15 unit cost of roughly $28 million (1987 dollars), of which some 60 percent, or $17 million, is the cost of the airframe, the U.S. Air Force spent about $4.5 million to give the F-15 its top speed, or $3.6 billion over the total buy of just over 800 aircraft. The opportunity cost of buying a top speed of questionable usefulness thus was roughly 150 more of the less expensive F-15s.[10]

Why did the Air Force press for a very high top speed in its new F-15? The service knew that high speed "would greatly affect the [aircraft's] structural design" and thus its cost.[11] Still, at that point the whole aircraft was expected to cost roughly $5.3 million (in 1968 dollars, or $15 million in 1985 dollars—about half the aircraft's average unit cost). With optimistic cost estimates paving the way, Air Force planners seem to have held to the traditional view that "high top speed insured adequate air superiority capability."[12] But contrary evidence was emerging from its experience against slow but maneuverable MiGs over North Vietnam, and from the innovative theoretical work on energy maneuverability then being done by Lt. Col. John Boyd.[13] So Air Force planners also absorbed Boyd's principles into the F-15's requirement, in the form of demands for maneuverability, a high thrust-to-weight ratio, and peak performance around Mach 1. The aircraft's requirement thus satisfied old and new theories of air combat.[14]

Some evidence suggests that even Air Force officials were uncomfortable with the F-15's full cost when it became clear in the early 1970s, since it threatened to enforce an unwanted reduction in the size of the service's tactical air force. Yet service support for the full range of F-15 capabilities never wavered over the course of the aircraft's development. Quite the opposite. Gen. Benjamin N. Bellis, the F-15 program manager, was castigated by his service chief as well as by members of Congress for unilaterally relaxing qualification test requirements for the F-100 engine.[15] Thus the Air Force purchased a very fine aircraft but one whose cost needlessly raised the so-called quality-quantity issue to the air staff as well as its critics.

Because consensus building, in the end, seeks to make a weapon that is all things to all people, it can produce the proverbial camel—a horse designed by a committee—that does nothing very well. Such would seem to be true of the Army's Bradley infantry fighting vehicle.[16] The Bradley was born in 1964 to fulfill the infantry's desire to trade its M-113 personnel carrier, a windowless, weaponless box on tracks, for a motorized infantry combat vehicle or MICV, an armored vehicle with gunports to allow those inside to fight while mounted. The choice, as well as the likely cost of the new vehicle, was widely debated over the next six years and not until 1972 did the service publish an RFP for the new system. By then the system had already acquired more complexity than the austere vehicle the infantry had originally sought. In particular, a complex stabilized turret had been added, despite associated weight and cost penalties.[17]

The MICV's design kept changing after development commenced. Systems analysts in the OSD were impressed by the Soviet Union's BMP, an infantry fighting vehicle equipped with firing ports, a cannon, and an antitank weapon. They were equally impressed with Egypt's success in using Soviet made antitank guided munitions (ATGMs) in the 1973 Arab-Israeli war. That war also impressed the Army's armor community, previously excluded from the Bradley requirements process. Armor officers now began touting the MICV with the Army's own TOW (tube-launched, optically tracked, wire-guided) antitank missile attached as a long-range tank killer. More important, members of the House Armed Services Committee, as well as the newly appointed secretary of defense, James R. Schlesinger, made clear their desire to see TOWs deployed in great numbers to U.S. forces in Europe. Many, including Schlesinger, saw the MICV as the perfect platform on which to hang TOWs.

Others made the costs of that plan clear. By the time of the 1973 war, for example, FMC Inc., the MICV's developer, had already begun to experience technical problems with the evolving vehicle. Its weight rose, raising questions about its ability to ford streams as required in the development contract. Gen. William DePuy, heading the Army's Training and Doctrine Command (TRADOC), noted that the addition of TOW missiles and the already required cannon would "add an unacceptable amount of weight to a vehicle which already exceeded the [required weight] . . . limit." The infantry branch, meanwhile, was on record as saying that an MICV with TOW would "require complete reorganization of the infantry force structure," since adding TOW would reduce the size of the infantry unit the MICV could carry.[18]

Evidently assessing the political situation more carefully than it assessed the technical situation, the Army's official study team nonetheless concluded that TOW and the cannon could be added to the MICV "without measurably degrading its primary role as an infantry fighting vehicle."[19] The technical costs of adding the TOW turret soon became apparent, as the system's weight rose to twenty-five tons while its cost finally topped out at well over twice the cost the service had hoped to pay for its original design MICV.[20] Weight growth rippled through the design, causing problems with the vehicle's power train and raising more concern about the Bradley's ability to swim across streams. Finally, despite the conclusions of the Army's study team, the TOW turret left less room for infantrymen, forcing a reduction in squad size to seven rather than the nine soldiers judged ideal in operational tests.

Technical problems aside, however, the real problem with the Bradley is the contradictory missions it is expected to perform. On the one hand, it is required to deliver troops to the forward area of the battlefield, moving in tandem with the Army's M-1 tanks. On the other hand, it has the job of firing antitank weapons, a mission safely handled well back and well covered. The Bradley is expected to be two places on the battlefield at once. Moreover, in becoming a tank killer the Bradley lost some of its utility as an infantry carrier. At best it can dispense seven rather than the doctrinally endorsed nine soldiers to the battlefield. Ostensibly that should make it necessary to buy more Bradleys, but the vehicle's higher than expected price tag makes this move unlikely.

Having purchased the Bradley, the Army has had to adapt to it. The vehicle's ability to swim remains questionable and controversial, prompting many to ask whether the swimming capability is necessary.[21] If, as has been suggested, the service adds 7,000 pounds of reactive armor to the vehicle, the requirement for fording streams may have to be dropped. Some service officials also argue that the greater firepower of infantry weapons makes a smaller squad size more appropriate. Finally, the whole question of the survivability of vehicles like the Bradley on battlefields littered with precision-guided antitank missiles is forcing the service to reconsider mechanized infantry doctrine in the broadest sense.[22]

There is no denying the weightiness of some of these issues, nor is it clear that doctrinal shifts imposed by the Bradley purchase are entirely without merit. Ideally, however, it would have made more sense to debate doctrinal issues rather than to have them decided by the purchase of a new weapon. Moreover, deciding doctrinal issues before or during the Bradley's development instead of after the design was embedded in fielded hardware would surely have simplified the vehicle's design. If the vehicle is required neither to swim nor to keep up with tanks, both weight and speed requirements might have been relaxed, leaving developers with greater leeway to focus on Bradley's armor, turret, and drive train.[23] It is difficult not to conclude that the Army would have been better served with a different vehicle, the product of a more flexible development process.

The Congressional Budget Office (CBO), interested in cutting waste from the defense budget and aware of the Bradley's contradictory missions, suggested in 1986 that the service buy two vehicles instead of one. The CBO would have canceled further Bradley purchases and instead bought an improved M-113, armed with a 25mm cannon, to serve as a troop carrier, and Improved Tow Vehicles (ITVs—basically M-113s armed with TOW-II missiles) to serve as a tank killer.[24] The CBO alternative would have saved $2.1 billion over five years, roughly 40 percent less than the cost of buying 3,200 Bradleys.

If gold plate means military capabilities not worth their cost, then the F-15 and the Bradley may be called gold plated. Still, this issue remains controversial. Given the uncertainty surrounding combat,

FIGURE 5-1. *The Problem of Gold-Plated Weapons*

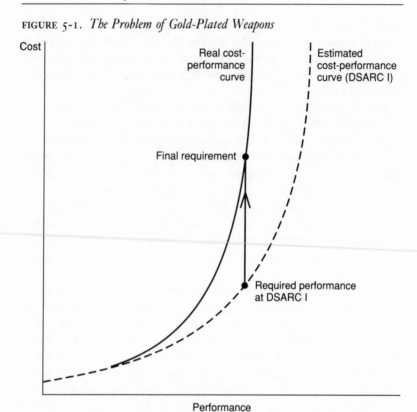

arguments about what is or is not gold plate go on endlessly, with the case for or against varying with each system or component under consideration.

Consequently the phrase gold plate is not to be used capriciously, nor is it here. But the developmental patterns outlined so far strongly suggest that the nation's acquisition process systematically errs in the direction of gold plating weapons (figure 5-1). Projects are initially aimed at a point on the cost-performance curve deemed cost-effective. But that goal is set on the basis of optimistic estimates. Cost turns out to be higher, often much higher, than expected, meaning that the real cost-performance curve for this particular system or component lies above and to the left of the estimated curve used to formulate the initial requirement. Ideally, project managers should sacrifice requirements in an effort to find a new balance between cost and effectiveness. But they are far more likely to pursue original performance goals at higher costs. If the original project goal reflected a sensible balance between cost and performance, the new goal almost certainly does not; the new weapon has some elements of gold plate. The problem is . acute if the initial goal is at the knee of the curve, since costs in this case will rise sharply with even small shifts in the location of the cost-performance curve.

Requirements enhancements could be said to rectify this systematic error by introducing new cost-performance curves farther to the right of the initial estimate. If optimism prevails in the formulation of enhancements, however, they too fall victim to the logic just described. Meanwhile, if enhancements complicate the design and the process of system maturation, they risk reducing reliability in the overall design. At worst, enhancements allow participants in a project to maintain the illusion that cost growth is not leading them into the realm of gold plate, when enhancements may in fact compound the problem.

Politics and Project Management

Recognizing the political and bureaucratic pressures that buffet project managers leads to an uncommon view of their role. In theory, project managers stand between the technical and military dimensions of the acquisition process and require technical skills, military experience, and managerial talent. In practice, project managers stand between the political system, the Pentagon's enormous bureaucracy, and their project. They tend to be bureaucratic interlocutors, salespersons, and game players. Unless they play these roles successfully, their technical talents may find scant outlet, since consensus building will crowd out the chance to make even the vaguest technical trade-offs.

Good project managers instinctively recognize this point. The Army's multiple-launch rocket system (MLRS) is widely seen as a technical success. MLRS program managers are reported to have spent "most of their time building and maintaining a consensus in favor of GSRS [an earlier acronym for the same project, standing for general support rocket system] within the Army, the Department of Defense, and in Congress." The project's first program manager referred to himself as an "advocate" and left the "crafting of an acquisition strategy, as well as its execution" to his deputy and to technical experts in the developing firm.[25]

Good project managers also can be adroit at manipulating events to protect the integrity of their projects. In interviews, many claim that, whatever other benefits competition may confer on a project, it has the added value of screening projects from outside interference. Once a competitive development project has begun, any attempt to alter requirements or project goals would alter the terms of the competition and force the project back to the start. Some project managers may ally themselves with a high-level official interested in their project as a means of keeping lower-level Pentagon agencies at bay.

Conversely, high-level officials who understand the consensus-building pressures at work in the acquisition process may stabilize and expedite projects by throwing their weight behind the project manager. As discussed in chapter 3, the Lightweight Fighter project got off to a good start partly because it was kept outside the established Air Force hierarchy until prototypes had been developed. Director of Defense Research and Engineering William Perry did virtually the same thing by creating a direct link between himself and the Joint Cruise Missile Project Office to ensure that the project was adequately protected. Aware of the disruptive effects of constantly changing requirements on a project's success, Navy Secretary John F. Lehman, Jr., established the policy that "no contract or engineering change can be submitted for negotiation without the signature of the Commandant of the Marine Corps or the Chief of Naval Operations and the Secretary of the Navy."[26] The policy made political and organizational sense, since with it Lehman effectively placed his power behind the program manager.

There are limits to how far even the most aggressive defense official can carry this approach, however. None has the time or technical talent to consider every change proposal to every project under his or her purview. And the wider that officials seek to spread the policy the more diluted it becomes. In protecting projects they are exercising political power, and political power must be used sparingly if it is to be used to effect. Still, while countless reforms have failed to streamline project management, high-level officials with clear priorities can intervene to simplify and stabilize a few key projects. Given the consistent failure of reforms to streamline acquisition management, simplifying life for a few project managers may be the best that can be hoped for.

Neither astute project managers nor political intervention can guarantee project success. Politically astute management cannot make a good weapon out of a bad requirement. And even technically successful projects like the TV-Maverick, discussed in chapter 4, can yield weapons of questionable combat value. Finally, no amount of political adroitness can produce technical talent and design wisdom if these do not already exist in the developing agency and firm.

But the converse is also true. The work of a talented design team can be rendered useless if the project manager cannot buy enough political support and bureaucratic freedom to sustain the project and leave designers with freedom to make some trade-offs. Without denying the need for project managers to have some training in the technical fields associated with their projects, it would be better to see them as buying the political and bureaucratic freedom in which the technical talent working for them can get on with development. Conversely, when a project moves along smoothly it may have less to do with the technical or business acumen of the project manager than with his or her political and organizational talents, or the similar talents of higher-level defense officials interested in that particular project.

POLITICS AND THE PLANNING PROBLEM

If project managers lack flexibility to make sensible trade-offs between cost and performance, then they transfer the need for flexibility to the planning process. Here weapons projects should be fitted into a sensible plan for modernizing the force posture as a whole. Planners at this level find it difficult to absorb higher-than-expected costs in individual programs as development proceeds, while both planners and project managers have to find some way to accommodate rising estimates of future costs. One way to do this would be to cancel some projects to make room for others. Yet it is never easy to cancel a vital requirement, and the services see almost all projects as vital. Besides, projects are organized in ways that make them politically difficult to stop in any case. Unless the defense budget rises to accommodate rising costs, something has to give. What usually gives, unfortunately, is any semblance of rational force planning.

Weapons Development and Force Planning

Confronted with developing weapons whose estimated costs are continuously rising, planners and project managers opt for commensurate cuts in the total number of weapons they had hoped to buy. Total program cost estimates remain remarkably constant even as the estimated cost of the finished product keeps rising, as Rand analysts documented in their study of weapons acquisition in the 1970s: "For the 31 programs in our cost analysis sample, reductions in quantity almost perfectly cancelled out the sum of the cost changes due to the other [cost] variance categories. In other words, the real flexibility in the acquisition process is found in the quantities of units procured, not in the aggregate cost of acquisition programs."[27]

Rand authors concluded cautiously that this finding raised important questions about "the manner in which quantity-quality tradeoffs are made," but the analysts did not press the issue.[28] Indeed, their finding stands as a serious indictment of the acquisition process, since it suggests that the steady decline in quantities of new weapons purchased has less to do with greater weapon effectiveness—the official explanation—than with the military's inability to plan effectively. The pursuit of quality in individual weapons overwhelms the effort to pursue balance and quality in the overall force posture.

But service planning documents do not tell the whole story. Quantities purchased may vary over the long run for reasons planners cannot foresee. Consider the following examples.

—Original plans called for the purchase of 650 F-16s, but late in the development program the planned buy was almost doubled, to 1,388 aircraft.[29] By 1987 the Air Force had ordered 1,535 F-16s of various models, and plans called for the Air Force to purchase a total of 2,729 F-16s by fiscal 1995.[30]

—Although the F-X (F-15) Decision Coordinating Paper was silent about the total planned size of the F-15 fleet, later decisions capped the buy at 732 aircraft. Yet with the Reagan administration's defense buildup and the approval of plans to procure the F-15E (configured for long-range interdiction rather than air combat), the Air Force was able to procure more than 800 air combat F-15s to keep the aircraft's production line warm while the F-15E was being perfected.

—When the Army canceled its MBT-70 tank project in 1971 it purchased the M-60A2 instead, largely at the insistence of Congress. Yet with its complex and unreliable turret, the M-60A2 proved unpopular with tank units and difficult to support in the field. The service quickly turned to the more sensible M-60A3, while Congress acquiesced in the purchase of only a few hundred M-60A2s.

These examples suggest that force planning in the United States does not take place on paper, despite the formal obeisance to the planning-programming-budgeting system imposed on the Defense Department by Robert S. McNamara. Rather, force planning unfolds as a political process, the result of decisions taken over time and in response to the full range of considerations that can affect political decisions in a democratic system. These considerations are neither confined to, nor necessarily dominated by, military and strategic calculations. They may emanate from the desire to keep a production line open, as when the Georgia delegation on Capitol Hill insists annually on the purchase of small numbers of C-130s, presumably as a favor to constituents employed by Lockheed Georgia, the plane's manufacturer.[31] Similarly, the Texas congressional delegation "kept the Fort Worth plant of General Dynamics open and producing F-111s for four years after the Defense Department requested termination."[32] On the margins, at any rate, political bargaining sets the size and structure of the nation's force posture, making the force structure a political outcome as much as the product of rational planning.

This does not mean, however, that the political process proceeds entirely without reference to analytical or technical criteria. The M-60A2's history, for example, suggests that the political process can identify and suppress truly poor weapons. Conversely, while the Air Force may not want more C-130s, many analysts within and without the Defense Department find its continued purchase a genuine blessing, especially in view of the Air Force's tendency to ignore transport requirements in favor of the more exciting fighter and bomber aircraft closer to mainstream service missions. Finally, in the case of the F-15 and F-16, it seems that the process has implicitly made a quantity-quality choice by opting for many more F-16s than were originally planned while holding the F-15 buy proportionately much closer to original plans.

Is this particular planning problem not really a problem? Unfortunately, no. Critics of the underlying quality-quantity bias in defense procurement remain largely correct. Force size may grow to levels only partially related to planning figures, but it rarely grows to the levels originally envisaged, nor in the mix originally sought. Force planning still takes second place to the pursuit of performance in weaponry. Equally important, if the political system seems able to make quantity-quality judgments, the acquisition process rarely presents it with alternatives on which such practical judgments can be made. The F-15 and F-16 were available for comparison and choice only because David Packard went outside the established acquisition process to produce the original F-16 prototype.

Production Rates and the Efficiency Problem

Whatever the ultimate size of the force or units within it, rising cost estimates in individual projects over the course of development forces planners to purchase weapons more slowly than planned. Whereas decreases in planned quantities may be rectified over an extended period, the costs of producing at lower-than-planned rates are real and immediate. Having prepared, on the basis of persistent optimism, to produce at a rate that rarely can be sustained when production begins, contractors find themselves producing inefficiently. This adds still more to the cost of the weapon.

In general, this problem is compounded by so-called instability in the defense budget. Congress sets overall defense budget levels in accordance with its own priorities, not necessarily those of Pentagon planners. Hence the defense budget rises and falls unpredictably from year to year. Because other budget categories—manpower, for example—are difficult to change in the short run, the acquisition budget often changes disproportionately in relation to swings in the overall level of the budget. Rolf Clark has shown, for example, that in response to an overall 5 percent cut in the Defense Department's proposed budgets between 1974 and 1980 the acquisition budget fell 14 percent below requested levels.[33] Unless the defense budget rises sharply, a lower-than-expected procurement budget will force planners to reduce production rates still further, adding to system cost.

There is no doubt that scheduling changes are a significant cause of cost growth in weapons projects. Rand's study of 1970s projects concluded that roughly 40 percent of total cost growth in the cases studied could be attributed to schedule changes.[34] Defense officials tend to blame Congress for budget instability and hence for cost growth. In so doing, however, they imply that politics should have nothing to do with setting defense budgets. And they overlook how much their own optimism also contributes to schedule changes, hence how much they contribute to cost growth. Although it would be useful to distinguish internally from externally generated cost growth, Rand analysts concluded that the data project managers collected on their projects did not allow for such distinctions.[35] All that can be said is that the two sources compound the problem of schedule changes and cost growth in weapons development.

Optimists might argue, only somewhat facetiously, that this problem is not so perverse as it sounds. In a backhanded way the nation has found a way to buy the surge production capacity defense planners and members of Congress often favor. Yet whether or not the nation needs a surge or mobilization production base remains a debatable issue that should be resolved by public choice, not as the offhand consequence of bad planning. As it happens, for much of the postwar era defense planners have thought in terms of a short war that left no time for mobilization, even as bad acquisition planning created excess capacity in the defense industry. Moreover, it is doubtful that buying excess capacity as a planning error is as efficient as buying it as a matter of choice. The nation has found an expensive way to buy mobilization capacity as well as weapons.

The Bow Wave

Historically, optimism has not been confined to weapons development, although it tends to be more pronounced there. Rather, planners have been optimistic about the costs of producing systems after they have left development. In the 1960s and 1970s, procurement budgets based on optimistic estimates suffered from a so-called bow wave of higher-than-predicted unit costs in individual projects. In many cases the bow wave enforced much the same behavior among planners as optimism in development. Production rates were lowered, increasing unit costs even more and leading at the least to a slower-than-planned buy if not to a smaller buy overall.[36] So badly were costs underestimated that even rising budgets could not accommodate rising costs. As Franklin C. Spinney showed, even as the tactical air procurement budget grew, the services "procured 9 percent *fewer* fighters than planned, with the exception of the A-6," while "the five-year average unit cost of each fighter *increased.*"[37]

With production as well as development budgets rising unexpectedly, however, the bow wave's effects spread beyond the acquisition process to other sectors of the defense budget. With the acquisition budget pushing constantly outward, for example, so-called readiness spending, on such things as spare parts and training, fell during the 1970s as a percentage of the capital value of the force then in being.[38] Spending for basic research also fell relatively during this period. As figure 5-2 shows, funding for basic research tends to rise and fall disproportionately in relation to the Pentagon's overall R&D budget, suggesting that when the defense budget is falling the services will raid this account, as well as the readiness account, to buy weapon systems.

During the Reagan era an important difference surfaced between cost estimation for weapons in production and costs that arise as

FIGURE 5-2. *Defense Department R&D Obligations, 1956–87*
1982 dollars

Index, 1972 = 100

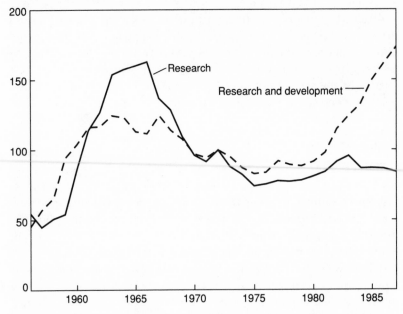

SOURCES: See Kenneth Flamm and Thomas L. McNaugher, "Rationalizing Technological Investment," in John D. Steinbruner, ed., *Restructuring American Foreign Policy* (Brookings, 1989), p. 148, fig. 54.

projects move through development. While cost estimates made during development tend to show a consistent optimism, cost estimates in the procurement budget as a whole are affected by broader budget trends. Production costs were consistently underestimated during the 1960s and 1970s, producing the bow wave. Facing the plentiful budgets of the early Reagan years, however, the services shifted to slightly overestimating production costs. A study by the Congressional Budget Office shows, for example, that unit production cost estimates for the systems in their sample rose sharply between President Jimmy Carter's fiscal 1981 budget submission and President Ronald Reagan's fiscal 1983 submission.[39] Actual unit costs for some of these systems were still higher than the fiscal 1983 estimate. The majority were produced for slightly less than the fiscal 1983 estimates (although far more than the fiscal 1981 estimates), even when the Pentagon purchased fewer systems than originally planned. Project managers and service staffs took advantage of the new administration's promise of vastly increased procurement budgets to pad their accounts.

Given the uncertainties that crop up in the production of new systems, not to mention their development, there is nothing wrong with providing additional funds to handle unforeseen contingencies. Indeed, one could only wish this occurred more frequently in the development process. Yet despite the budget plenty of the early Reagan years the services still purchased fewer weapons than they planned to buy in the fiscal 1981 five-year defense plan (FYDP).[40] Moreover, many of the systems purchased were still produced at lower than optimum rate. In its study of procurement stretch-outs during the Reagan era the Congressional Budget Office found that of forty systems in its sample, half were produced at inefficiently low production rates, and six (15 percent) were produced at rates below that required to sustain an active production base.[41] Although the cost of lowering production rates varied by system, overall the CBO found that "decreasing the basic rate of production for major weapons by 50 percent would increase real unit costs by from 7 percent to more than 50 percent, according to data supplied by the military departments and weapons producers."[42]

This confirms the argument that unit costs of production systems were generally overestimated during the early Reagan years. But the question arises, why didn't the Pentagon purchase all the weapons it planned to purchase at the beginning of that period? Spending on procurement doubled, in real terms, between 1980 and 1985, while the CBO report shows that weapons costs rose but generally not by a factor of two. Absorbing much of the difference between high weapons costs but still higher procurement budgets were new procurements like the B-1B, the F-15E, and ships for the 600-ship navy, which the Defense Department had not planned to buy under President Carter but added to its plans soon after the Reagan administration took office.[43] Given the money to buy according to its original plan, the Defense Department changed its plan.

The Pentagon, no more than Congress, should be held to past plans simply because those plans exist. Arguably the world changed in the late 1970s, making it necessary not only to raise the defense budget but to buy a panoply of new weapons. Here again, however, it is important to see that budget instability, inefficient production rates, and hence higher than necessary weapons costs were generated largely by the Pentagon. Indeed Congress gave the Defense Department more than it asked for in fiscal 1980 and 1981. Although support for Reagan defense budget requests declined after 1983, the Pentagon still received more overall than it had planned on getting in its last Carter five-year plan. If the Defense Department still could not carry out its original plans, it has itself, not Congress, to blame.

Reagan administration officials claimed that they had eliminated cost growth, at least for systems under production rather than those in development. The CBO's study confirms this claim. While some systems still rose in cost, the cost of others fell below estimates. But the elimination of cost growth did not result from significant advances in the science of cost estimation. Rather, sharply rising procurement budgets confronted the services with incentives to overestimate rather than underestimate future costs. The lesson for the future is limited. The defense budget rose, more gently, in both the 1960s and the late 1970s, yet underestimation persisted during these periods. And this suggests that unless procurement spending increases at the unprecedented rates achieved during the early Reagan years, cost growth will quickly return to the defense planning process.[44] The Reagan administration's solution to the problem of cost growth is not one the nation is likely to try again for some time.

The Emerging Procurement Bias

If in the plentiful years of President Reagan's first term the Defense Department still did not buy what it planned to buy, it set up conditions that have already begun to make sensible planning more difficult in the lean years that began in 1986, as the defense budget headed gently downward for the first time since 1978. This planning problem is the product of two forces. First, defense planners have assumed that budgets would continue to rise. The Reagan administration's last defense budget (for fiscal 1990) assumed a 2 percent real increase in defense spending even as most observers argued that the Pentagon would be lucky if it could avoid a real decrease in spending power. Second, new procurement projects begun early in the Reagan era are still ongoing, while development projects launched at that time are now coming due. Most have behind them a good deal of political momentum, making cancellation difficult. The nation is returning to the 1970s in budgetary trends, but the gap between the funding required to buy the currently planned force and the funding the Pentagon can expect to get is so large that the standard approaches to dealing with the bow wave will be of doubtful help.[45] The acquisition budget thus is exerting enormous pressure outward against the rest of the defense budget.

Readiness has already been victimized by these pressures. The CBO reports, for example, that starting in fiscal 1985, operations and support spending as a percent of the capital value of the nation's weapons inventory began to decline sharply, arriving in fiscal 1987 at a level still lower than it reached in the 1970s, when there was widespread talk of a "readiness crunch." If changes in Soviet security strategy and the tenor of the U.S.-Soviet relationship are ending the cold war, then U.S. forces will not need to be as ready as they have been through most of the postwar era. But the decline in readiness spending began just as Mikhail Gorbachev rose to power. And it has continued even though official U.S. policy has been hopeful but also skeptical of the changes that Gorbachev has imparted to Soviet strategy and forces. Pressures in the defense budget thus are undermining official policy.

Meanwhile, a much broader trade-off is being considered, that between modernization and force structure. Former secretary of defense-designate John G. Tower and various members of Congress have argued that "military manpower might be cut rather than arms to meet budget restraints," leading some to talk of fielding a "leaner and meaner" force.[46] William W. Kaufmann has countered by arguing, "It would be difficult to demonstrate in any persuasive way that the United States has acquired excessive insurance (in terms of force structure) against the key planning contingencies on which its force structure is based." Thus from Kaufmann's perspective, modernization "is the central issue for decision." He would hold the size of the nation's forces constant while canceling new weapons or delaying their purchase.[47]

This debate is certainly worth having. For members of Congress anxious to escape the technical detail of project review, the debate is of great strategic importance. Yet representatives are hardly in a position to debate objectively. Rather, the political context in which the debate will take place is sharply biased toward buying hardware that has acquired too much political momentum to be easily stopped.

Instability versus Inflexibility

No one should expect the Defense Department to plan weapons acquisition perfectly. The undertaking is too big, too uncertain, and too buffeted by pressures beyond its control to submit to precise bookkeeping. Among many other problems that haunt planning is the fundamental fact that the department cannot predict its budget from year to year—neither in the grand sense of overall funding levels nor in the narrow sense of choosing weapons and quantities each year. Congress will always provide for the common defense with only partial reference to the executive's budget submission. In so doing it will continue to give defense officials a ready excuse for their department's many planning problems.

Yet budget instability, as Pentagon officials refer to it, is hardly unique to the Defense Department. Few businesses can predict sales in advance, and many individuals—consultants, for example—experience wide and unpredictable swings in annual income. All employ approaches to budgeting that leave options open for handling uncertainty. They may leave reserve funds cached away in the budget, or they may hold open choices involving the rapid sale or purchase of assets in order to cope with changing fortunes. Facing uncertainty, not surprisingly, one seeks to preserve flexibility.

Clearly the Pentagon functions in the opposite way. It is hard to find any level of the acquisition process that can respond quickly and positively to changing budget fortunes. Project managers have little room to trade performance for savings as development proceeds. Planners find it equally difficult to cancel some weapons to make room for others. Given the optimism that pervades development, and even production except under the most luxurious budget circumstances, the acquisition process presses constantly outward. It is run not to maximize flexibility but to demand it from its external budget environment.

It makes little sense under these circumstances to complain about budget instability. Such instability is unavoidable in a democracy. Moreover, the instability has been an established fixture in defense budgeting for years. The real problem is not lack of control over the budget, but lack of control at the opposite extreme—over individual projects, where the ability to make sensible trade-offs begins to erode almost as soon as the new project begins to take shape.

TIME AND POWER IN THE PENTAGON

With everyone fighting for control over ongoing weapons projects, no one has full control. Instead there is an annual battle for budget space, driven by optimism and budget instability on the one hand, and the priorities and choices of policymakers and service officials on the other. In establishing new budget levels for individual projects each year, in approving or rejecting proposed changes in requirements for evolving weapons, and perhaps in canceling a system occasionally, policymakers effectively register their acquisition priorities. Yet the politics of setting priorities is set up so that the services, rather than civilian policymakers, have greater control.

Behind this imbalance in power lies the enormous time required to develop new systems. Political appointees like the secretary of defense, his deputy, and service secretaries are rarely in their jobs long enough to sustain their own or their administration's priorities. They take office to find weapons about to enter production that are for the most part difficult if not impossible to stop, and they set in motion new projects on the basis of data that will be proved wrong only sometime after they leave office. They can make decisions about projects already in development, but that only adds another layer to the process of consensus building, with negative results for weapons design. High-level military officials suffer the same liability. They often come and go even more frequently than Pentagon civilians and have only limited power to shape the priorities and programs of their service.

Under conditions in which individuals come and go as a weapon evolves, military organizations have decided advantages in the politics that surround weapons procurement. On the one hand, military leaders, coming from similar backgrounds and experience, are likely to exhibit more continuity of view than political appointees. Air Force chiefs of staff may come and go, but most of them probably want a new manned bomber. Meanwhile, if high-level officials are not in position long enough to influence organizational priorities, choices will implicitly be delegated to lower levels of the service staff. Again no single individual is in control. Rather, control flows less to people than to service priorities, which tend to be more consistent within each service than among civilians who may belong to administrations with different goals.

This helps explain how projects powerfully backed by service traditions often survive political opposition and analysis that question their usefulness. The Air Force's twenty-year quest for a new manned bomber after Robert S. McNamara canceled the B-70 is a most impressive example. There was never much analytical support for such an aircraft outside the service itself, while political support tended to be strong in Republican administrations, weak in Democratic administrations, with President Carter finally canceling the B-1 program in 1977. By this time, however, the B-1 had strong backing on Capitol

Hill and the industry as well as the Air Force. Working together, these groups kept the B-1 option alive until Ronald Reagan took office and the B-1B program was given the nod.[48]

Continuity of service traditions and the advantages this confers on service officials in playing politics with procurement also help explain why, after four decades of trying to eliminate service independence, the Defense Department still underinvests in areas that fall outside areas of traditional interest to particular services. The Air Force's lack of interest in providing close air support to the Army and the disinterest of both the Navy and the Air Force in providing transport for ground forces are the most notable illustrations. Missions crucial to national defense but less than crucial to individual services tend to remain unfilled.

These gaps in the nation's force posture remain unfilled despite repeated attempts to fill them. But no one is around long enough to see such attempts through to their finish. The effort to begin a project of this sort will create a call for studies that consume more time than most high-level officials are likely to spend in office. Such studies may be seen as a legitimate requirement by all concerned. But given the absence of hard numbers on costs and performance, the studies are unlikely to resolve the debate. And they may be nothing more than a way to buy time until personalities change. Even if studies end and development begins, the officials responsible are likely to leave office before a project acquires momentum. Then service priorities are likely to reassert themselves, at which point the bow wave looms as a ready excuse to cancel an unwanted system or at least lower it on the list of priorities.

An example is the purchase of sealift to support the Rapid Deployment Joint Task Force in its mission of projecting military force to the Persian Gulf region. Capitalizing on political interest in the Gulf generated by the energy crisis, the fall of the shah of Iran, and the Soviet invasion of Afghanistan, Under Secretary of Defense Robert W. Komer was able to allocate money out of the fiscal 1980 and fiscal 1981 defense budgets to use in purchasing supplies and transport for this regional command. He planned to purchase two sets of eight fast deployment ships, each capable of transporting an Army division rapidly to the Gulf region. The first set was built in Great Britain and was for sale on grounds that the ships consumed too much fuel to be of commercial use. These ships were purchased before Komer left office, along with the rest of the Carter administration, in 1981. The second set remained to be purchased, but, with Komer replaced by officials anxious to allow the services to do their own planning, the ships were quickly dropped from the Navy's procurement plans, which reverted to traditional priorities.

In the mid-1980s a search began for a replacement for the Air Force's aging A-10 close air support aircraft. Aware that his service was far more eager to launch the development of a new fighter (the advanced tactical fighter) than it was to begin work on a follow-on to the A-10, Air Force Secretary Verne Orr dictated in April 1985 that "until the Air Force makes good on its promise to provide the Army with close air support . . . the advanced tactical fighter will be relegated to the bottom of the service's list of tactical priorities."[49] But Orr left office at the end of 1985, at which point the Air Force submitted close air support to a massive cost-effectiveness evaluation. This move effectively shelved the issue, prompting one Defense Department official to assert that the service "just has not been paying attention to this mission."[50] Meanwhile contracts for development of the ATF were let to Lockheed and Northrop in late 1986.[51]

The problem of control is evident during, as well as at the start of, development. Clearly making cost-performance trade-offs during development is difficult. Project managers are encouraged instead to pursue performance while letting costs rise. When military and civilian priorities for a project differ, however, the need to make trade-offs may be a genuine opportunity, since whoever controls such trade-offs controls, within limits set by the basic design, the shape of the weapon or component that will reach fielded units. Over time, the services are in a much better position than civilians who come and go to control those trade-offs. Witness the application of Air Force priorities to the lightweight fighter as it evolved into the F-16A.

Recognizing this possibility, Pentagon civilians concerned about a system's final shape are encouraged to keep close track of development projects even if their own priorities are reflected in the initial requirement. Herein lies the fallacy of the notion of "centralized control, decentralized execution," a managerial concept frequently voiced by high-level Pentagon officials. Who controls execution controls project outcomes. The incentives to micromanage development should be clear.

Approaches to acquisition that create viable hardware alternatives enhance civilian control. McNamara's ability to pick and choose among weapons stemmed largely from the fact that real alternatives existed. Decision and implementation were compressed in time, and real data existed to support the choice. Packard and Schlesinger were also able to make good use of available alternatives to effect decisions in what were far shorter tenures than McNamara's. Weapons choices remained political choices in these cases, as well they should be. But civilians constitutionally charged with controlling the nation's military fought these political battles on even grounds with the military. It is an advantage few other defense secretaries have enjoyed.

Generating real choices costs money, however, which is one reason why politicians and policymakers have, since the early 1960s, consistently sought to eliminate alternatives. In so doing they have weakened the ability of civilian officials in the Pentagon to do precisely what they are supposed to do—exercise control over acquisition, with an eye especially toward promoting cooperation among the services. The irony is that those who helped create this situation were trying to strengthen civilian control in the Pentagon.

CONCLUSION

Starting with the simple truth that soldiers, policymakers, technicians, and politicians all have a right to some say over weapons acquisition, the nation has arrived at a process in which these groups fight for control continuously over the course of development. And because everyone has partial control over part of the process, no one has control over all of it. Weapons and forces are political outcomes, just like policy choices in other areas of government activity.

This way of organizing acquisition has not prevented the nation from fielding weapons or organizing forces. But it has made it almost impossible to do these things in a sensible way. Wars are won by forces, not by weapons. Yet the Pentagon systematically sacrifices its ability to integrate and train its forces in the pursuit of weapons capabilities. All too often, in doing so it pushes weapons capabilities beyond the point at which they are worth their cost. In the process, force planning occurs almost as an afterthought. Although official descriptions depict a defense planning process that works from the top (strategy) to the bottom (weapons that support that strategy), the opposite would be more accurate; weapons drive force structure and strategy.

This problem is likely to grow worse rather than better in the future. Political pressures on individual development projects can be expected to increase as the number of projects continues to decline while political and bureaucratic oversight of projects grows. Thus pressures to hold to performance are likely to mount rather than subside. But forces have grown more complex and interactive over time, raising the importance of force planning and integration as well as training in relation to the pursuit of individual weapons capabilities. Never easy, force planning and integration are getting harder. The vicissitudes of weapons development are likely to make the job of force planners and policymakers harder still, the nation's defense priorities more perverse than ever.

CHAPTER 6

The Accidental
Industrial Policy

IN ANY given year the Defense Department deals with about 30,000 firms. The aerospace giants are among them, but so are manufacturers of shoes, uniforms, baked goods, paper clips, and toilet paper who do only a small share of their business with defense. Even in the high-technology sector there is variety—among electronics, aircraft, engine, and armaments firms, for example.

Yet when one thinks of the defense industry one thinks mostly of the aerospace primes and a few large engine and electronics firms, and for good reason; the industry is and always has been heavily concentrated. Since the Korean War the top one hundred defense contractors have consistently garnered more than 60 percent of all defense contract dollars awarded, while the top twenty-five contractors have consistently carried away more than 45 percent of the dollars awarded. Nor have the top ten defense firms (by total sales each year) changed much, especially after note is taken of mergers and diversifications. McDonnell Douglas, Lockheed, General Dynamics, Boeing—these familiar names can be found on almost every list of top ten defense contractors since 1960. The only notable change in industrial structure at the top has been the growth in importance of electronics firms, paralleling the increasing use of electronic components in weapon systems.

These firms do not face a market. They are private firms in the sense that they sell stock, borrow money in commercial markets, and seek an adequate return on investment. But the similarity to a private firm stops there. Defense firms sell unique products to what has always been a single buyer, the U.S. government.[1] The defense sector thus involves a monopsony in which prices are negotiated rather than set by market forces. Defense firms also face qualitatively different risks than most private firms. They engage in "winner take all" competitions rather than a fight for market share. Their sales are politically determined. And they face a constant demand for very high levels of technological advance. Thus risks are heavily subsidized if not covered entirely by the government. In short, defense contractors, especially those at the top of the defense industrial hierarchy, constitute a unique quasi-private, quasi-public sector of the nation's economy. The point should be obvious, yet often criticism and reforms are based implicitly on a market model.

In the absence of market forces, the big defense firms respond mainly to the signals, incentives, and regulations provided by the government. Sizable Defense Department bureaucracies oversee profit levels, industrial base issues, and so forth. Given the defense sector's importance, however, as well as how power is divided and shared among branches and agencies of the government, the structure and behavior of the big defense firms are shaped in important ways by forces flowing from the political system as a whole, often as the unintended result of the tugging and hauling that mark American politics. In this way the nation arrives at an accidental industrial policy toward its defense sector.

The important question is not how the nation arrives at what passes for a defense industrial policy, but whether that industrial policy serves the nation's security. Does it encourage creative and militarily appropriate R&D? Does it encourage efficient production? Does it supply an industrial base that can handle expected wartime needs? Given the somewhat accidental quality of policy in each of these areas, there are problems in each. Surprisingly, however, the defense sector's principal problems have less to do with efficiency, which remains the concern of most critics, than with R&D, where conflicting incentives and pressures have slowly undermined the rewards attached to this critical function.

THE DEFENSE MARKET MECHANISM

In the absence of a real market, something still has to play the marketlike role of directing resources more or less efficiently toward more or less useful ends. Presumably the Pentagon's huge planning and policy bureaucracies do so, in the manner of the state planning apparatus of a socialized economy. Yet this analogy is no more appropriate than the market analogy. Defense firms are private and independent. They have stockholders, show profits or losses, and are free to invest what private money they have as they wish. Yet they have had mixed results investing those funds outside the defense sector. They remain largely dependent on the government as buyer and thus are responsive to incentives that stem from the way the government operates. This hybrid form of organization has a similarly hybrid market mechanism, combining competition, reminiscent of the private sector, and administrative pricing based on extended negotiations between the government and client firms.

Negotiations depend on power or leverage, which, as already discussed, changes over the course of a project. As a project begins, the government has most of the leverage. Competition early in development is an important component of that leverage, and the buy-in is one of the more notable symptoms. As a project evolves, sunk costs rise, competitors are eliminated, and the winning firm moves into a monopoly position from which it can deal with the government with increasing authority. From this position it seeks to get well or recoup investments borne of earlier optimism. As in most negotiations in which power is shared, this one includes a good deal of gaming, as each of the two parties seeks to maximize its interests. Insofar as the game forms the core of the relationship between risk and reward in defense projects, the game is, for practical purposes, the Defense Department's market mechanism.

Markets, for example, communicate consumer needs to private firms. In the defense sector, needs are communicated through elaborate and detailed requirements documents and contracts, which firms accept because they have no alternate market. More broadly, however, what the Defense Department wants is innovation, and competition for development contracts is widely thought to produce it. The prospect of competition encourages firms to scour the technological horizon for new ideas, and perhaps to invest their own research funding to bring those ideas to reality. Some of those investments will later be reimbursed by the government as allowable independent R&D expenses. When firms buy in, they extrapolate from this early development work, albeit exaggerating somewhat to win the contract. By tying firms into those exaggerated promises, the government can force them past existing technical horizons, precisely what the nation needs if it is to stay ahead of the Soviets.

Competition for development contracts also serves the marketlike function of placing downward pressure on prices in the defense sector. Large bureaucracies and elaborate administrative guidelines come into play, yet the theory is simple: "good pricing," as a recent Defense Department study of industry profits said, "has the advantage of encouraging cost control, because a contractor must underrun tight costs to earn a high profit."[2] Prices may be the result of competition, but in most projects competition ends early. Prices then depend on the outcome of negotiations between government agents and specific firms. Project managers and contract officers enter negotiations with weighted guidelines by which they attach allowable profit margins to estimates of the costs that their client firm expects to incur in performing a stated amount of work.[3] The government's goal is to base profit estimates on tight, that is, low-cost, estimates.

The government's success in achieving this goal in price negotiations will vary according to the skill of negotiators on both sides, the transparency of costs, and so forth. Overall, however, the project manager's ability to hold the industry to tight cost estimates depends on his leverage, and leverage is highest when competition is encouraging optimism among client firms. Aware of this fact, and aware as well that their leverage declines sharply once competition has ended, project managers have good reason to encourage a buy-in early in development, seeking to lock a firm into an especially "tight" cost estimate. Indeed, managers may even elicit production cost estimates during the competitive phase of development. All parties to such negotiations realize that contracts so negotiated will no doubt have to change, not just in response to continuing technical problems and requirements enhancements but in response to externalities like unforeseen inflation. Still, each change will take off from a baseline established under competitive circumstances. The buy-in thus is the project manager's way of trying to carry the benefits of competition over into the monopolistic phase of a project.

A recent Defense Department study of profits in the defense sector concluded that competition-induced optimism about costs also encourages defense contractors "to share in the development costs with the government."[4] Academic studies reach the same conclusion. Applying regression analysis to R&D spending data taken from the years 1979 to 1984, Frank R. Lichtenberg of Columbia University confirmed that "the prospect of . . . future noncompetitive contracts awarded to the winner of the design competition makes firms willing to make [private] R&D investments which are large, relative to the value of the initial competitive contracts." Because he found no similar private investment in the case of noncompetitive contracts, he concluded that "the entire stimulus to private R&D from government procurement comes from competitive acquisition."[5] Using a somewhat different model in his study of profits in the defense sector, David E. Kaun also found that "R&D spending clearly has had a statistically significant negative effect on current profits during the period under study."[6] The buy-in forces firms to share the financial risks of development with the government, and confronts firms with marketlike incentives to make good on past promises.

As a market mechanism for the Defense Department, the buy-in is important and constructive. Given how major projects are organized, the buy-in may well be crucial. In a perfectly competitive situation firms have no power over the market. In the defense marketplace, power flows from the government to the firm over the course of a project. Consequently, the buy-in enables government to capitalize on its leverage when it has some. How else can the government, and implicitly the public, hold a monopoly producer's feet to the fire than by locking that producer into its early optimism?

THE DEFENSE GAME AND THE R&D SQUEEZE

The use of the buy-in to discipline defense firms is politically costly. Ironically, although politicians see cost growth as evidence of waste, it may instead be evidence of the project manager's initial attempt to hold costs down. Thus the prevailing relationship between the government and its client firms invites political intrusion into the weapons development process. Yet even without political intrusion, this approach to organizing the government-industry relationship is costly. The costs have less to do with wasteful production, however, than with the way defense firms carry out research and development.

Innovation versus Marketing

Costs begin to mount early in a project, even before the negotiating game gets under way. These early costs spring from the questionable relationship between competition and innovation in the defense firms. Most observers agree that competition is a useful spur to innovation. Yet Merton J. Peck and Frederic M. Scherer noted years ago that design competitions tended to promote marketing over solid development work.[7] In large part, the problem occurred because defense firms were competing with ideas, technical notions that had yet to become technical artifacts in all but the slenderest sense. Design competitions became the "competition in dreams" noted in chapter 2.

In a later work, Scherer suggested that budgetary assumptions prevailing early in the development process exacerbated marketing tendencies. "When competition takes place at the outset of or during the early developmental stages of a program," he noted, "military officials deciding which weapon system to choose do not worry about over-all budgetary constraints." Instead they tend to select winning contractors on the basis of quality, without reference to cost. This in turn, however, "encourages contractors to build too much quality into their weapon systems."[8]

Prevailing economic assumptions are hardly the only forces that encourage the pursuit of too much quality. Consensus building during requirements formulation has the same effect. So do longstanding perfectioneering tendencies in the services and industry. Clearly many forces contribute to the overzealous pursuit of quality in weapons. Scherer's argument, however, suggests that the stress on quality early in development arises as well from the nature of the relationship between the government and defense firms, making it that much harder to achieve a better balance between cost and performance.

The Costs of Getting Well

Historically, firms got well from profits on production, normally carried out under monopoly conditions. To some extent this process is carried out today. But getting well is no longer as simple and straightforward as it was in the early years, when R&D was relatively cheap and production runs were long and fairly stable. Almost from the birth of the aircraft industry, for example, R&D (in commercial as as well as military aircraft programs) has grown steadily more expensive, while production runs, especially for military aircraft, have lost whatever resemblance they once had to mass production and have instead acquired the character of customizing operations. These trends can be found in the other principal defense industrial sectors as well. While the pressures and possibilities for buying in remain roughly the same, the chances to get well from production profits alone have diminished. If buying in and getting well still mark the government-industry relationship, getting well has become a more complicated undertaking over time.

The effort to get well begins as soon as competition ends. With competitive pressures abating, firms can begin to recover earlier investment, seek higher profits, or both. Government project managers will seek to use the low bids extracted during competition to contain the firms' efforts. Given that many of the numbers that underlie profit calculations are uncertain—determining allowable overhead levels for a defense firm is far more complicated and imprecise than determining allowable tax reductions for the average citizen—the stage is set for the game of getting well.

The principal vehicle for playing this game remains the engineering change proposal, which can make even fixed-price contracts flexible over time. In his study of competition and private investment in R&D, Frank Lichtenberg found that private R&D investment stopped when noncompetitive contracts were used. Indeed, noncompetitive R&D contracts tended to "crowd out private R&D investment."[9] In short, the reverse buy-in sets in as soon as conditions that encourage the buy-in end.

But the reverse buy-in is only one vehicle for getting well. Another means to do so is through overhead loading, when contractors, like citizens at tax time, take the most liberal interpretation of the phrase "allowable cost" in submitting their requests for government reimbursement. As David Packard once put it, contractors and the Defense Department at this point are "basically playing games with each other. The contractors . . . put every expense that they [can] get away with in a contract, because it [will] later be negotiated with the contracting officer."[10] Given that historically such negotiations have resulted in "pretty much a 50/50 split" of the costs being negotiated, contractors have been encouraged to start the negotiations at as high a level as possible.[11] It may not be honorable, but it also is not too surprising when they add to their overhead claims the cost of "conferences in Hawaii, plush suites at the Plaza Hotel in New York, . . . and . . . kennel fees for Furston, a dog belonging to one of General Dynamics' top executives."[12]

The lateral shift is a third vehicle for getting well. Contractors shift their costs to other components of a project, or even to other projects, rather than to overhead. Arguably this occurrence should be more prevalent in low-risk projects when ECPs are based on fewer technical uncertainties. An analysis of the M-1 tank's development, for example, shows that production contracts negotiated at the end of the project's competitive phase exerted positive control over cost growth during production. But ceiling prices in the initial contract did not include the price of spare parts, which had to be negotiated under sole-source conditions and "effectively raised the tank ceiling price because the allowance for cost overruns on the spares contract could now be used to offset cost overruns on the tank contract." An estimated $2.6 million loss on the first tank production option became a profit of approximately $3 million (besides the $3.2 million profit for the spares contract).[13]

The rules of the get well game make it difficult to evaluate true costs in a project. Is a high-priced spare part evidence of massive waste across a particular factory or of losses taken elsewhere? Is low overhead on one project evidence of efficiency, or has overhead merely been shifted to other projects? Judgments about efficiency and waste must comprehend a project in all its dimensions. This is hard enough in a single project, which may include hundreds of small contracts. It is more difficult when a single defense plant has two or three major projects under way simultaneously.

THE COSTS OF CONTRACTING. Contract officers on any given project are probably negotiating several contracts at any given time, as well as renegotiating or modifying any given contract repeatedly over time. This process is less true for the early competitive phase of development, when project managers and contract officers can rely on competition to discipline contractors. But competition ends early, and thereafter discipline, if it is to be imposed at all, must be imposed through contracts.

Robert S. McNamara's effort to use incentive contracts as a disciplinary tool produced massively detailed contracts and pressures toward litigation that seriously constrained the speed and freedom of development. McNamara was applying such contracts at the start of development, when uncertainties were especially high. More recent practice is to rely on tight contractual devices only after early development work resolves basic technical uncertainties, thereby relieving some of the problems McNamara experienced. Nonetheless development is far from over at Milestone II. Even putting aside requirements enhancements, unexpected engineering problems continue to plague development through most of full-scale engineering development. Hence the basic tensions that surfaced during development of the F-111 are still in evidence. Detailed contracts must change but cannot be changed quickly or, given the antagonistic interests of the contracting parties, easily. This situation is hardly conducive to good R&D. And, in the end, its real costs raise questions about whether it protects the taxpayers' interest.

Incentive contracts have become more sophisticated and complex since McNamara left office. Starting in 1971, the Defense Department launched a continuing effort to encourage firms to invest in more efficient capital equipment by adding formulas to the basic incentive contract that would base the industry's profit markups on return on investment (ROI) as well as on sales.[14] This effort initially produced contracts so complicated that the directive on which they were based was phased out in 1975.[15]A new and somewhat simpler directive, promulgated late in 1976, has been in force since then.

Despite the complexity of incentive contracts, Defense Department officials maintain that they save money. They can point to empirical evidence that final costs have tended to underrun cost targets more often when incentive contracts have been used than when the old cost-plus arrangements prevailed. Yet critics find "little evidence of significant behavioral changes when the organization moved from a CPFF [cost-plus-fixed-fee] situation to the kind of fixed price incentive contract customarily negotiated."[16] These critics point out that contractors change their negotiating behavior as the risk sharing formula of the contract changes. If the government insists that the industry cover most cost growth, as it does with incentive contracts, then firms will negotiate for a target cost that leaves them some elbow room. If the government agrees to cover costs, as it does with cost-plus contracts, then firms can buy in more aggressively. Firms may do the same work in both cases, but the empirical data will suggest that the incentive contract enforced more efficient behavior. As a rule, studies of incentive contracting in the 1960s found that the type of contract had little real effect on costs.[17]

Nor is it clear that encouraging capital investment has been very useful. The Defense Department's *Defense Finance and Investment Review* (DFAIR), published in 1985, found abundant evidence of increasing capital investment by defense firms after 1978, when the new ROI-based contracts took effect. Using various measures, the DFAIR team found that capital expenditures and capital employed had increased faster for defense than nondefense firms, though defense firms were usually starting from a lower base.[18] Yet 1978 was also the year that defense procurement budgets started to rise steadily, and with the election of Ronald Reagan in 1981 the way was clear for several more years of rising defense budgets. The defense business base expanded, and confidence increased about future defense business, a change from the previous decade. Thus the DFAIR team was forced to conclude that "it was not possible to definitively relate defense sector capital investments to the profit policy changes alone."[19]

More important, perhaps, it was not possible to equate capital investment levels to investment in efficient capital. The DFAIR study found, for example, "an increasing percentage of capital expenditures went to buildings at the expense of equipment" and suggested that such investments produced assets that firms could "substitute . . . between defense and nondefense work."[20] In this sense, ROI contracts might reward defense contractors for what amounts to hedging against uncertainty in future defense funding. What the contracts do not seem to do is encourage efficiency. The program manager's most important source of leverage, the contract, is a relatively weak reed.

Unfortunately, this weak reed is not a cheap reed. The contracting game imposes costs on the development contractor, as well as on the taxpayer, that, if difficult to quantify, are in the opinion of informed observers substantial.[21] Indeed, as former defense official Ronald Fox points out, the contractor's incentive under an incentive contract is to "document every departure from the original contract and to blame anyone and anything possible for these departures. Hundreds or thousands of contract changes are then negotiated. This process . . . raises contract target costs substantially."[22]

Clearly the effort to impose contractual discipline under the uncertain conditions that mark most development projects adds to overhead charges against development. The effort to lock unrealistic promises into the print of contracts ensures that later development will be littered with transactions, "the doing and undoing of logistical, balancing, and quality transactions that result from change," contributing directly to overhead.[23] But overhead is not strictly attributable to the firm. As services build huge bureaucracies to negotiate contracts and ensure their implementation, the Pentagon's overhead is likely to match that in the firms it manages.

A more important cost of doing business this way, however, is measured in technical flexibility rather than overhead. Contracting occurs over the life of a project—research, development, and production. But the costs of contracting as just outlined are highest during development, when uncertainties are high, ECPs frequent, and speed essential. Insofar as ECPs become the vehicle for renegotiating cost and performance commitments, the ECP game is an integral part of the technical design process. Technical changes must be funnelled through an imposing bureaucracy, much of it outside the firm, which takes time and adds rigidity to the development process. Ironically, it was in the interest of saving time and obtaining flexibility that the services turned to commercial firms in the first place.

A final cost has to do with the atmosphere in which development takes place. At the level of politics, industry may cooperate with the military services in lobbying for a project. At the project level, however, the need to negotiate and renegotiate contracts can create powerful animosities, deep-seated suspicions, and distrust. Unfortunately, it is at this level that the military and its developers should cooperate most congenially if the weapon that finally emerges from development is to meet the military user's needs.

POLITICS AND THE GET-WELL GAME. Contract negotiations usually unfold at relatively low levels, hidden from public view. But the broader game of which they are a part has a natural tendency to burst into public relief. When news surfaces that General Dynamics, for example, has experienced sizable cost growth on spare parts, the public tends to see waste and abuse if not fraud. Starting in 1983, horror stories about incredibly expensive spare parts and tools helped precipitate the most recent wave of acquisition reform.[24] Clearly, however, spare parts prices by themselves have little meaning. The game is played out over many contracts. The way the game is played certainly creates the appearance of waste, however, whatever the reality. Thus the interactions at the core of the industry-government relationship stand as a built-in source of controversy and an invitation to political intervention.

The game makes cost growth inevitable. Indeed, project managers looking out for the public's interest and aware of their waning leverage over contractors as a project evolves have a positive interest in locking client firms into their early optimism. Yet increasingly since the 1950s national political figures have come to equate cost growth with waste, or worse, with dishonesty. Senator William Proxmire began his book on America's military-industrial complex, for example, with the simple statement that the book was "about cost overruns and military waste." Later in the book he equated cost overruns with deceit.[25] Proxmire has been joined by a number of scholars, as well, in condemning cost growth.[26]

Meanwhile, if cost growth looks like waste, negotiations about allowable overhead costs look all too much like criminal attempts by contractors to bilk the government. In the early 1980s the latter view was embodied in the law. As David Packard has put it:

Suddenly Congress called for the establishment of a DoD inspector general, and he was given authority over the defense contractors. The defense contractors weren't warned and suddenly they found that procedures that had been traditionally accepted were now criminalized. Although the situation was very bad, it did have the result of making contractors recognize that they have a responsibility that goes a bit higher than the average commercial business.[27]

Arguably congressional attitudes and actions strengthen the government's hand in its negotiations with industry. Aware that overhead claims are being scrutinized more carefully or that cost growth provokes negative reactions on Capitol Hill, management in the industry recognizes its higher responsibility and reduces costs and claims accordingly. In fact, experienced project managers have even used the political system as part of a strategy for forcing industry to absorb more of the costs of weapons programs.

Clearly that was the case with Admiral Hyman Rickover's handling of General Dynamics in construction of the SSN-688-class submarines.[28] There is little question but that David Lewis, CEO of General Dynamics at the time, bid low in 1973, lower than many of his subordinates thought advisable, to win the SSN-688 contract, a fixed-price contract at that. Yet Lewis felt strongly that Rickover had encouraged the low bid, coached him in the art of winning the contract, and rewarded him for bidding correctly by awarding General Dynamics a $300 million Navy contract for the first Trident submarine.[29] Within three years Lewis was forced to admit publicly to cost growth in the SSN-688 project of more than half-a-billion dollars, the result principally, in his view, of frequent changes in the Navy's design requirements.[30] By this time, however, Rickover had stopped coaching and started castigating Lewis and his firm for failure to live up to their contract.

Moreover, Rickover took this argument to members of Congress sympathetic with it, essentially using Congress to buttress his own position. Public statements by Senator William Proxmire strongly suggested that negotiations with General Dynamics would lead to a "corporate handout" to the firm.[31] These were not idle threats. In the end the SSN-688 settlement required a restructuring of the government's contract with the firm that required congressional approval.[32] But the SSN-688 restructuring was not only approved at the political level, it was adjudicated there as well. Senators like Proxmire backed Rickover. Senator Abraham Ribicoff of Connecticut, home of the

SSN-688 construction site, tried to help an important constituency, and Representative George Mahon of the House Appropriations Committee sought a compromise between the two. Rickover's approach to project management helped suck the political system into project management.

THE GREAT GAME AND ITS COSTS. Politicians and policymakers recognize that defense firms buy in to win contracts. Official Defense Department studies admit as much. Their refusal to acknowledge the buy-in during the get-well phase of a project is part of a sensible negotiating strategy. Defense firms have their own negotiating strategy. No doubt they overstate their original investment, pad overhead accounts, and shift costs around to more pliable contracts. The ensuing negotiations may include complex litigation, possibly serious recriminations. But in the end an equitable compromise may be reached.

Politicians participate in these negotiations, either directly, as in the SSN-688 case, or indirectly, as when they champion an end to cost growth or the criminalization of overhead loading. This too, however, is justifiable given the stakes. The public's representatives can hardly stand by idly while technical experts negotiate blame for cost growth of nearly a billion dollars, as occurred with the SSN-688. Politicians echoed various sides in the more technical debate about the SSN-688. Some opted to protect constituents, some tried to protect an essential component of the nation's defense industrial base, and some sought to blame General Dynamics for the whole problem. The political vituperation may be noisy. Careers may be sullied, and individuals vilified, some rightly, perhaps, but some wrongly too. The political system is not capable of great precision in such things. Still, in the end the large defense firms survive intact to go on to new projects. All's well that ends well, and arguably even the SSN-688 ended well.

So is there a real problem here? In fact, there are several. This way of doing business adds substantial overhead costs to weapons procurement. Only a small part of this overhead is incurred at defense firms, where time and talent must be directed to litigation, hosting auditors, and so forth. The rest is spread around the government, with a large share falling to the Pentagon and its subordinate agencies, but some falling to the law firms that specialize in contracting. There is no precise estimate of the size of this overhead, but Under Secretary of Defense for Acquisition Robert Costello has said that "as much as a quarter of the cost of some weapon systems goes into red tape."[33]

A second problem is less obvious but more pernicious, and arises because in the development of weapons the end is determined by the road taken to it. Adjudication may produce a sharing of risks and rewards that in the end is politically and financially acceptable. But the process of adjudication, not to mention the political fireworks that may surround it, clutters the road that developers must take in the technical pursuit of new systems. The government's role in contract negotiations adds to the animosity that haunts the military-industrial relationship at the project level. If politicians see waste where project managers see necessity, then project managers are likely to find themselves squeezed into taking a more antagonistic attitude toward their client firms. Some will even use the political system's aversion to cost growth to their advantage, following Admiral Rickover's example. Perhaps in Rickover's case this approach worked. But no one should expect fine weapons to emerge from the atmosphere that came to haunt the SSN-688 project.

Nor does the negotiation process—the game in its political as well as technical and financial dimensions—bode well for the broader goal of retaining the nation's overall technological advantage. Increasingly, the political system confronts industry with incentives to reduce the risk they take. The services, by contrast, continue to push client firms to take greater risks. And competition for development contracts ensures that firms have little choice but to comply. From the industry's point of view, this is a no win situation. Defense firms can be brutally honest about costs and feasibility in the interest of avoiding later cost growth, but then they risk losing big contracts. Or the firms can be optimistic and win the contract, at the risk of being vilified in the effort to get well. R&D is the most important function these firms perform. Yet R&D feels the squeeze when politicians react to waste in the defense sector.

In rough outline, at least, the nation has reached the same impasse in its defense industry that it reached in the 1920s, when the effort to introduce competition into the production of new aircraft threatened the ability of fledgling aircraft firms to recoup their earlier losses. Then as now, the society wishes to save money at both ends of the acquisition process. Insofar as firms buy in, the nation saves money on development. But the nation also wants to save money on production. Both are legitimate desires. But when paired they would make sense only if production were a separate enterprise, financially disconnected from development, and that has never been the case. Nor can it be if the government implicitly relies on the buy-in as part of its negotiating strategy for holding costs down.

THE EFFICIENCY ENIGMA

Obviously the United States has settled on a very expensive way of conducting what would be a very expensive undertaking anyway. To make matters worse, the process as a whole is expensive in ways that make it difficult to determine whether or not the industry is wasteful. Cost growth is not necessarily evidence of waste. It may be a sign that the government is protecting the public's interest. And cost growth is not totally the industry's responsibility. The industry carries high overhead costs but not entirely by choice. Moreover, the broader overhead costs that stem from the established way of doing business are not registered in the firms or the cost of weapons but in the overall defense bill to society.

Critics of the defense industry do not dwell long on cost growth as evidence of waste, since there are more than enough other data to support their case. For example, critics cite the apparent failure of contractual incentives to spur more capital investment in the defense industry as a sign of inefficiency in defense production. They can also point to seemingly damning comparisons between defense and commercial firms. Wages paid to defense production workers, for example, run higher than the wages of production workers in the average U.S. manufacturing firm.[34] Worse, defense workers seem to do less for their higher wages, since by things such as standard hour measures they are less productive.[35]

Yet there is no necessary relationship between the failure of contractual investment incentives and inefficiency in the defense sector. Contracts may produce few changes in a firm's behavior, for example, because the firm is already efficient. Or perhaps defense firms invest in capital for reasons having nothing to do with contracts. In their study of the 1950s acquisition experience, for example, Peck and Scherer found that defense firms had done an "outstanding" job of improving their production methods.[36] Engineers at McDonnell Douglas calculate that they could produce the F-4A more cheaply today than they could when it first came off the production line twenty years ago, suggesting process improvements at the McDonnell Douglas plant.[37] And the Defense Department's DFAIR study certainly found evidence of capital investment, whether or not it was the result of incentive contracts.

There seem to be higher-level incentives, having to do with a firm's long-term competitive position, that encourage some capital investment, some effort to lower costs. The capital investment decision is an important and complex one for both commercial and defense firms, and is normally made on the basis of considerations that have little to do with specific projects. Rather, as the DFAIR study pointed out, the decision depends on "the rate of inflation, the interest rate, changes in the level of aggregate demand or sales, tax policies, expectations or uncertainty concerning future demand levels, and technological change."[38] From this perspective, surges in capital investment in the defense sector in the 1950s and again starting in the second half of the 1970s had less to do with profit policies or contracting techniques than with the fact that both eras were marked by an expectation of higher future defense spending and hence a relatively assured return on capital investment. Conversely, lack of capital investment in the early and mid-1970s probably resulted from low business expectations, owing to falling defense budgets and high inflation, that could not be countered by complex incentive contracts promising higher profits on specific projects.[39]

If there is no necessary relationship between the failure of contractual incentives and capital investment in the defense sector, neither is there much usefulness in commercial comparisons. Private firms neither would nor have to put up with most of the strange practices that are standard in the defense business. Private firms are free from continuous external audits. They are relatively free from externally imposed design changes. Internal incentives discourage such changes rather than encourage them, in contrast to the defense industry. In private industry, incentives also encourage a balance between price and performance, while defense firms have traditionally been prodded to deliver performance with little regard to cost. It should hardly be surprising that labor productivity is lower in the defense sector than in the average commercial industry.

The shift toward customizing and away from long production runs exacerbates the problem of making comparisons between the Defense Department and commercial firms. The constantly changing nature of the defense design process has encouraged the defense industry to become a leader in adopting numerically controlled (NC) machinery, which can be quickly reprogrammed while production continues.[40] Computer-assisted design and manufacturing devices also facilitate the industry's response to shifting requirements. But the machinery gives an upward push to overhead, since it demands a full complement of white-collar computer programmers. Production workers disappear, replaced by programmers and computer maintenance personnel whose salaries go into overhead.[41]

This way of doing business also drives wages up and productivity down. So-called learning curves are the effect of workers learning how to assemble a piece of equipment more efficiently as they repeat their functions over a full production run. If the product changes frequently, however, little learning can take place. That, of course, happens in key sectors of the defense industry. Standard hour measurements normally are taken only after a firm has reached the mature level of production, usually "the point at which a company produces its thousandth item."[42] What does this measure have to do with labor productivity at McDonnell Douglas, whose F-15 line, opened in 1972, had barely produced its thousandth item in 1988?

The popular perception of waste in the defense industry is based on simpler comparisons. In the Reagan era, horror stories about $435 hammers and $640 toilet seats were taken as seemingly irrefutable evidence of waste and inefficiency in the defense industry. Yet the presence of waste in the production of sophisticated weapons is much more difficult to establish than these cases suggest. Efficiency implies a point of reference. A hardware store hammer, for example, tells one that $435 is far too much to pay for a hammer. But what should an F-15 cost—not today, but in 1973, when it first entered the nation's inventory as the world's most advanced fighter aircraft? Ironically, so long as the United States stays technologically ahead of its adversaries (and its allies), U.S. weapons will forever be without firm points of comparison.[43]

Moreover, given its national strategy, the United States should be willing to pay a premium to get the best new technologies to the field quickly; that is what it takes to stay ahead. In this sense, the Soviets, much more than the United States, should be concerned about the efficiency of their defense industry. Previous chapters have made clear that the United States pays such a premium. There could hardly be a less efficient way to move new weapons to the field than the rush currently imposed on that process. Yet the military routinely justifies this practice as essential to staying ahead, and Congress routinely funds the rush to production, presumably for the same reason. Efficiency, in short, is less important than national security.

In certain cases, efficiency is also less important than domestic politics. For every member of Congress who criticizes waste in the defense industry, there is one who ensures that a defense firm in his or her state or district remains open, even though production rates are inefficiently low. Others hold up production of a new system by forcing the Defense Department to consider yet again a production award fairly granted some years before, thereby forcing taxpayers to carry the cost of an idle production line. Meanwhile, legislation that mandates the allocation of defense procurement funding to small business ensures that production awards will not always be made on the basis of economic or technical merit alone. Here again, commercial comparisons will no doubt surface evidence of waste but not avoidable waste.

With commercial comparisons of little use, a better way to get a grip on the question of waste in the defense industry is to compare like commodities. Rough but useful comparisons do exist. For example, one can compare the cost of U.S. weaponry with the cost of comparable European systems, on the assumption that European systems are not likely to be far behind U.S. systems in their degree of technical sophistication. Occasionally production competition is introduced into a U.S. weapons program. Both comparisons offer only ballpark estimates of efficiency and waste. But if the $435 hammer is any indication of the waste found in the defense sector, even ballpark estimates should be useful.

European Comparisons

Finding European points of reference is not as easy as it sounds. The costs of European weapons are difficult to find and interpret. Moreover, because European governments and defense firms depend on weapons exports far more than their U.S. counterparts (since their domestic military markets are much smaller), they tend to hold costs secret, the better to compete in the international market. European production runs are usually smaller than those in the United States, raising overhead costs, and hence average costs, per unit. Finally, fluctuating exchange rates complicate attempts to convert European prices to dollars for purposes of comparison. This makes precise comparisons almost impossible. But rough comparisons do not suggest that massive waste is present in U.S. weapons procurement.

For example, most observers consider West Germany's Leopard II tank and the U.S. Army's M-1 close equivalents in performance. For a brief period in the mid-1970s the U.S. Army considered buying the Leopard II, hence that vehicle's cost became a matter of some concern. Testifying before Congress during this period, the XM-1 program manager noted, "based upon the best information that we have available from the Germans, the Leopard II today in 1975 dollars would cost a little over $1 million. Our XM-1 cost in those same 1975 dollars, under the same terms, we estimate to be somewhere between $700,000 and $750,000."[44] Cynics would argue that U.S. Army cost estimates for a tank competing with the Army's XM-1 should not be trusted. Yet the U.S. firm that would have produced the Leopard II on license had it been purchased came to roughly the same conclusion. In a detailed cost analysis, FMC, Inc., determined the Leopard's unit production cost as $520,000 in 1972 dollars, compared with the U.S. Army's XM-1 unit driveaway cost estimate at the time of $507,000 in 1972 dollars.[45] While one might expect the cost estimate of a U.S. firm to include all the waste for which the defense industry is criticized, for this comparison the presence of competition would be expected to control for these extra costs.[46]

Although data for comparisons of aircraft are more difficult to find, a study of cost and performance trends among U.S. and European aircraft by analysts at the Analytic Sciences Corporation (TASC) found no evidence suggesting gross price disparities between U.S. and European aircraft. Whereas U.S. fighter aircraft costs have risen at an annual rate of about 6 percent since 1950, costs of similar European aircraft have risen at about 8 percent a year over the same period. TASC analysts found that although both Europeans and Americans are paying more now for percent increases in performance than they did two decades ago, the rate of increase has been higher in Europe than in the United States. In general, when the Europeans pay less for aircraft, they ask for less, and indeed the study found that European technology lags slightly behind U.S. technology.[47] For relatively ambitious projects like the Tornado and the Harrier aircraft, however, the Europeans seem to have paid the same or even slightly more than the United States paid for comparable aircraft.[48]

The Nimrod project, Great Britain's attempt to build a radar early-warning aircraft like the U.S. AWACS (airborne warning and control system) aircraft, is another example. Aimed to be deployed before AWACS, Nimrod instead became a procurement nightmare. "The equivalent of $1.17 billion has been spent on Nimrod, about three times the projected cost. The government blames inflation. But Nimrod needs up to $1 billion more to bring it up to snuff. And the planes aren't expected until 1988—six years late. The 12 NATO nations that ordered 18 Awacs in 1978 received them all by last April [1985] at a cost of $1.7 billion."[49] For the Nimrod, quantity and delivery date differences muddy the comparison considerably. Yet even controlling for these differences would not yield a much different final comparison.

U.S. Comparisons

Perhaps there is little reason to be delighted that the Europeans pay roughly as much as the U.S. military for sophisticated weapons. Given productivity problems across Great Britain's commercial economy, one might even be embarrassed that the U.S. F-15 is not much cheaper than the Tornado, the A-10 cheaper than the Jaguar or the Harrier. This suggests that one look at internal U.S. comparisons. Most critics assume that the absence of competition in the defense sector, especially among the large prime contractors, almost guarantees waste, not to mention fraud and abuse. Thus another approach to the question of how much waste plagues defense procurement is to ask whether competition has lowered prices much more than would have occurred as a result of so-called learning curve price decreases at the sole-source plant.

Perennially strong political interest in competition suggests that prices do drop, and this conclusion seems borne out by a wide range of studies. In 1979, for example, the Institute for Defense Analyses (IDA) examined thirty-one cases in which competition was introduced into defense procurement after an initial period in which the items were produced by a single firm. It found that in twenty-seven cases competition produced savings over what would have been expected from continued sole-source production. Overall savings in these twenty-seven cases varied greatly, from 64 percent to just over 1 percent (losses in the other four cases varied from 4 percent to 24 percent).[50] Such data support the notion that, once they are safely ensconced in a monopoly position with regard to a specific project, defense firms are able to bilk the taxpayer to finance waste and inefficiency.[51]

But interpreting data about competition is as problematic as interpreting the cost of European weapons. A Defense Department study conducted in 1976 demonstrated that learning curves are highly volatile in the early stages of production. On the basis of seventy-nine case studies, the study concluded that at least eight price-quantity data points are needed to establish a statistically valid learning curve. In examining the forty-seven competitive procurements commonly used to document the benefits of competition, however, Donald Pilling found that in none of these cases had more than six data points been used to establish a learning curve. Moreover, in twenty-one cases learning curves had been established on the basis of one or even no sole-source production data points.[52] Thus none of the forty-seven cases can be proved statistically valid. Since small variations in the slope of the learning curve can yield large differences in downstream price predictions, estimates of savings are soft at best.

Studies of competition in defense procurement also suffer from excessive focus on changes in the price the Defense Department pays for a system, rather than the system's cost to the producer. But the relationship between a system's price and its cost is indirect. Competition may induce an impressive drop in a system's price, for example. This drop may mean that the contractor has adopted more efficient production methods. Alternatively, however, the firm may have done nothing more than accept a temporary loss in an effort to stave off or foreclose further competition.[53] Or perhaps overhead has been shifted elsewhere in the plant. Or perhaps the price of spare parts or tools has increased commensurately. A defense contractor's income is based mostly on profits from system sales, so over the long run decreasing system prices probably reflect decreasing production costs, the result of learning curve or capital improvements. But the nation's most expensive systems no longer enjoy long production runs.

The Pentagon's typical approach to planning and production can also falsely confirm popular impressions of the inefficiency of defense firms and, conversely, the efficacy of production competition. Given the bow wave and its effects, the situation Michael Beltramo depicts is not unusual:

> The government capitalizes sole-source Firm A to produce 1,000 units per year. The program is cut back and A produces only 600 units a year. Its costs are higher than estimated. The government established Firm B as a second source to produce up to 60 percent of the annual buy (360 units). Because it is capitalized for the appropriate rate, B bids lower than A and wins the larger share of the initial split-buy competition causing a savings to be credited.[54]

Given the consistency of production stretch-outs, it would be surprising if second source producers failed to come in lower than the original developers.

Finally, competition among American defense firms probably does nothing to eliminate the costs of red tape and other accoutrements of the American way of buying weapons. Testifying before the House Industrial Base Panel, for example, one defense subcontractor whose firm did commercial as well as defense business said, "When bidding on government contracts, we factor in the regulatory and administrative requirements, and increase the price quite substantially." The Panel heard from other witnesses that "the price difference for performing Government contracts ranged from 25 percent to double the price charged for comparable commercial contracts."[55] Whether or not competition among American firms encourages efficient production arrangements, it leaves this artificially high base untouched.

Clearly conclusions drawn from studies of competition in defense procurement must be taken with some caution. In their conclusions, IDA analysts argued that "conservative figures for the projection of post competitive savings are 10 percent for split-award buys [in which each firm wins a share of the production run] and 20 percent for winner-take-all buy outs."[56] This suggests that competition can be useful in cutting defense costs. And it suggests that there is some room for savings in the way monopolistic firms operate. But it hardly suggests the kind of massive waste that most critics have in mind when they castigate the defense industry.

Competition between Close Equivalents

The IDA study, and most other studies of competition, focus on smaller defense items, since these items are often purchased in quantities large enough to make competition pay off. The studies overlook the prime contractors, since the weapons these firms build are often too expensive, and production runs are too short, to justify the cost of a second production line. Competition among prime contractors may nonetheless be induced through the use of rough or functional equivalents. One example is the U.S. Air Force's Alternate Fighter Engine program, in which General Electric's F-110 engine was brought on line to compete with Pratt and Whitney's troubled F-100. Another example is Northrop's effort to bring its F-20 fighter-bomber into competition with the F-16 made by General Dynamics. In both cases, critics say, competition saved, or could have saved, money. If true, this means that prime contractors also lowered prices, suggesting inefficiency in the original sole-source situation.

The so-called great fighter engine war was spawned by continuing minor, but bothersome, performance and reliability problems with the Pratt and Whitney F-100, the very high performance engine developed in the early 1970s to power both the F-15 and the F-16.[57] The competition also arose, indirectly, from President Jimmy Carter's decision to cancel the B-1 bomber, which left General Electric with a partially completed engine assembly line for that aircraft. With part of the competing engine's cost already sunk, the Air Force and Congress found it fairly easy to fund continued development at General Electric for the F-110, which would be roughly the same size and power as the F-100. The F-110's emergence from development in the early 1980s was greeted with great excitement: Air Force officials predicted that competition would yield savings of $3 billion to $4 billion over the next twenty years.

More recent briefings on the subject have made clear, however, that these savings are not derived from any decrease in the price of the F-100. Rather, they stem from estimates of lower operating costs, the result of improvements in the F-100's reliability, and the high estimated reliability of General Electric's F-110. Officials argue that only the threat of competition prompted Pratt and Whitney to make these improvements, yet between 1975 and 1985 the Air Force paid Pratt and Whitney nearly $700 million to improve the F-100's reliability, which may also have something to do with lower operating costs. In short, competition did not lower prices and may not have had much to do with improving reliability. In recent testimony before Congress, Air Force officials have lauded the great fighter engine war less for money saved than for the greater mobilization base for engine production it has created.[58]

Competition between Northrop's F-20 and the Air Force's F-16 stemmed from the Carter administration's decision to allow Northrop to develop a relatively simple and reliable fighter-bomber for export. But Northrop's intended market shrank greatly as the Reagan administration offered the F-16 to friends and allies that Northrop's F-20 (formerly the F-5G) was meant to serve.[59] Moreover, other nations interested in the F-20 were leery of buying a major aircraft not already in the U.S. inventory, since only a U.S. buy was seen as ensuring other customers of a steady supply of spares and support. Northrop thus was forced to seek a U.S. buy for the aircraft. After having failed to sell the F-20 to the U.S. Navy, Northrop turned in 1985 to the Air Force, offering a "multiyear price and utilization competition" between its F-20 and the F-16C. The offer meant the sale of 396 F-20s for a fixed unit price, including initial support, of $15 million (1986 dollars) and a guaranteed support price per flying hour of $475 (1985 dollars).[60]

Interest in the offer from Air Force and Air National Guard officials as well as members of Congress prompted General Dynamics to make a counteroffer. Arguing that the F-20 was no match for its F-16C, General Dynamics offered a slightly stripped-down aircraft, the F-16SC, at a unit cost (with spares) of $10.9 million (1985 dollars, or roughly $11.3 million in 1986 dollars) and a guaranteed flying hour cost of $554 (1985 dollars).[61] This came to roughly half the F-16C's unit price at the time, suggesting massive savings. But the F-16SC was more like the F-16A, whose cost was roughly $13 million and still falling when General Dynamics shifted production to the more expensive F-16C.[62] As for the alternative fighter engine, it is difficult to find evidence of enormous waste in the F-16's production.

Public Perception, Defense Realities

How can one square these arguments with the reality of $435 hammers and $1,000 stool caps? Part of the explanation lies in the practice of buying tools and specialized components in very small quantities, forcing producers to allocate special production costs over a small production run. This hardly accounts for the $1,000 markup on stool caps. Nor does it apply to common items like the hammer. The practice was wasteful, but the source of waste was procedural—the failure to purchase spares in efficiently sized bundles—not waste and abuse in defense firms.

By far the more serious procedural error, however, was ordering parts through the prime contractor for whose system the spare or tool was required. This opened the part's price to three incredibly disproportionate influences. First, labor connected with modifying, packing, or processing the part was paid at wage and benefit levels of skilled aerospace workers. Second, both packing and processing were controlled by military specifications far more stringent than required for most tools and spares. Third, the item was forced to carry part of the prime contractor's overhead.[63] Indeed, even if contractors do not engage in the lateral shift of overloading spare parts to compensate for lower profits elsewhere, overhead loading will add greatly to spare parts costs.

Procedural waste is still waste, and spare parts horror stories prompted the Defense Department to institute reforms designed to "break out" small components, tools, and spare parts, that is, they would be purchased directly by the services, usually under competitive conditions. Yet it remains unclear how much will be saved by reform. Prime contractor overhead will not disappear. It will be reallocated to larger components where it should have been allocated in the first place. Wage rates are not likely to decline in the aerospace industry, nor will workers be laid off because of the absence of stool cap production requirements. Meanwhile, Jacques Gansler argues that reform created problems: "Not only did this [the addition of 6,000 people to check the prices of each spare part] shift valuable defense resources from the high-cost items to the low ones, but the added time required . . . doubled the lead time for the military to acquire spare parts. This will mean either spending more money to fill the longer spare parts pipeline or suffering reduced force readiness."[64] The effort to eliminate procedural waste in one area created it in another.

Gansler's argument provides a metaphor for the larger problem of waste in defense procurement. Nothing in the data analyzed suggests that defense firms are losing money. If the game were producing losers, more defense firms would be going out of business. More important, some data support the idea that monopoly production is not entirely efficient. Yet there is little support in the data for the argument that the defense industry alone is massively wasteful. The contracting game can produce $435 hammers, and defense firms can run up standard labor hour costs several times the size of those found in similar private firms. But the excess cost of U.S. weapons in comparison to European weapons, or conversely the savings induced by competition among American defense manufacturers, is often measured in small fractions. This reality may be nothing to be happy about, but it is far from the levels that horror stories often suggest.[65]

The more important point, however, concerns procedural waste. No doubt some of the fat exposed in the preceding comparisons is the result of avoidable waste at defense firms unmotivated to find a cheaper way to produce weapons. And the government has successfully prosecuted enough cases of fraud in the defense sector to confirm its presence there as well as elsewhere in the nation's economy. But much of the fat exposed must be attributed to the complicated, bureaucratically encrusted way the nation buys weapons. The current weapons acquisition process is neither an accident nor the result of manipulations by pernicious industrialists. Rather it results from a long process of political adaptation in which Congress, the Defense Department, and the defense industry have all participated.

POLITICS AND THE INDUSTRIAL BASE

Thus far the discussion has focused mostly on the efficient allocation of resources within individual defense firms. Efficiency across the entire defense industry is also at issue. In theory, the market encourages allocational efficiency in the private sector. Given the presence of free and open competition, falling demand in one sector depresses profits, slowly driving some firms out of business. Rising demand in another sector promises profits, which draws firms into that sector. A market economy's industrial base thus adapts to changing societal requirements and desires. Demand in the defense sector has shifted over the past forty years. What mechanism shapes the defense industrial base?

In the defense market, as demand for a particular defense good declines, competition for new contracts increases, producing more optimism, a larger buy-in, and, potentially at least, larger private investment in development. If procurement spending in defense declines over the long-term, there will not only be fewer new project starts in this sector, but the ability of these firms to get well will decline too. The resulting squeeze between increasing risk taking by contractors and declining compensation should force some firms to leave the business (or move into other lines of defense work), bringing supply into line with demand.

That dynamic helps account for the closings, consolidations, mergers, and diversifications that have marked the nation's defense sector since the 1950s. And the dynamic may be at work currently in the tactical aircraft industry, where recent events suggest that reduction may be in order. In taking bids for the prototype phase of the advanced tactical fighter (ATF) project—one of only two major tactical aircraft projects likely to be under way during the next decade—the U.S. Air Force was able to use fixed-price contracts for the simple reason that several firms needed the business. As one high-ranking Air Force officer said, "We looked at the marketplace, we saw what the marketplace was willing to do, and we took advantage of it. Any prudent businessman would do the same bloody thing."[66] Five major aerospace prime contractors teamed three-on-two for the project, mostly to share the obvious risks of this kind of contracting arrangement. By all accounts each team bought in to the tune of $300 million to $400 million.[67] Given the prospect for stable or even falling defense budgets during the next five years, members of the losing ATF team will face the prospect of having to recover that investment in lean years. The losing team risks going out of business or at least losing tactical aircraft business for good.

Many would argue that the nation must preserve excess capacity sufficient to support a surge in production driven by a long war or serious mobilization. The same argument arises in slightly different garb when defense firms go overseas to purchase components. Foreign suppliers may be the economically efficient choice, but many individuals argue that it is not in the national interest to depend on foreign suppliers for critical defense needs.[68] Purely economic logic should fall before the logic of national security in organizing the nation's defense industrial base.

At one level this argument is largely technical and strategic. What kind of a war does the United States plan to fight? What constitutes a critical defense need? How is the best balance achieved between the need for efficiency and the need for a large and thus inefficient industrial base? These questions have been analyzed and debated for years, though no convincing resolution has been achieved.[69] The debate received new impetus early in the Reagan administration, when increased emphasis was given to planning for a long war in Europe.

Like everything else connected with acquisition and the defense industry, the question of a proper industrial base for defense is and should be a political issue. Whether a big defense firm lives or dies is rarely a question that bureaucrats or economic forces are free to address. And though it may be left to strategists to determine how long a war the nation is likely to face, the nation's willingness to take risks—that is, how much hedging the nation is willing to buy—is eminently a political decision. As it happens, U.S. military officials and civilian strategists have never agreed on the length of any war for which they are planning, so this issue, too, is often left open for political as well as technical and strategic debate.

The political system subjects issues related to an industrial base to conflicting pressures born of a marked ambivalence among politicians and the public they represent toward the defense industry. The nation wants an efficient defense industry. Why else would politicians savage firms for what they see as wasteful practices? Yet when a defense firm, especially an important prime contractor, faces the risk of going out of business, politicians come to see it as an important national resource. Protectionist feelings may be strongest among politicians in whose district and state the firm is located but need not be confined to them. There is a broadly shared sense that the failure of a defense prime contractor somehow damages the nation's security.

There is no simple formula for predicting which of these views will dominate. Often the political system can take both views of the defense industry at the same time. Cost growth and technical flaws in its C-5A project brought Lockheed enormous criticism but also a federally guaranteed loan to help it survive immediate problems. Similarly, the government negotiated a sharing formula for repaying the billion-dollar cost overrun General Dynamics ran up on its SSN-688 project, despite accusations of a bailout by some representatives on Capitol Hill. And in the mid-1980s, as Congress passed the Competition in Contracting Act, presumably to enforce efficiency in defense production, other members of Congress joined those in the industry and the Defense Department in lamenting the defense industry's growing dependence on foreign, perhaps cheaper, suppliers. Given the size and complexity of the issue, the industrial base, and the nation's political system, both sides of this debate are almost always in evidence.

Still, the political mood shifts slowly over time in concert with peaks and troughs in defense procurement spending. As defense spending falls, the defense industry experiences economic problems that tend to evoke the "national resource" argument, while rising defense budgets bring higher profits but also more criticism. The defense industry was subjected to almost constant criticism at the end of the 1960s, but as the 1970s progressed, political concern shifted to support as falling defense budgets, combined with unprecedented inflation, rippled perniciously through the industrial base. By the end of the decade the House Armed Services Committee produced a small volume entitled "The Ailing Defense Industrial Base" that received wide attention.[70]

Yet by the time that study appeared the defense budget had already begun to rise, only to rise much faster once the Reagan administration took office. By 1983 not only had some of the spare parts horror stories hit the press, but it was clear that profits in the defense sector were much higher than elsewhere in the nation's economy. This event should have been neither surprising nor cause for concern, since the nation's commercial sector experienced a recession in 1982-83 while defense spending soared. Nonetheless, the industry's high profits became another element in the broad critique of the industry's performance.[71]

By 1986 three separate studies—one each from the Navy, the General Accounting Office, and the Defense Department—had produced conflicting conclusions about defense industrial profits. The Navy and GAO studies claimed that profits were excessive, while the Defense Department's DFAIR study asserted that the profits differential between defense and commercial firms during the early 1980s had "not been unreasonable."[72] Yet the DFAIR nonetheless recommended a slight (1 percent) lowering of allowable profit markups on defense contracts, suggesting that the Defense Department was responding to political pressure more than its own analysis. Steps were then taken that resulted in the lowering of industry profits. A somewhat lower ceiling was placed on the amount of independent R&D that defense firms could claim for reimbursement, while the traditional markup on general and administrative (G&A) expenses was canceled. Meanwhile the level of progress payments, paid by the Department of Defense to firms as their work progresses, was lowered from 90 percent to 80 percent in May of 1985, and then to 85 percent in October of 1986. Each move forced defense firms to absorb the cost of an increasing amount of private capital required to finance their operations.[73] Combined with the Competition in Contracting Act (CICA) and falling defense procurement budgets, these policies work to decrease profits in the defense industry.[74]

The defense industry was quick to claim injustice, especially when lowered profit prospects were combined with what seemed to be a trend, exemplified by the ATF, of using fixed-price contracts for R&D. In fact, decisions in various quarters suggest that the profit policy pendulum has been reversed. In mid-1988 the under secretary of defense for acquisition raised progress payment levels to 80 percent. And despite the ATF contract, or perhaps in response to the fears it generated, U.S. Air Force officials asserted early in that same year that "if the U.S. government wants to develop a [weapon] system, it is our responsibility to provide funds to the industry," signaling the demise of fixed-price R&D contracts.[75]

As in the case of the get-well game, the interplay of political, industrial, and bureaucratic forces, and especially the political system's tendency to operate countercyclically to economic and budget trends, might seem to produce a balance, over time, that effectively preserves a certain excess capacity in the nation's defense industrial base. Without solid analytical resolution of this complex issue, in other words, the political system muddles through to a compromise. This is true as far as it goes; the presence of excess capacity among the nation's prime aerospace contractors is a well-noted and longstanding fact.[76]

Yet the presence of excess capacity among the primes has perverse consequences for R&D. With the presence of excess capacity cutting into profits, prime contractors are likely to feel more pressure to win the next big contract. Competition for projects will be more intense if the procurement budget is stable or falling. Willingness to buy in will increase, as clearly occurred with the advanced tactical fighter. Arguably the firm's tendency to market aggressively will increase as well, and with it the proclivity to make rash promises, dedicate engineering talent to proposal writing rather than solid component development, and so forth. Thus indirectly the nation's dealings with the defense industrial base reinforce the R&D squeeze discussed earlier.

CONCLUSION

The defense industry's ambiguous, quasi-public, quasi-private status leaves it open to criticism and policymaking from opposite directions. Critics who see defense firms as fraudulent and wasteful implicitly treat the industry as private, something separate and apart from the society it serves. They want more competition, as if competition could play the same role in the defense sector that it plays in the private sector. Yet they recognize the socialized nature of the industry when they send more auditors out to scrutinize each firm's books, or when they assert, as David Packard did, that managers in these firms have higher responsibilities than the private sector manager. The socialized quality of the defense sector is especially visible when a large defense prime seems on the verge of financial ruin.

The industry cannot be treated as private. Its structure and behavior have been shaped by a sustained and necessary interaction with the political system that remains the principal market these firms confront. Many of the defense industry's most controversial behavioral patterns, the buy-in, cost growth, and various get-well games, for example, are deeply ingrained features of that interaction. Some of these patterns even protect the public's interest.

Indeed, these patterns may be more of a reflection of American society and politics than critics care to admit. In a narrow sense, the buy-in is an unavoidable industrial response to competition under conditions of uncertainty and part of a government negotiating strategy designed to counter the industry's monopoly power. But in a broader sense the buy-in systematically understates the costs of R&D to a society whose short-term political perspective makes it uncomfortable with the real investments required for good R&D. Having bought in, firms collaborate tacitly with the services in understating the costs of R&D until the political system's attachment to sunk costs effectively commits it to carrying the project forward despite its true costs. If this way of doing business is inherently controversial politically, it may also be the only way that the American political system can do business.

Yet it is undeniably a costly approach to weapons acquisition. Even if the industry were perfectly efficient, the costs of auditing, contracting, and administering—in short, the costs of political control—would still add greatly to the price that society pays for weapons. The only way to avoid the cost of red tape is to find an alternative to direct controls. But that solution seems unlikely so long as development and production remain largely monopolistic undertakings. Without a basic change in organization, the government-industry relationship will continue to foster controversial behavior patterns, drawing political fire and ensuring that the trend toward micromanagement and political intrusion will continue.

The industry is not perfectly efficient. But then one should hardly expect it to be. Some of these firms make unique, advanced products whose production eludes common measures of efficiency. The government often purchases quantities so small that monopoly is the only reasonable means of production. This sector is so far from the free market of economic theory that even the effort to impose competition on defense procurement seems artificial, however useful in specific cases. If comparisons are made to similar items rather than to the private sector, there is little suggestion of massive waste in production.

The truly worrisome costs of this way of organizing the defense industry are taken from R&D, not production. Defense firms must promise to do good R&D to win contracts. Over the long haul they have to deliver on those promises to stay in business. Yet in encouraging them to understate the costs of R&D, the nation leaves them little choice but to skimp on R&D as well. Better said, the firms are encouraged to transfer undone R&D to the production phase of a project. That may be in keeping with the need to create political momentum, but it is hardly the best way to generate quality development work. Meanwhile, with the rewards for good R&D still tied mainly to production profits, the incentives for doing quality R&D rise and fall with the defense budget and generally fall as production grows less and less important in individual weapons projects. Ironically, the more critics seek to increase production efficiency the more pressure they inadvertently bring to bear on the way these firms do R&D.

Perhaps none of this should be surprising. The industry merely reflects the broader values and incentives of the society of which it is a part. Attention should be focused on American society. Arguably, the United States, as the nation seeking to rely on quality rather than quantity, should be less concerned about inefficiency in production than about the quality of its R&D. Instead, Americans focus almost exclusively on production efficiency. Yet in trying to promote it they reduce incentives for good R&D. There is perhaps no better example of the tensions between the needs of R&D and basic values and norms of American society.

CHAPTER 7

Toward Meaningful Reform

IF THERE were an easy way to solve the problems discussed in this book, surely a nation as bent as the United States on reforming its acquisition process would have found it. But the political system handles acquisition reform as it handles most other issues, by muddling through, to use Charles E. Lindblom's famous phrase.[1] Lindblom saw much wisdom in this approach to policymaking. Perhaps that is true for many areas of social policy, but muddling through reflects the short-term perspectives of the political system. Muddling through acquisition reform is simply another way of imposing political values on a technical process that functions best in their absence.

No reform would be better than muddling reforms. Effective reform will have to be radical by comparison. Ironically, socializing the acquisition process, often presented as radical reform, is neither radical nor helpful. Those who recommend it forget that military R&D was socialized in arsenals and bureaus through most of the country's history. The services broke with these socialized R&D centers in the 1920s because the centers could not keep pace with fast-moving technologies. The private defense firms that handle most of the nation's military R&D today are now mostly socialized and evince many of the problems that hampered the work of arsenals and bureaus. Socialization is the problem, not the cure.

Choices about national defense and public expenditures will always be social choices; in this sense the issue is not whether the acquisition process is socialized but how. The problem is that the country has socialized the process from top to bottom. The first goal of reform must be to desocialize development: reform must seek to remove political incentives from an elaborate technical process whose proper workings they can only disrupt. Yet reform must also respect the right of those politicians and policymakers to have real choices. There is a way to do both. That way is not cheap, but in some ways it is far more compatible with national traditions and culture than the prevailing approach to acquisition. It means using competition differently and more extensively than is normally the case in developing weapons.

EXTENDED COMPETITION

It would be hard to imagine a less productive use for competition in weapons acquisition than the way the Defense Department normally uses it. Competition should encourage creativity and efficiency. Employed early in development, however, competition is more likely to encourage optimism and marketing, while detailed requirements sharply limit creativity. Competition early in development may enforce efficiency, but it ends long before development ends, and at this point further financing becomes a matter of time-consuming litigation that slows development and raises overhead costs. Reintroducing competition during the production process may generate savings, but it also reduces the rewards for good R&D. Competition in the commercial sector presents consumers with choices. Yet detailed requirements narrow the range of choice, while the early elimination of alternatives, coupled with political momentum, makes the possibility for informed choice in the defense sector remarkably small.

If that were the only way to use competition in weapons acquisition, it might be better to socialize the process and handle development and production monopolistically. But doing so would ignore the real potential that competition has to solve many of the problems that currently plague weapons acquisition. Historically, competition has been the only politically viable alternative to direct political controls on developers. In practical terms, competition satisfies the political system's demand for accountability. Meanwhile, to the extent that competition defers choices to some future date, it defers the politician's quest for access to that point as well. In short, competition has the potential to keep the political system out of development—that is, to separate the technical and political dimensions of the acquisition process.

But because important parts of the design process unfold so late in development, even early in production, competition must be carried further than it currently is. Competition should end only after early production models of competing new designs have been subjected to operational as well as technical testing. The need to conduct such testing before selecting a winner would make it essential to slow the current rush to production, both to give designers the flexibility to respond to the kind of information that often surfaces during force integration and to minimize costs and hence commitment to competing candidates. Doing so would also give military users a chance to explore the potential of competing new designs far more extensively than they do now. And it would give politicians and policymakers the unique opportunity to survey real alternatives and to debate them on even ground with the military services.

Extending competition in this way would dramatically change the incentives facing the nation's weapons developers. It would present them for the first time with the prospect of a real final exam at the end of development, with the choice of a winning developer uncertain until testing had surfaced information about reliability and military utility as well as about technical excellence. This should replace marketing tendencies with a more conservative approach to developing or selecting components that work well and reliably. To the extent that prime contractors deal with subcontractors in developing subsystems and components, as they do now, the primes would have to take a more judicious view of these products as well as their own. Extended competition would also encourage them to use commercially available, so-called off-the-shelf items, something the Defense Department has tried unsuccessfully to encourage in the past.[2]

Although a production decision would come more slowly than is currently the case, developers would have to develop the tools to produce their products as they developed the product. Given the increasing sophistication of production processes as well as weapons and components, and the tight interaction between the two, there is no other practical way to develop working products or believable test data. Under these circumstances, competition would encourage innovation in production processes, as developers explored ways of lowering the cost of their product. Continuing competition until a production decision has been made might be the only way to encourage process as well as product innovation.

In a sense, extended competition would create a more marketlike defense sector in the United States. The effort is artificial, of course;

the sector will never sustain a real market. But the more the government can recreate some of the marketlike incentives found in the private sector, the more it can relax its suffocating embrace of these firms and let them do the things private firms do so much better than either the government or the quasi-socialized companies that now populate the defense sector. At the same time, by creating an artificial market in the defense sector, the government can create for itself the possibility of making informed choices among alternative technologies and systems.

It would be wasteful, however, to restrict that choice with the kind of detailed requirements that currently govern weapon system development. Extended competition conducted on this basis would yield two F-15-like aircraft, or two M-1-like tanks. Neither the competition nor the choice would be meaningless, since one product might be markedly higher in quality or more ingenious in design than the other. But this approach would fail to exploit competition's full potential. The government could use extended competition to explore conceptual differences in weaponry or different technical approaches to a mission, for example. Given the persistence of budget uncertainty as well as questions posed by the quality-quantity debate, extended competition might also be used to produce items of disparate cost. Development projects run in these ways would leave politicians, policymakers, and service officials in a position to deal with budgetary as well as military uncertainty when it came to source selection. The force planning process would benefit commensurately, but only if the requirements process were fundamentally changed.

Project financing would also have to change in order to realize the full potential of extended competition. The uncertainties and risks of technology development have traditionally called for the use of flexible, cost-plus, or incentive contracts. But these arrangements make American politicians extremely uncomfortable and anxious to verify, drawing the political system into development. Meanwhile, administering such contracts normally produces the cumbersome litigation and negotiation process described in chapter 6. Like detailed requirements, the administrative approach to contracting would make even less sense in the presence of extended competition, because competition itself should be expected to discipline contracting firms.

Clearly the development process would still need some initiating impulse and guiding direction, some way of relating the military user to the technical developer, the technology under development to the budget and the nation's broad military needs. Just as clearly, developers would need government funding if they are to handle the costs and uncertainties of most military R&D projects. How does the government launch and fund R&D without creating contractual barriers to speed, flexibility, and efficiency? The answer varies according to whether the government is buying weapon systems about which it knows a great deal, or less certain technologies about which it wishes to know more.

BUYING SYSTEMS

The Defense Department is reasonably familiar with the weapons under development in most system development projects. Often long procurement histories offer data on cost and performance trends. The Defense Department also knows, or at least ought to know, that such systems have reached a point in their evolutionary cycles where dramatic performance increases come only at great expense, and where system integration poses special demands at the end as well as the beginning of the development cycle. It is neither wise nor necessary to rush into large system projects. Nor should the push for performance be allowed to undercut sensible cost priorities.

Setting System Requirements

With mature and costly systems chiefly in mind, William W. Kaufmann once spoke of an investment strategy for force modernization. "An investment strategy," he remarked, "can focus on more than the merits and defects of a particular system. It can choose the length of time between replacements, the sequencing of those replacements, and the real cost growth to be allowed from one generation of equipment to the next."[3] That possibility is based on the knowledge of such systems. Often, for example, modernization decisions are replacement decisions; hence timing can be set with reference to when existing systems are expected to wear out. With an understanding of evolving cost curves for a particular system, the acceptable cost of a replacement can be set in advance.

The requirement for a new system would focus principally on a unit production cost the government finds acceptable. To open options for dealing with budget uncertainty, competing contractors might be aimed at different cost targets. In a sense, the nation had that competition in the 1970s, with the F-15 and the F-16. While the nation purchased both aircraft, in the end it settled predominantly on the F-16. In this sense, extended competition would formalize what now occurs only through the manipulation of events by adroit defense officials. In all cases, competition would encourage developers to deliver their best effort within a cost target.

Systems like the advanced tactical fighter (ATF) or the Army's LHX helicopter would be meaningful candidates for this approach. Indeed, extended competition against a stated unit cost may be the only way to bring the spiraling cost of tactical aircraft under control. If the F-15 experience has anything to say about the ongoing ATF project, for example, the ATF's stated price of $35 million (1985 dollars) will at least double, in real terms, before development is complete, at which point the nation will have little alternative but to buy the aircraft in whatever numbers it can afford.[4] If the Air Force thinks that $35 million in 1985 dollars is reasonable for a new fighter aircraft, why not aim developers at that price now, while eliminating detailed requirements that would force costs up later? It would make even more sense to aim one developer at that price and another at a unit cost of $25 million—still enough for an impressive aircraft but a level that allows the choice of a winning candidate to be based on quality-quantity considerations.

Major system components could also be handled in this way. Experience with the F-100 jet engine program, for example, suggests that performance-oriented requirements in this technology can easily get out of hand, especially if those writing the requirement expect more than technology can deliver. A better approach would be to set as the principal requirement a final engine cost, calculated on the basis of engine cost trends and with reference to expected future budget trends and force levels. Competition through extended testing of essentially finished products would encourage developers to pay attention to reliability as well as performance.

Clearly price alone is insufficient guidance for developers. But how much more guidance do they need? Systems are becoming more complex, as are the organizations they will enter if purchased. Surely that calls for more rather than less detail in requirements. Military users understandably feel strongly about the importance of certain capabilities and also about their general right to control what developers do. And service technical agencies like the Air Force Systems Command are filled with technical experts who advocate, often justifiably, precise technical solutions to every technical problem. So strong are such feelings that even when contractors are competing with one another and competition is ostensibly providing design as well as financial discipline, service "Program Offices tend to 'manage' each contractor as if it were a sole source."[5]

The problem with such controls is not that military and technical officials are wrong, although they may be, but rather that they cannot set priorities. They ask for everything, and political forces make it difficult to back away from debilitating cost increases. Could developers do any better? Merton J. Peck and Frederic M. Scherer were skeptical. Years ago they questioned the usefulness of market surveys from developers to determine appropriate product characteristics for a new system, noting that "the preferences expressed [in such surveys] might well be in conflict with one another, and without official machinery to resolve these conflicts the best the seller could do would be to make his own assessment of the strategic situation and proceed accordingly."[6] Yet clearly the official machinery that in their view should resolve incompatibilities among requirements is incapable of doing just that.

The services are reluctant to turn detailed requirements choices over to developers because they assume that developers are ignorant of their real needs. In saying this, they confuse the intricate detail that emerges from the requirements process with real military needs, of which neither they nor contractors are likely to be fully cognizant. Even ignoring the uncertainty that surrounds most military operational issues, it would be more correct to say that military users are ignorant of the developer's needs. Defense industrial personnel interact constantly with military users. Many may be retired military personnel. They are far more aware of prevailing user debates than military users are of the intricacies of the latest technology. Particularly for mature systems, the industry has long experience with what the services want, with minute technical design features, and with milspecs. What designers need is the freedom to pick and choose among them in accordance with technical and military, rather than bureaucratic and political, logic.

One could hardly argue, for example, that Northrop and General Dynamics, placed into competition in the Lightweight Fighter program starting in 1972, proceeded in blithe ignorance of Air Force needs. The program went forward on the basis of a requirement document that was in substance only ten pages long and specified only general performance goals. Contractors had been working on designs for this type of aircraft for some years, often in close consultation with the U.S. Air Force. Both operated on the assumption that the winning prototype would enter production, although there was no formal promise from the government when the program began. Contractors even "tended to abide by MilSpecs as a matter of course—but . . . extensive compliance documentation was avoided."[7] At the same time, however, General Dynamics in particular took some innovative design risks—use of fly-by-wire with a relatively unstable airframe design— that might well have been ruled out in a formal, service-sponsored project.[8] In short, competing contractors balanced their own technical requirements with a well-honed sense of what the service would want if the project entered production.[9]

The LWF competition ended at Milestone II. After that the Air Force added a level of detail to the aircraft's full-scale engineering development RFP that should have no place under extended competition. Brief requirements documents that specify broad performance goals and service priorities should govern development through the extended testing phase before a winning contractor is selected. The industry must be allowed to add and subtract design detail with great freedom. Clearly it must be able to interact with military users and weigh their design suggestions against the technical and cost problems associated with responding to such suggestions. Military officials, meanwhile, must be willing to let competition enforce a sensible responsiveness from the industry.

Under these circumstances design detail will be added toward the end of the development process rather than at its beginning. There is no way to avoid some reengineering during the transition to production. The demands of force integration will be felt during operational tests prior to source selection. Yet these arguments only reinforce the need for continuing competition through extensive operational as well as technical testing of preproduction prototypes. By slowing down development and retaining competition, military officials can be far more certain than they are today that the design detail they wish to add makes technical, financial, and military sense.

Financing System Projects

Just as it is possible to specify a reasonable unit cost for the next tactical aircraft or tank or gun, it is also possible to calculate a rough cost for developing the system. At the same time, developers unconstrained by detailed and overly ambitious requirements will be in a position to control costs as they cannot under current arrangements. Thus it is possible to think of subsidizing the development of a new tank or tactical fighter with a fixed-price development contract. The government employs fixed-price contracts frequently, of course, but normally these are exceptionally detailed so that both the seller and the government buyer know exactly what is to change hands. In this case, by contrast, contract detail would be held to a minimum, with competing contractors being asked instead for their best effort.

As they do now, the use of fixed-price contracts for development work would encourage competing developers to add private capital as a marginal addition to the federal subsidy. This approach would have several advantages. Leaving room for private investment would give developers both the incentive and the freedom to make investment choices quickly and in response to technical information that they are best positioned to have. Forcing developers to absorb some of the risks of development would also submit them to some market discipline.

There is absolutely no sense calling for more private investment in weapons development, however, without offering commensurate private profits in return. This raises the crucial question of how profits are calculated and who performs the calculations. The current practice of basing prices, hence profits, on costs opens both the developer's costs and his profit levels to negotiation. That opens the way to extensive government intrusion into the developer's internal structure in a contentious and often disruptive effort to validate costs. And it shrouds the whole question of return on investment in uncertainty until development has been completed. This is likely to discourage risk-taking by the developer, or, ironically, it may encourage too much risk-taking, as developers compete in adding needless frills to their products in an effort to attract service buyers notoriously prone to buying "quality" at any price. In short, though extended competition may make the supply side of the acquisition process a bit more marketlike, the demand side remains unavoidably monopsonistic and thus must provide an artificial signal to producers as to what the market will bear.

The best way to do so would be to reverse the prevailing relationship between prices and costs in the defense sector. Rather than basing prices on costs, the government should state a price it would be willing to pay for the final product and allow developers to base their costs on that price. Prices could be calculated as described in the previous section on requirements, which suggested a move toward the "design to cost" approach to development. Because the government is in no position to be specific about production start dates, quantities, or rates, it could present prospective developers with a present value based on an estimated production run.

Clearly this approach would work only under conditions of extended competition. Without it, developers would lack incentives either to absorb private risk or to develop innovative designs. A monopolistic developer on a fixed-price development contract would deliver his best effort, or perhaps something less, at the stated contract amount. With extended competition, developers would be encouraged to maximize investment in relation to potential reward, in the manner of private business firms. And so long as it was willing to trust the disciplining effects of competition, the government would be able to pay the stated price without replicating the developer's accounting apparatus.

But if extended competition can be expected to hold contractors' feet to the fire, who will hold the government to its promises? Overall, the reforms outlined here will increase the risks that defense contractors take. As much as they might be interested in freeing themselves from bureaucratic and political oversight, however, they are likely to be wary indeed of sinking more private funds on the basis of a mere promise from so finicky a political system. Yet the government should be able to change its mind, in response to changing international conditions, for example, or changing budgetary circumstances. How can the government at once ask defense firms to absorb greater risk during development while it demands and deserves the right to retain flexibility?

The only feasible solution is for the government to engage in a contractual relationship with developers, with penalties should it renege on its promise to pay a stated price for a stated quantity of merchandise. The Defense Department negotiates such penalty clauses all the time; doing so is often seen as one way of locking the government into a certain choice by raising the cost of cancellation. Penalties would be calculated along a sliding scale tied to the extent of development work completed when the project was canceled. If cancellation were to occur at the end of the development process, the winning contractor would be awarded the present value of the profit stream promised in the contract. Risk-reward calculations in competing firms thus would go unchanged, while the government would remain free to change its mind.

Setting the Subsidy

At what level should the U.S. government subsidize a new R&D project? Sometimes a subsidy may not be necessary. Firms like FMC, Inc., and Cadillac Gage develop wheeled and tracked combat vehicles, including light tanks, largely with private risk capital. These are relatively inexpensive and low-risk products for which there is a fairly large international market. The U.S. military will no doubt want more sophistication and will have to pay for it. But, conceivably, in some sectors of the arms market, development costs will be small enough and alternative outlets attractive enough that the Defense Department could expect candidates to be forthcoming even without government subsidies.

How far up the risk ladder can "privatizing" be pushed? Northrop claims to have invested nearly a billion dollars of its capital to develop the F-20. And, having lost its bid to develop the C-5 for the U.S. Air Force, Boeing teamed with Pan Am in raising private capital to develop its famous 747 passenger aircraft. Indeed, the whole commercial aircraft business is fraught with risk; "a new airplane program," John Newhouse tells us, "will devour $2 billion long before deliveries begin."[10] These examples suggest strongly that developers of military aircraft could absorb more risk than they do now.

Yet one must not push these examples too far. Neither the F-20 nor the 747 were aimed expressly at the high-technology end of the military market. Northrop developed the F-20, for example, to replace its F-5 series overseas. Moreover, it began the project with a reasonably optimistic assessment of potential profits, having gotten the Carter administration's backing for overseas sales. But that market withered away when the Reagan administration approved F-16 purchases for what had previously been seen as key F-20 customers. Had it faced from the start the correct market signals, Northrop would probably never have taken the risks it took. Meanwhile Boeing's 747 was developed against a market niche that, if won, promised a much longer and more stable production run than the U.S. military market. And the sizable business both firms have with the U.S. Defense Department no doubt provided each with a reasonable base from which to take occasional risks. Indeed, the sizable risks of what Newhouse calls the "sporty game" of building commercial aircraft would be higher still were not most of these firms also engaged in defense work.

This suggests that for most of the weapons that enter the U.S. arsenal, and certainly those like fighter aircraft, helicopter gunships, and air defense missiles, on which the nation's technological lead is likely to depend, the use of fixed R&D subsidies is warranted. The size of the subsidy can be roughly established based on historical data about the relationship between unit cost, which would be highlighted in the initial requirement, and likely development cost. The U.S. Air Force apparently had no problem fixing the level of the ATF's initial fixed-price development contract. The Air Force was also able to estimate the amounts that competing teams of developers would probably invest in their designs.

Clearly developers are going to have to bid on specific projects, and those bids will cite likely development costs for the product they have in mind. Firms might seek to buy in, as they do now, by understating costs. They might assume that rising sunk costs over the course of development would create the same kind of momentum that it does now, opening the possibility for raising the subsidy later. Or they might see a much larger international market down the road that justifies taking more risk. There is also some danger that initial bids will take on the character of today's initial RFPs, with design detail and potential gold plate added to each firm's proposal for the same reason it is currently added to the government's RFP—namely, in an effort to win the widest possible political and military support for a particular design. Firms might calculate that they could even risk overshooting stated cost goals, on the premise that political lobbying could erode the government's adherence to its stated price and quantity goals.

Still, extended competition should greatly change developers' calculations relative to what they are under current arrangements by sharply reducing their leverage over the government until they have actually delivered on their promises. Under these circumstances, pressures to buy in would be balanced by reasonably powerful incentives to overstate costs in an effort to minimize private risk. The government would probably receive more realistic development cost estimates as a result.

In any case, however, a firm's past performance should figure as importantly in a contract award as the specific design advanced for that contract. For smaller, high-risk components new firms should of course be encouraged to enter the competition; thus the services will benefit from the natural creativity of American capitalism. But subsidies are likely to be small in this case, and the nation can afford to gamble on a new and untried commodity. Subsidies will be large for major systems—tactical aircraft, heavy tanks, and so forth. But the firms likely to bid in such cases are well known, having been dealing with the Pentagon for years. Thus when the stakes are large, the participants have histories. Those histories should be weighed heavily in the Pentagon's selection process.

The arrangements would seem to be getting increasingly complicated, perhaps counterproductively so. Yet such financial arrangements are not unusual for the commercial world. Firms contract with one another every day. Much of this is routine, but often the focus of such contracting is high technology, a product or component that must be developed in support of some larger project the contractor has in mind. The contractor may even offer progress payments as work progresses, based always on some idea of what the market will bear and hence what should reasonably be spent for a development. Progress payments advanced under these conditions are not much different from the fixed subsidies under discussion here.

There are crucial differences between the commercial setting and the context in which weapons acquisition proceeds, to be sure, but these do not lie in the financial area. They lie instead in the military's preference for capability over cost, in the propensity of both the political system and the military organizations that are part of it to reach out to control the development process, and, finally, in the individual firm's efforts to manipulate these organizations to raise profit margins. These problems add an unavoidable artificiality to defense procurement. Commercial firms can obtain a sense of what the market will bear from the market itself; in defense acquisition, it is necessary to impose that notion. Commercial firms may deal with trusted firms on a sole-source basis; in defense acquisition, competition keeps political and organizational pressures to a minimum while developers do their work.

Developing Expertise

While the winner of an extended system competition will move on to produce its candidate, the loser will shift into other areas of its business. Given the size and diversity of most of the important defense contractors, it is unlikely that losing firms will go out of business. Still, the design expertise that assembled and integrated the losing candidate will fall into disuse. In areas such as tank design this may be of little national concern, since it does not seem to be too difficult to reestablish design expertise. In the tactical aircraft business, by contrast, the business base is now small enough, and competitions can be expected to occur rarely enough, that the losing design team will be dismantled and the assembly plant closed. In this particular realm, at least, the nation is slowly but surely moving toward the day when the winner of a service competition will assume a monopoly position in the business.

Until tactical aircraft are proved beyond a doubt to have no military utility, it is essential to sustain the design talent capable of competing for the next major aircraft project. This is not the same thing as keeping production lines intact. Indeed it would be useful to eliminate much of the longstanding excess capacity at the prime contractor level. Production processes will change with each new production aircraft, as firms find new ways to produce new designs. The government can buy as much capacity for a particular design as it thinks it needs. What it cannot buy is expertise, which takes time to acquire and must be cultivated over the long term.

How many expert teams are required to sustain real competition? With only two such contractor teams the chances for collusion seem high. Yet competition involving only two firms has been standard Defense Department practice and as such has been instrumental in encouraging firms to invest their own funds in weapons projects. One finds little evidence of collusion in the ATF project, for example, despite the presence of only two competitors. Indeed, competition involving "the limiting case of only two rivals," Frederic M. Scherer has argued, "may be just as effective . . . as competition among a few firms. . . . For optimal incentive effects the number of competitors needs to be only large enough to pose a distinct threat of project cancellation, but should not be so large that the chances of surviving are considered so small that a company finds it preferable to divert its resources to less competitive programs."[11]

One way to keep teams alive and active is to keep them in competition for product improvements to the winning design. Although this would involve a good deal of component development, in the end it would also entail systems integration work. Another approach is simply to recognize that hardware alternatives can be put to good use more widely than is currently the case. The ongoing debate about a replacement for the A-10 close support aircraft, for example, is being carried out largely on paper. Critics speak of a so-called Mud Fighter that would be smaller and better protected than the A-10, but the cost and military utility of such an aircraft remains uncertain.[12] Developing competing Mud Fighter candidates would allow for real tests of operational utility while putting aircraft design and integration expertise to good use.

Another approach would be to run design competitions to the prototype stage as a means of exploring new design and integration concepts. The Lightweight Fighter competition stands as an example and suggests that the costs of such competitions need not be prohibitive.[13] Such competitions would also allow firms to reduce the risk and uncertainty associated with new concepts that could be incorporated into candidates developed for the next major system competition. Such competitions could be run on the basis of fixed-price, best effort contracts. In the absence of a production promise and thus a profit motive, competitors could not be expected to invest their own funds. Rather, they would be motivated by pride in their own technical expertise and by the assumption that the prospects for winning future production contracts will depend importantly on technical work performed in the years between competitions.

Finally, relatively small amounts of seed money might be awarded to sole-source firms for exploratory work on new aircraft design concepts. Such has been the case with Grumman's X-29, developed in the early 1980s to test the advantages of forward-swept wings. Funding in this case came from the Defense Advanced Research Projects Agency and the National Aeronautics and Space Administration. It totaled $80 million for two experimental prototypes—a fairly small amount by tactical aircraft standards.[14]

BUYING INFORMATION

Systems and their development consume most of the Defense Department's research, development, and production budget. Between such large projects and the technology base lies a middle level of technology that is smaller in financial terms but in many ways even more important in military and technological terms. The middle level is populated by fast-moving technologies crucial to the nation's technological advantage. The challenge is to get to know them well enough to make sensible choices about their future.

That takes a lot longer, and a lot more work, than the present acquisition process allows. Currently much of the work on such technologies falls to service laboratories, the Defense Advanced Research Projects Agency (DARPA), or the National Aeronautics and Space Agency (NASA), which focus quite properly on basic technical exploration. Technologies that show promise in such early exploratory work may be inherently unreliable, however, yet evidence of reliability will show up only late in development. Prototypes of such technologies may be impressive, but production tooling for the new device may pose significant technical uncertainties that may affect the performance of the new device and will certainly add to its cost and delay its delivery. Most important, questions about the device's operational utility exist wholly apart from its technical characteristics. And because operational testing must be realistic, it requires test articles far beyond the so-called brass board level of development. For the TV-Maverick, discussed in chapter 4, it is not clear that utility could have been thoroughly explored in advance of full-scale development.

Under current arrangements no one has an interest in exploring technologies this extensively. And there is no flexible means for doing so. For the services, developing new ideas to fairly advanced levels means generating hardware alternatives that policymakers may use to gain power over service choices; the services would prefer to make fundamental judgments about maturity and potential at an early stage and then rush through development to production. Neither the services nor Congress is comfortable spending large amounts of money and then shelving a project; momentum tends to carry such projects into production. That sits well with defense firms that still make most of their money from production contracts. Meanwhile the size of such investments combined with the uncertainties of the technology usually make it necessary to use cost-plus or incentive contracts that burden the development process with litigation and artificial constraints on speed and flexibility.

The result is bad choices, like TV-Maverick, or foregone choices, as the services artificially constrain the nation's technology base by imposing project-related goals on basic research. In a sense the nation pays for much of this information anyway, in maintenance costs for unreliable equipment, in the cost of useless devices, and in the cost of retrofitting fixes to fielded systems. But the nation pays for the information when it is too late to respond to it decisively and efficiently. And because funds for these activities come from operations and maintenance or production accounts, major actors in the acquisition process normally fail to recognize that they are really paying for inefficient R&D.

The nation can avoid such wasteful practices only by spending much more money fully exploring new technologies before making commitments. The need to do so will be still more apparent and important if the system acquisition reforms just outlined are implemented. Confronted with cost targets and the prospect of extensive testing under competitive circumstances, system developers would have the incentive to reduce risk by scouring the technological horizon for proven technologies and components. Unconstrained by rigid and detailed requirements, developers are likely to search far more widely than occurs under present arrangements. But the horizon they search must be populated with options that have been explored past the levels commonly achieved in current practice.

The industry's increased interest in component development opens one method for doing more exploration. When new technologies form part of a larger system, prime contractors might be allowed to handle component development. Often they do this now, but funding levels would have to increase. This might be incorporated into the fixed-price contract for a system development project. But it would make sense to subsidize the industry's search for components. Such a subsidy could take a form similar to that of independent R&D. Critics of independent research and development (IR&D) have been rightly concerned with lack of accountability, since firms do not submit detailed investment data for their IR&D spending. Critics also cite lack of independence, since often IR&D money is used to fund early development of specific projects rather than basic research.[15] Extended competition would at least partially allay the first concern, although it would be necessary to ensure that the subsidy was spent on military or dual-use technology rather than on work to advance a prime's commercial operations. Meanwhile the second concern may be a blessing in disguise. In effect, the industry would acquire a greater role in bringing new technologies out of the technology base and converting them into militarily useful components.

Another institutional approach to increasing exploratory development is to use the Defense Advanced Research Projects Agency (DARPA) more aggressively and broadly than has normally been the case. This is clearly what the Packard Commission sought to do in calling for a greater role for DARPA in prototyping. DARPA's problems in obtaining funds for such work, discussed in chapter 3, bear witness to the difficulties the current process has in handling exploration. Arguably, with industry looking for more mature components, there may be more pressure in a reformed process to give DARPA larger budgets. But it will probably always take active participation by the secretary of defense to ensure that the funding remains not only high but relatively stable.

In general, the Defense Department's goal should be to create a stable environment, over a reasonably long period—say, five years—in which developer teams can explore and test a new device. Though service officials speak fondly of the need for budget stability in funding system projects, stability is probably even more important in exploratory work. It would be useful to think of five-year, fixed-price contracts with civilian developers offering an interesting new device or idea. Judgments about continuing work or turning elsewhere could then be made on a relatively long-term basis. Given the industry's interest in component development, it would be useful to let interested firms participate in making such judgments.

Competition can be useful even at this level of exploratory work. Although the Sidewinder missile was developed at a government R&D center (the Navy's China Lake facility), the project chief later noted the important role competition played in moving the project along. "We were not commissioned to design Sidewinder; we had no externally imposed specifications, and we started with no time scales *other than those imposed by competition*. Our prime motivation was to avoid the construction of the Aircraft Fire Control System Mk 8 involving an air-to-air rocket weapon system [the Falcon] which we felt would produce an inferior result."[16] McLean's motivation was not profits, in short, but pride, prestige, and a sense of mission. These can be present without competition, of course, but competition provides discipline and efficiency—an eye to deadlines, costs, and user requirements as well as technological perfection.

Competition might also be used to provide decisionmakers in industry as well as the government with a wider range of choice, much as extended competition is meant to do for system development projects. Long-term contracts could be let in pairs or triplets to firms exploring conceptually or technologically different approaches to the same military mission. Or developers could be aimed at different levels of cost and effectiveness for the same technology. In this way the overall program would define the cost-effectiveness curve (or surface, in the case of a range of several different technological approaches to the same mission) reasonably well while offering the concerned service several choices lying along that curve.

The goal of such programs is to bring new technologies, components, and systems to a level where it would be appropriate to include them in a system development project carried out under the reforms described earlier in the chapter. But inclusion in such projects, or the organization of a project around a new device, must be left open. Some technologies will turn out to be basically flawed in some way, while others will simply be less cost-effective overall than a competitor. Even a perfectly useful technology or device might be passed over because the nation's security situation did not call for such a device or because the technology was moving fast enough to warrant waiting to a later point in its evolution.

All of these suggestions presuppose institutional changes to the current approach to acquisition. More important, they require a basic change in the way the nation as a whole conceptualizes what is going on in R&D. It is not surprising that a political system with inherently short-term perspectives and military services anxious to get weapons to the field would underfund exploratory development. But the United States has been doing this for some forty years, and the cost of this way of doing business has grown increasingly clear. The political system must understand that information about sophisticated new technologies is not cheap. Paying for that information up front and without commitments, however, is far cheaper in the long run than the nation's current approach.

THE POLITICAL CHALLENGE

Implementation of the reforms just discussed would produce a marked shift in emphasis in U.S. defense investment away from production and toward R&D. This shift would result from nothing more than an honest recognition of the real costs of military R&D. It would signal an end to the systematic optimism and understatement that marks the nation's current approach to weapons development, and explicitly recognize that technical exploration and system design take more time and money than the current approach allows. But the shift would be larger than what would be required from a purely analytical or technical point of view. The political environment in which weapons acquisition unfolds is not conducive to the long-term perspective or flexibility that underpins investment in R&D. Extended competition serves the political purpose of freeing development from these political constraints. If Congress and the nation's taxpayers really want good development and freedom of choice among alternatives, they will have to pay for them.

Can the Nation Afford It?

It may make perfect sense to increase R&D funding in comparison with current levels, and in comparison with production funding. But the nation still must arm a force able to meet real military threats. Will the production funding that remains after paying fully for R&D be sufficient for this purpose? There is no way to make a precise calculation. But analysis suggests that the shift would be far from momentous. Spending more on R&D would allow the nation to spend procurement dollars far more wisely than is currently the case.

First, a development process relatively free of requirements and accounting strictures, a process that encouraged trade-offs rather than prevented them, would produce weapons generally less expensive to buy and support. Taxpayers paid $641 million (1987 dollars) to develop the Bradley fighting vehicle through early production. The Congressional Budget Office's M-113-based alternative to the Bradley promised a savings of $2.6 billion over five years. Assuming that extended competition in the development of infantry fighting vehicle projects would have eliminated much of the Bradley's hackneyed requirements process, it seems likely that the costs of extended competition could have been easily compensated in the purchase of a cheaper vehicle. The F-15's excessive top speed cost taxpayers more than a billion dollars over the course of that aircraft's production. The aircraft's initial development cost just over $4 billion (1987 dollars). The trade becomes less favorable as developers move into projects with higher R&D content. But it remains fair to say that a large share of the additional money going into R&D will be reimbursed with savings from the production side of the acquisition process.

Extended competition aims not simply to enforce technical trade-offs within projects but also to allow policymakers and programmers freedom to deal with budget uncertainty. To the extent that reform produces a better planning process by reducing unit cost growth and introducing variety in the price of available options, it will create additional savings from the production end of the acquisition process. The CBO's study of the relationship between production rate and weapon program cost concluded that increasing production rates from 19 to 127 percent over Reagan-era rates would reduce program costs between 5 and 11 percent, depending on the system.[17] Bringing production rate into closer alignment with plant capacity, which under the reforms envisioned here would be built up more slowly than is currently the case, would be expected to impart similar savings.

Finally, the costs of better choices must be factored into the calculation. By rushing TV-Maverick into its inventory the Air Force spent $1 billion that could have been better spent elsewhere. The same phenomenon is replicated across the defense budget, especially in the high-technology areas where uncertainties remain high and rushing tends to promote bad choices. These may in general be less expensive systems and subsystems. But the cumulative savings of shelving many of them would not be trivial.

The Dilemma of Choice

These arguments may be convincing in purely analytical terms, but they are meaningless if the political system cannot handle reform properly. On this issue there are two major grounds for skepticism. First, arguments about better production choices assume that politicians will actually choose. Clearly they do not like to say no to a project with substantial sunk costs. They failed to say no in the lightweight fighter competition, for example, when the Navy chose the YF-17 candidate despite congressional pressure to choose the Air Force's favorite, the YF-16.[18] And they failed to say no repeatedly during the 1950s. Recall Michael Armacost's conclusion, based on his study of the Thor-Jupiter controversy, that "political obstacles to clear-cut decisions emerge as the intellectual obstacles are being removed."[19] Given the uncertainties that surround warfare, it may not be entirely bad to have a variety of production-ready candidates available for testing and purchase. Yet clearly the use of competition makes sense only if it can lead to exclusive choices.

There is no way to allay completely the fear that, presented with multiple choices, the political system will pick "all of the above." Obviously the use of extended competition will make it impossible to do so across the board, since the costs of producing all candidates will be impossibly high. But there are no guarantees that in certain cases political pressures will not produce an expensive refusal to choose.

Yet this problem may be less imposing than it first seems. The momentum that carries weapons into production results partly from sunk costs but also partly from the early elimination of alternatives, which confronts policymakers with the choice of buying something or nothing. Extended competition would eliminate the latter source of momentum by providing a choice between two working options. Moreover, although "wasteful duplication" was clearly a problem in the 1950s, the Defense Reorganization Act of 1958 gave the defense secretary more statutory power, which Robert S. McNamara used decisively. As Alain C. Enthoven and K. Wayne Smith later noted, the secretary's power is "largely negative," the ability to "stop the services from doing something he does not want done. . . . by withholding funds."[20] Extended competition plays to this kind of power. Indeed, it enhances it by creating competing momentums that an adroit defense secretary might use with some success.

Much will depend on the managerial and political skills of the secretary of defense. The need for the secretary's involvement in acquisition will be more obvious than is the case under current arrangements; as in the 1950s, duplication in development will demand some overarching intelligence for its resolution. Moreover, extended competition will provide the tools for realizing the fabled "centralized control, decentralized execution" that under present arrangements either invites intense civilian involvement in service projects (so-called micromanagement) or serves as an excuse for not managing the department. Secretaries of defense who fail to use those tools astutely in the politics of procurement that will surround source selection, however, will have little greater chance of creating order in acquisition and the nation's forces than is attainable today.

The Long-Term Vision

The more powerful basis for skepticism is the long-term perspective required to fund extended competition in the first place. The case for reform makes sense only over a period of years that stretches far beyond the practical horizon of politicians and policymakers. Reform thus wreaks of 1950s-style wasteful duplication. Extended competition might be politically feasible when development costs are relatively small, but politicians can be expected to shrink from funding full development of two expensive systems—manned bombers, for instance—even though at this end of the spectrum reform promises its greatest long-term benefits.

It is surprising, however, how often the political system makes such investments without really admitting to them. Arguably, manned bombers represent a system too expensive to be developed using extended competition. Yet between 1965 and 1985 the nation financed the development of two hugely expensive bombers, the B-1 and B-2. Although the Carter administration implicitly placed the two in competition at an early stage, preferring to cancel the B-1 and wait for the B-2, in the 1980s the continued development and production of both bombers were handled in a way that explicitly excluded the possibility of competition between them. The B-1B program, as one Air Force official said, was meant to "buy time for ATB [B-2] development."[21] It is questionable that the mission in this case was sufficiently urgent to warrant such an approach. Yet somehow the phrase wasteful duplication has yet to be heard.

Manned bombers are not the only example. The United States developed four tactical aircraft during the 1970s rather than the two the services set out to develop in the late 1960s. Originating outside

official service procurement channels, both lightweight fighter prototypes were nonetheless fully developed and purchased. Meanwhile
interservice rivalry continues to produce duplicative development,
much of which goes unrecognized. The political system funds more
duplications than it likes to admit. Extending such duplication in
accordance with the reforms just outlined would not produce a wholesale
doubling in defense R&D investment. And formalizing the competition
among duplicative alternatives would only increase the chances for
making sharper choices among them, saving money downstream as
well. The basic trade-off underlying reform, in short, is not so extreme
as it might seem at first glance.

THE CONUNDRUM OF REFORM

Still, there is no denying the enormity of the challenges these
reforms pose to the political system. Political momentum is an
established fact of American politics; politicians have difficulty backing
away from bad investments in other areas besides that of advanced
weapons. Consensus building is an equally well-established way to
resolve social differences, with the same expansive implications for
federal budgeting that are found in weapons projects. The conflicting
signals that confront defense firms spring partly from the tension
between specific and general interests that lies at the heart of representative government. And the short-term perspective that dominates
political behavior is written into the Constitution.

The nation handles acquisition well in war and crisis because such
moments of recognized national peril move the political system to a
resolve normally unattainable in peacetime. The arrangements generated by such circumstances have been ad hoc and often wasteful. But
overall they have worked, and in crises that is all anyone has asked of
the acquisition process. The nation has yet to prove that it can devise
an approach to acquisition that works over the long peacetime haul in
which the political system's resolve quickly fragments into contentious
debate. Unfortunately, the conditions that call most urgently for reform
do not breed the political resolve necessary for it. Therein lies the
conundrum of acquisition reform.

The real challenge to American arms procurement is not war but
peace. Nonetheless, peace may provide the impetus for genuine reform.
The United States and its allies seem poised at the edge of a new
security era. Changes in the Soviet Union's approach to security now
hold out the promise of a great relaxation of international tension. The

risks of war may lessen seriously in the years ahead. Soviet force levels in Europe, in particular, may approach parity with those of the West, acquiring a more defensive character in the process. With the cold war ending, it is said, the superpowers and their allies may direct their attention away from preparing for war and toward peaceful economic development.

All this is well and good. Yet it poses near-mortal challenges to the prevailing approach to weapons acquisition. A genuine lessening of the risk of war, for example, would remove any pretext for rushing weapons through development and into production. That makes imminent sense from technical and military perspectives, even in the current security environment. But it raises a formidable challenge to the service's control at a point in the development process when projects are the most vulnerable politically. To the services, the alternative to rushing is not more time to do things right but more time for the political system to intervene in ways that make things worse rather than better.

A serious lessening of the risk of war would also encourage a basic change in the balance among research, development, and production. Strengthening basic research and buying information about new developments will be more important than buying weapons, especially in fast-moving technologies where new systems and technologies may quickly become outdated. Yet the U.S. political system has enormous difficulty investing large sums of money for nothing more than information, while the nation's defense firms still expect to be reimbursed for R&D with profits from production. The alternative to buying new products thus may be a reduction in the resilience of the nation's underlying technology base, just the reverse of what is required.

Finally, the emergence of rough parity between Soviet and U.S. forces would undermine the rationale for pushing technology to extremes, encouraging instead a much more judicious approach to balancing cost and performance in new systems. Yet consensus-building pressures in the requirements process, reinforced by long-standing service preferences, prevent politicians, policymakers, and often even project managers from working toward such a balance. Those pressures are likely to grow even worse as projects are slowed. Ironically, a relaxation in international tension might make it even more difficult to balance cost and performance sensibly.

In short, America's weapons acquisition process is not organized to handle new and more pacific international conditions. The rationale for the current organization harks back to the 1950s. Though military officials may not necessarily believe the world is as dangerous now as it was then, the appeal to crisis is always politically useful for protecting an undertaking that otherwise cuts so sharply across the grain of American politics.

The issue for the future is not whether the United States has a weapons acquisition process or dispenses with one, although many see isolationism as the only alternative to cold war. There will be good strategic reasons to maintain an acquisition process even under benign international conditions, though the pace and purpose of its operations should change. Moreover, the process has become too deeply ingrained in the American political economy to disappear. The real question is whether the nation can manage weapons acquisition sensibly in a more relaxed strategic setting.

Clearly it is not currently organized to do so, nor is it anxious to take on real reform. Yet in removing the excuse for maladies that currently afflict the acquisition process, changing international conditions will make the costs of this approach steadily more obvious and inexcusable. In the event that real peace arrives, the impetus for basic reform may finally emerge from the troubled workings of the acquisition process itself.

Notes

NOTES TO CHAPTER ONE

1. Speech delivered to the National Security Industrial Association, Washington, October 6, 1988, C-Span transcript, October 24, 1988, p. A-11.

2. Thomas J. Peters, "The Mythology of Innovation, or a Skunkworks Tale," pt. 1, *Stanford Magazine*, vol. 11 (Summer 1983), pp. 3, 14.

3. Norman R. Augustine, "Managing the Cost and Schedule of Major Development Programs," in NASA Program Management and Procurement Procedures and Practices, Hearings before the Subcommittee on Space Science and Applications of the House Committee on Science and Technology, 97 Cong. 1 sess. (Government Printing Office, 1981), p. 82. (Emphasis in original.)

4. Burton H. Klein, "Policy Issues Involved in the Conduct of Military Development Programs," in Edwin Mansfield, ed., *Defense, Science, and Public Policy* (W. W. Norton, 1968), p. 103. See also Robert Perry, *The Interaction of Technology and Doctrine in the* USAF, P-6281 (Santa Monica, Calif.: Rand Corporation, 1979), p. 17.

5. The British experimental engine was developed "only because a British investment company decided a jet-powered airplane would have an enormous advantage for carrying airmail." The demonstration engine's cost was "something like twenty or twenty-five thousand dollars." Klein, "Policy Issues," p. 107.

6. Klein, "Policy Issues," p. 104.

7. See Institute for Defense Analysis, IDA/OSD Reliability and Maintainability Study, vol. 2, *Core Group Report*, R-272 (Washington, November 1ᵣᵣ p. II-9.

8. There is a large body of literature on the management of research and development, much of it drawn from empirical work done at the Rand Corporation during the past four decades. The best short statement is B. H. Klein, W. H. Meckling, and E. G. Mesthene, *Military Research and Development Policies*, R-333 (Santa Monica, Calif.: Rand Corporation, 1958). See also Klein, "Policy Issues"; Charles J. Hitch and Roland N. McKean, *The Economics of Defense in the Nuclear Age* (Atheneum, 1967), pp. 243–65; and Richard R. Nelson, "Uncertainty, Learning, and the Economics of Parallel Research and Development Efforts," *Review of Economics and Statistics*, vol. 43 (November 1961), pp. 351–64.

9. The classic expression of the need for parallel projects under conditions of technical uncertainty is Nelson, "Uncertainty, Learning, and the Economics of Parallel Research and Development Efforts."

10. See Leonard Sullivan, Jr., "Q3: The Quality/Quantity Quandary," unpublished briefing, October 1981, p. 3.

11. See Norman R. Augustine, *Augustine's Laws* (New York: American Institute of Aeronautics and Astronautics, 1983), law 15.

12. See, for example, Edward L. Katzenbach, Jr., "The Horse Cavalry in the Twentieth Century: A Study in Policy Response," in Richard G. Head and Ervin J. Rokke, eds., *American Defense Policy*, 3d ed. (Johns Hopkins University Press, 1973) pp. 406–22; Edmund Beard, *Developing the ICBM: A Study in Bureaucratic Politics* (Columbia University Press, 1976); Thomas L. McNaugher, *The M16 Controversies: Military Organizations and Weapons Acquisition* (Praeger, 1984); and Morton H. Halperin, with the assistance of Priscilla Clapp and Arnold Kanter, *Bureaucratic Politics and Foreign Policy* (Brookings, 1974).

13. Katzenbach, "Horse Cavalry," p. 421.

14. R. Douglas Arnold, "The Local Roots of Domestic Policy," in Thomas E. Mann and Norman J. Ornstein, eds., *The New Congress* (Washington: American Enterprise Institute for Public Policy Research, 1981), p. 250.

15. Arnold, "Local Roots," pp. 261–62.

16. Richard E. Neustadt, *Presidential Power* (New York: New American Library, 1964), p. 42. (Emphasis in original.)

17. Thomas E. Mann, *Unsafe at Any Margin: Interpreting Congressional Elections* (Washington: American Enterprise Institute for Public Policy Research, 1980), pp. 102–03.

18. U.S. Department of Defense, Office of the Assistant Secretary of Defense (Comptroller), *National Defense Budget Estimates for FY 1983* (March 1982), p. 56, table 6-2.

19. See *What Have We Got for $1 Trillion? Report of the Staff to Accompany H.A.S.C. No. 99-66*, Defense Policy Panel of the House Committee on Armed Services, 99 Cong. 1 sess. (GPO, 1987), especially pp. 7–16.

20. *Defense Acquisition: Major U.S. Commission Reports (1949–1988)*, Committee Print, House Committee on Armed Services, vol. 1, 100 Cong. 2d sess. (GPO, November 1988), p. v. See also Robert F. Coulam, *Illusions of Choice: The F-111 and the Problem of Weapons Acquisition Reform* (Princeton University Press,

1977), p. 379; and Bill Keller, "A Familiar Face, a Familiar Problem," *New York Times*, June 20, 1985, p. B-12.

NOTES TO CHAPTER TWO

1. For a discussion of changes in artillery and ammunition as well as small arms, see Trevor N. Dupuy, *The Evolution of Weapons and Warfare* (New York: Jane's Publishing Company, Ltd., 1980), pp. 292–95.

2. The Krag was purchased only after Congress insisted that the Army buy a multishot rifle. The U.S. Army modernized its inventory more slowly than European armies, reflecting the hidebound traditionalism of the Army's Ordnance Department but also the nation's rather benign strategic situation. Still rifle modernization did not proceed appreciably faster or further in Europe than it did in the United States.

3. Of the aircraft used during World War I, Bernard Brodie noted that "a single advance in fighter performance could bring one side or the other virtual domination of the skies." Brodie, *Strategy in the Missile Age* (Princeton University Press, 1959), p. 80. When introduced in the spring of 1916, for example, the DeHavilland DH-2 easily outclassed the Fokker E-IV Eindecker fighter that had been the scourge of allied aircraft the previous year. By fall of 1916, however, the DH-2 had fallen prey to the German Albatros D-III. See Laurence K. Loftin, Jr., *Quest for Performance: The Evolution of Modern Aircraft* (Washington: National Aeronautics and Space Administration, Scientific and Technical Information Branch, 1985), pp. 10–27.

4. Michael J. H. Taylor, *Warplanes of the World, 1918–1939* (Charles Scribner's Sons, 1981), p. 4.

5. Robert Schlaifer and S. D. Heron, *Development of Aircraft Engines and the Development of Aviation Fuels* (Harvard University, Graduate School of Business Administration, 1950), p. 16.

6. On British policy see Irving B. Holley, Jr., *Buying Aircraft: Matériel Procurement for the Army Air Forces* (Washington: Office of the Chief of Military History, 1964), p. 51. On U.S. naval practice, see Archibald D. Turnbull and Clifford L. Lord, *History of United States Naval Aviation* (Yale University Press, 1949), p. 256.

7. Holley, *Buying Aircraft*, pp. 70–72.

8. Irving B. Holley, Jr., *Ideas and Weapons: Exploitation of the Aerial Weapon by the United States during World War I* (Washington: Office of Air Force History, 1983)), pp. 175–76. (Emphasis in original.)

9. See the discussion in Holley, *Buying Aircraft*, pp. 72–76, quotation on p.76.

10. Holley, *Ideas and Weapons*, p. 104.

11. One commission member noted "almost daily improvements in allied designs were being made as a result of practical experience in combat." See Turnbull and Lord, *History of United States Naval Aviation*, p. 113.

12. On testing time, which could run from "six months to two years," see Holley, *Buying Aircraft*, p. 108.

13. The Ordnance Department published a requirement for a semiautomatic rifle in 1902 but did not consider the need seriously until after World War I, when Springfield hired inventor John Garand to work on the project. After a stormy decade of tests, when the department rejected commercial competitors, it finally settled on Garand's prototype, which became available in 1930. It was two more years, however, before the model was standardized, and four more years before production placed the new rifle in the field. See Major General Julian S. Hatcher, *The Book of the Garand* (Washington: Infantry Journal Press, 1948).

14. Schlaifer and Heron, *Development of Aircraft Engines*, p. 20.

15. Schlaifer and Heron, *Development of Aircraft Engines*, p. 16. See also Turnbull and Lord, *History of United States Naval Aviation*, p. 56.

16. Holley, *Buying Aircraft*, p. 107.

17. For a more recent assessment of competitions that "may actually be . . . noncompetitive selection action in disguise," see Merton J. Peck and Frederic M. Scherer, *The Weapons Acquisition Process: An Economic Analysis* (Harvard University, Graduate School of Business Administration, 1962), pp. 328–29.

18. As one naval officer noted just after World War I in arguing for the creation of a bureau for naval air, "creation of a separate bureau of aeronautics [would avoid] . . . the long delays, misunderstandings and frequent lack of final decision . . . [attributable] chiefly to the requirement that all questions be submitted to the conflicting views of seven bureaus." Turnbull and Lord, *History of United States Naval Aviation*, p. 137.

19. Schlaifer and Heron, *Development of Aircraft Engines*, p. 23.

20. As Schlaifer says, "a government establishment tends to become a collection of specialists, each promoting his specialty whatever the effect on more necessary objectives." Schlaifer and Heron, *Development of Aircraft Engines*, p. 24.

21. See Turnbull and Lord, *History of United States Naval Aviation*, p. 113.

22. Turnbull and Lord, *History of United States Naval Aviation*, pp. 10–12, 21, 211. Manufacturers lobbied for good reasons: aircraft were quickly reaching a complexity that made it increasingly difficult to finance R&D strictly out of commercial sales. Military sales thus became "the most important element of the aircraft market even during the years of peace from 1928 to 1938." Holley, *Buying Aircraft*, p. 11. See also David C. Mowery and Nathan Rosenberg, "The Commercial Aircraft Industry," in Richard R. Nelson, *Government and Technical Progress: A Cross-Industry Analysis* (Pergamon Press, 1982), pp. 104–08.

23. See Paul Y. Hammond, *Organizing for Defense: The American Military Establishment in the Twentieth Century* (Princeton University Press, 1961), pp. 94–95.

24. Holley, *Ideas and Weapons*, p. 105.

25. Holley, *Buying Aircraft*, pp. 97–99.

26. W. D. Putnam, *The Evolution of Air Force System Acquisition Management*, R-868-PR (Santa Monica, Calif.: Rand Corporation, 1972), p. 2. The laboratory

at Wright Field had responsibility for systems support as well as research, although the laboratory personnel preferred research. In practice, the relationship between project officers and laboratory personnel seems to have been tenuous. Research at Wright Field was organized along functional lines, while individual development projects spanned an array of functions. The contrasting approaches could not be reconciled. Robert Perry notes that a "major shortcoming" in the project office system was "inadequate technical support for immediate program management." This lack helps account for turning to the industry, which only encouraged the development of technical and management expertise there rather than in the Air Corps. See Robert L. Perry, *System Development Strategies: A Comparative Study of Doctrine, Technology, and Organization in the USAF Ballistic and Cruise Missile Programs, 1950–1960*, RM-4853-PR (Santa Monica, Calif.: Rand Corporation, 1966), pp. 23, 27.

27. See Mowery and Rosenberg, "Commercial Aircraft Industry," p. 128.

28. Holley, *Buying Aircraft*, p. 113.

29. Holley, *Buying Aircraft*, pp. 142–143; and Schlaifer and Heron, *Development of Aircraft Engines*, p. 10.

30. Holley, *Buying Aircraft*, p. 85.

31. Quoted in Clarence H. Danhof, *Government Contracting and Technological Change* (Brookings, 1968), p. 25.

32. For both quotations, see Holley, *Buying Aircraft*, p. 89.

33. Danhof, *Government Contracting and Technological Change*, pp. 25–26. For a detailed description of the 1926 act's crucial section 10, see Holley, *Buying Aircraft*, pp. 89–93.

34. Holley, *Buying Aircraft*, pp. 116–17.

35. "During the years from 1926 to 1938 the practice among virtually all manufacturers seeking Army contracts for experimental air matériel was to bid as low as possible, even accepting a loss, on experimental work in the hope of recouping later with high-volume production contracts." Holley, *Buying Aircraft*, pp. 24–25.

36. In practice, the relationship was more complex because no neat line separated research, development, and production. Much development work was done on the production line, and designs changed accordingly. Design and production engineers thus mingled on the production line. The mingling of design with production funding reflected what was going on in the industry.

37. Funding for Army Air Corps research, for example, started falling in 1926, reached its lowest point in 1932, and then rose greatly each year thereafter. See Martin P. Claussen, *Matériel Research and Development in the Army Air Arm, 1914–1945*, Historical Study 50 (Army Air Force Historical Office, 1946), p. 49.

38. A book by that title, written by H. C. Engelbrecht and F. C. Hanighen, appeared in that year (Dodd, Mead, and Company, 1934) and generated great interest. The book helped precipitate the famous Nye Committee (formally, the Special Senate Committee to Investigate the Munitions Industry) hearings, which ran from 1934 to 1936. For more on the Nye Committee, see Paul A.

C. Koistinen's, *The Military-Industrial Complex: A Historical Perspective* (Praeger Publishers, 1980).

39. For a longer discussion of the 1934 hearings and an assessment of the validity of the charges raised, see Holley, *Buying Aircraft*, pp. 119–22.

40. See Holley, *Buying Aircraft*, pp. 130–43.

41. Small firms favored competition, since sole-source contract awards usually went to the larger firms capable of conducting sophisticated aeronautical research. The small firms and subcontractors pushed for more competition during the 1934 hearings.

42. See Holley, *Buying Aircraft*, pp. 144–46.

43. Holley, *Buying Aircraft*, chap. 13.

44. An exception seems to be the famous B-17 Flying Fortress, a product of a sample competition. Holley notes, however, that the B-17's design drew heavily on Boeing's XB-15, which had been developed earlier as an experimental aircraft. *Buying Aircraft*, pp. 148–49.

45. Quoted in Peck and Scherer, *Weapons Acquisition Process*, p. 43.

46. See Herman O. Stekler, *The Structure and Performance of the Aerospace Industry* (University of California Press, 1965), pp. 14, 17, tables 12, 16.

47. See Marcelle Size Knaack, *Encyclopedia of U.S. Air Force Aircraft and Missile Systems, Volume I: Post-World War II Fighters, 1945–1973* (Washington: Office of Air Force History, 1978), pp. 1–11, 13–21, 53–81. That war gave birth to most of the jet aircraft procured during the 1950s.

48. Samuel P. Huntington, *The Common Defense: Strategic Programs in National Politics* (Columbia University Press, 1966), pp. 382–83. On p. 157, Huntington notes that "between 1955 and 1959 . . . , in acting upon twenty-three split JCS [Joint Chiefs of Staff] papers, the Secretary of Defense supported the Air Force in seventeen cases and the Army in only three."

49. U.S. Department of Defense, Office of the Assistant Secretary of Defense (Comptroller) *Defense Budget Estimates for FY 1983* (March 1982), pp. 61–62, table 6-5. James L. Clayton notes that research, development, and production funding for aerospace products rose throughout the decade, while money spent to produce "tanks, conventional ordnance and commercial types of military hard goods" dropped from $11 billion in fiscal 1953 to roughly $2 billion in fiscal 1957. Clayton, *Economic Impact of the Cold War: Sources and Readings* (Harcourt, Brace and World, 1970), p. 58.

50. Members of the Air Force Scientific Advisory Board, especially Louis N. Ridenour and Theodore von Karman, were important in pushing for the new command. See Edmund Beard, *Developing the ICBM: A Study in Bureaucratic Politics* (Columbia, 1976), pp. 107–28; and Putnam, *Evolution of Air Force System Acquisition Management*, pp. 3–4.

51. Having risen to the rank of the nation's largest single industrial employer by 1944, the aircraft industry watched sales decline from a wartime high of $16 billion to about $1 billion in 1947. In 1946 the industry produced only 1,417 military aircraft—fewer than it had produced in 1939. The impact of this decline was eased for a time by a surge in demand for commercial aircraft.

In 1946, for example, the industry produced nearly ten times the number of commercial aircraft it had produced in 1939. But by 1948 the market for commercial aircraft was saturated, and the industry fell further toward its prewar status. See Stekler, *Structure and Performance of the Aerospace Industry*, pp. 4, 12–15.

52. On the "diversify or die" impulse produced by declining airframe demand, see G. A. Busch, "Some Emerging Developments in the Airframe Industry," in J. A. Stockfisch, *Planning and Forecasting in the Defense Industries* (Belmont, Calif.: Wadsworth Publishing Company, Inc., 1962), pp. 175–191. Busch was director of market research at Lockheed Aircraft Corporation at the time.

53. Peck and Scherer, *Weapons Acquisition Process*, p. 122, fig. 5.1. The decline in contracts to the automotive industry accounts for most of this change. Clayton notes that "the value of production of tanks, conventional ordnance, and commercial types of military hard goods dropped from $11 billion in fiscal year 1953 to about $2 billion in fiscal 1957, a cut of 85–90 percent in 4 years." Clayton, *Economic Impact of the Cold War*, p. 58.

54. Stekler, *Structure and Performance of the Aerospace Industry*, p. 21, note 41. On pp. 83–84, Stekler notes that in the second half of the 1950s the ratio of R&D to sales in the aerospace industry averaged more than five times the comparable ratio for all manufacturing industries. For aerospace firms, the ratio rose from roughly 19 percent in 1957–58 to more than 24 percent in 1961.

55. Peck and Scherer, *Weapons Acquisition Process*, pp. 129–30.

56. The ten were the F-84, F-86, F-89, F-94, F-100, F-101, F-102, F-104, F-105, and F-106. See Knaack, *Encyclopedia*.

57. Knaack, *Encyclopedia*, p. 159.

58. On early moves toward system development, see Schlaifer and Heron, *Development of Aircraft Engines*, p. 12; and Margaret A. Kennedy and Robert L. Perry, *The Establishment of Wright Air Development Center*, vol. 1, *Text* (Wright Patterson Air Force Base: Historical Divison, Office of the Assistant Chief of Staff, Wright Air Development Center, 1953), pp. 68–69. The contrast with the Army's arsenal system could not have been more pronounced. Although the Army was struggling to come to terms with science and warfare, R&D was still dominated by the Ordnance Department, whose arsenals developed systems components separately and sequentially. In developing rifles, for example, Frankford Arsenal would develop and classify a new cartridge, after which Springfield Arsenal would design a rifle for that cartridge. This fairly simple, linear approach left designers at each stage free to focus on one set of uncertainties. And it was well suited to meeting the requirement for massive production of items not likely to change for some years. But that was precisely the opposite of what the Air Force was doing.

59. Putnam notes, for example, that the turn toward weapon system development resulted partly because the Air Force's acquisition agency at Dayton "had neither the experience nor the expertise to perform the requisite management" the new systems required. Hence, "these complex systems

problems were offered to industry as a package." *Evolution of Air Force Acquisition Management*, p. 6.

60. While the Air Force blithely turned management over to industry, Army generals anxious to exploit new technologies labored mightily between 1946 and 1955 just to create an R&D staff agency (the chief of R&D, a position first occupied by Lt. Gen. James M. Gavin) that was separate from the J-4 (Logistics). This move did little, however, to break the Ordnance Department's grip on weapons development. That grip would be formally broken only in the early 1960s, less through the action of service generals than the decisive intervention of the secretary of defense. See James E. Hewes, Jr., *From Root to McNamara: Army Organization and Administration, 1900–1963* (Washington: U. S. Army, Center of Military History), pp. 242–58, 363–64.

61. Knaack, *Encyclopedia*, pp. 113–14.

62. Knaack, *Encyclopedia*, pp. 115–17, 119–32.

63. Holley, Jr., *Ideas and Weapons*, p. 105.

64. Kennedy and Perry, *Establishment of Wright Air Development Center*, p. 15.

65. See, for example, Thomas Marschak, "The Role of Project Histories in the Study of R&D," in Thomas Marschak, Thomas K. Glennan, Jr., and Robert Summers, *Strategy for R&D: Studies in the Microeconomics of Development* (Springer-Verlag, 1967), pp. 59–60, especially p. 60, note 9, which quotes ARDC manual 80-4, ARDC *Program Management Procedures* (August 1957), on processing design changes. See also Kennedy and Perry, *Development of Wright Field Development Center*, p. 67.

66. Marschak, "Role of Project Histories," p. 63.

67. These points are discussed in detail in Peck and Scherer, *Weapons Acquisition Process*, chap. 12, especially pp. 325–26.

68. At various times Lockheed, North American, Convair, and McDonnell rejected letter contracts to build prototypes "because of a clause forfeiting all patent features to, and permitting, the government to assign the new airplane's production to others." See Knaack, *Encyclopedia*, p. 175, note 2.

69. Burton H. Klein, "Policy Issues Involved in the Conduct of Military Development Programs," in Edwin Mansfield, ed., *Defense, Science, and Public Policy* (W. W. Norton and Company, 1968), p. 99.

70. This led Klein to suggest that a missile was "a system mainly made up of components and subsystems initially developed for other missile systems." See "Policy Issues," p. 98. Making the same point from the other direction, Lt. Col. Jon S. Eckert notes that for the F-106 "the requirement really was not made final until 3 months before first flight, a sure way to have the requirements and performance nearly match." See his insightful "Trends in U. S. Air Force Tactical Fighter Life Cycles," Occasional Paper 11 (Cornell University Peace Studies Program, April 1979), p. 7.

71. Knaack, *Encyclopedia*, pp. 122–23.

72. Klein, "Policy Issues," p. 99.

73. Knaack, *Encyclopedia*, p. 162.

74. Robert L. Perry, *System Development Strategies, A Comparative Study of*

Doctrine, Technology, and Organization in the USAF Ballistic and Cruise Missile Programs, 1950–1960, RM-4853-PR (Santa Monica, Calif.: Rand Corporation, 1966), p. 116. On pages 114 and 122, Perry argues persuasively that the ICBM project succeeded largely because it "embodied the most comprehensive application of deliberate system parallelism of the postwar period."

75. Perry, *System Development Strategies*, p. 71. See also Beard, *Developing the ICBM*, pp. 153–94.

76. Perry, *System Development Strategies*, pp. 77, 71–72.

77. See Robert F. Coulam, *Illusions of Choice: The F-111 and the Problem of Weapons Acquisition Reform* (Princeton University Press, 1977), pp. 359–61.

78. See Edward A. Kolodziej, *The Uncommon Defense and Congress, 1945–1963* (Ohio State University Press, 1966), p. 127.

79. Attitudes began to change even before Sputnik. Before the missile gap came the bomber gap. Concern reached its peak during, and largely because of, the Symington hearings of 1956. Those hearings, only the most prominent among several investigations into the status of aircraft and missile R&D, were prompted by complaints by Air Force generals during routine hearings concerning the fiscal 1957 defense budget. They were also prompted by the resignation of Trevor Gardner, special assistant to the secretary of the Air Force for R&D. Gardner was frustrated with the ceiling imposed by the Eisenhower administration on missile R&D. See Beard, *Developing the ICBM*, pp. 198–200. On the hearings and their effects on the administration, see Huntington, *Common Defense*, pp. 138–39; and Kolodziej, *Uncommon Defense and Congress*, pp. 233–36.

80. Perry, *System Development Strategies*, p. 88.

81. Quoted in Huntington, *Common Defense*, p. 369.

82. Huntington, *Common Defense*, pp. 412–13.

83. A story described in detail in Michael H. Armacost, *The Politics of Weapons Innovation: The Thor-Jupiter Controversy* (Columbia University Press, 1969).

84. Armacost, *Politics of Weapons Innovation*, p. 129.

85. Huntington, *Common Defense*, p. 416.

86. Beard, *Developing the ICBM*, p. 125.

87. The noisy resignation of Trevor Gardner, special assistant for R&D to the secretary of the Air Force and a major force in that service's ICBM program, on grounds that "intolerable" interservice rivalry was undermining the nation's missile program, helped focus congressional concern. See Raymond H. Dawson, "Congressional Innovation and Intervention in Defense Policy: Legislative Authorization of Weapons Systems," *American Political Science Review*, vol. 56 (March 1962), p. 50.

88. Quoted in Dawson, "Congressional Innovation and Intervention," p. 50.

89. See Dawson, "Congressional Innovation and Intervention," p. 49.

90. They were invited to help by Secretary of Defense Neil H. McElroy, who noted to Senate Committee Chairman John C. Stennis, Democrat of Mississippi, that "it would not bother me if you held our feet to the fire and

forced us in connection with this budget." Dawson, "Congressional Innovation and Intervention," p. 52.

91. John C. Ries, *The Management of Defense* (Johns Hopkins University Press, 1964), p. 186. Ries notes that members of Congress expressed their ambivalence on this score by ensuring that "civilian [service] secretaries and service chiefs were still permitted direct access to Congress, if they first notified the secretary of their intention."

92. "Once these programs get under way," Secretary McElroy said to the Senate Armed Services Committee, "the problem of diverting that very vigorous attention that is being given by an individual service is not a simple one." Quotations in Armacost, *Politics of Weapons Innovation*, p. 227.

93. Huntington, *Common Defense*, p. 399. Huntington was referring to Navy as well as Air Force aircraft projects and also to Navy shipbuilding firms.

94. Glenn L. Martin, whose Baltimore-based aircraft firm lost contracts when the Air Force shifted more funding toward the B-36, apparently contributed to the Navy's case against the aircraft. See Paul Y. Hammond, *Super Carriers and B-36 Bombers* (Bobbs-Merrill, 1963), p. 496; and see especially Huntington, *Common Defense*, p. 401.

95. John K. Galbraith, *The New Industrial State* (Houghton Mifflin, 1967), p. 317.

96. Quoted in Armacost, *Politics of Weapons Innovation*, p. 154.

97. Frederic M. Scherer, *The Weapons Acquisition Process: Economic Incentives* (Harvard University, Graduate School of Business Administration, 1964), p. 27.

98. Peck and Scherer, *Weapons Acquisition Process*, pp. 429–44.

99. See his "Air Force Planning and the Technology Development Planning Process," p. 160. See also Robert Perry and others, *System Acquisition Strategies*, R-733-PR/ARPA (Santa Monica, Calif.: Rand Corporation, 1971), pp. 6, 11.

100. Peck and Scherer, *Weapons Acquisition Process*, p. 413. On pp. 415–16 the authors note "some evidence that the degree of competitive optimism in contractor proposals increases with the intensity of competition . . . [and] is undoubtedly correlated positively with the degree to which the firm is interested in obtaining a particular contract."

101. Frederic M. Scherer, *The Weapons Acquistion Process: Economic Incentives* (Harvard University, Graduate School of Business Administration, 1964), p. 28.

102. As Burton Klein said at the time, "Economists can iterate and reiterate that past investments should not be considered in making future decisions, but they will be." See "Policy Issues," p. 113.

103. Quoted in Hammond, *Super Carriers and B-36 Bombers*, p. 517–18. On p. 491, Hammond notes the convenient leaking of reported improvements in the bomber's performance, or the passing of development milestones, to coincide with congressional consideration of the fiscal 1950 defense budget.

104. Charles J. Hitch and Roland N. McKean, *The Economics of Defense in the Nuclear Age* (Atheneum, 1967), p. 255.

105. Perry, *System Development Strategies*, p. 93.

106. Interview with Air Force officer in initial group of Thor trainees, Washington, December 1986.

107. Knaack, *Encyclopedia*, p. 163.

108. Klein, "Policy Issues," p. 110.

109. Hitch and McKean, *Economics of Defense in the Nuclear Age*, pp. 256, 258.

110. Stekler, *Structure and Performance of the Aerospace Industry*, p. 51.

111. Huntington, *Common Defense*, pp. 378–79.

112. Quoted in Huntington, *Common Defense*, p. 400.

113. Armacost, *Politics of Weapons Innovation*, p. 167.

114. Armacost, *Politics of Weapons Innovation*, pp. 174–75; and Huntington, *Common Defense*, p. 414.

115. Armacost, *Politics of Weapons Innovation*, p. 17.

NOTES TO CHAPTER THREE

1. Systems analysis was located initially in the Office of the Comptroller, run by Rand economist Charles Hitch. In 1965, however, the activity was raised to the level of an assistant secretary, and Alain Enthoven became the first assistant secretary of defense for systems analysis. According to Enthoven, it was not until 1965 that his office "had the charter and the manpower to review systematically the requirements aspects of proposed engineering development programs." Still, from the start systems analysts were helping to make judgments about weapons already under development or in production. See Alain C. Enthoven and K. Wayne Smith, *How Much Is Enough?: Shaping the Defense Program, 1961–1969* (Harper and Row, 1971), pp. 262–63.

2. See John Crecine, "Making Defense Budgets," in *Report of the Commission on the Organization of the Government for the Conduct of Foreign Policy*, vol. 4 (Government Printing Office, 1975), pt. 1, especially pp. 97–100. (Hereafter *Murphy Commission Report*.)

3. Kennedy was briefed soon after he took office on the Strategic Air Command's plans to deploy 10,000 Minutemen. See "U.S. Strategic Offensive Forces in the 1960's," based on a case study by Graham Allison, edited by Frederic A. Morris, in the *Murphy Commission Report*, vol. 4, especially p. 147.

4. Richard A. Stubbing and Richard A. Mendel, *The Defense Game: An Insider Explores the Astonishing Realities of America's Defense Establishment* (Harper and Row, 1986), p. 271.

5. See Richard G. Head, "Doctrinal Innovation and the A-7 Attack Aircraft Decisions," in Head and Ervin J. Rokke, eds., *American Defense Policy*, 3d ed. (Johns Hopkins University Press, 1973), pp. 431–45.

6. Leon H. Dulberger, "Advanced Fighter-Attack Aircraft," *Space/Aeronautics*, vol. 45 (April 1966), pp. 80–81.

7. See Enthoven and Smith, *How Much Is Enough?*, p. 263.

8. See Thomas L. McNaugher, *The M16 Controversies: Military Organizations and Weapons Acquisition* (Praeger, 1984), especially pp. 75–114.

9. The most laudatory expression came from Senator Richard B. Russell, chairman of the Senate Armed Services Committee, in early 1961: "I have been listening to statements from officials of the Department of Defense now for almost thirty years . . . and I have never heard one that was clearer, more definitive, and yet more comprehensive." Quoted in William W. Kaufmann, *The McNamara Strategy* (Harper and Row, 1964), p. 2.

10. House Armed Services Committee Chairman Carl Vinson agreed to rephrase his legislative directive, authorizing rather than directing the Defense Department to spend money on the bomber, in return for an agreement to study the bomber issue. See Michael E. Brown, "Flying Blind: Weapon Acquisition in the U.S. Strategic Bomber Program," Ph.D. dissertation, Cornell University, May 1983, pp. 413, 491.

11. See Raymond H. Dawson, "Congressional Innovation and Intervention in Defense Policy: Legislative Authorization of Weapons Systems," *American Political Science Review*, vol. 56 (March 1962), pp. 42–57.

12. See Andrew Mayer, *The Authorization Process*, a brief history of authorizing legislation, with particular reference to its use by the Armed Services Committees (Washington: Congressional Research Service, December 22, 1976), pp. 25–28, 35–37.

13. Mayer, *Authorization Process*, pp. 22–25; and Dawson, "Congressional Innovation and Intervention," p. 53.

14. Louis Fisher, "Annual Authorizations: Durable Roadblocks to Biennial Budgeting," *Public Budgeting and Finance*, vol. 3 (Spring 1983), p. 33.

15. See Arnold Kanter, *Defense Politics: A Budgetary Perspective* (University of Chicago Press, 1975), p. 55.

16. Enthoven and Smith, *How Much Is Enough?*, p. 310.

17. See Richard B. Crossland and James T. Currie, *Twice the Citizen: A History of the United States Army Reserve, 1908–1983* (Washington: Office of the Chief, Army Reserve, 1984), pp. 165–67. See also Martin Binkin, *U.S. Reserve Forces: The Problem of the Weekend Warrior* (Brookings, 1974), p. 26.

18. Aaron Wildavsky, "The Political Economy of Efficiency: Cost-Benefit Analysis, Systems Analysis, and Program Budgeting," *Public Administration Review*, vol. 26 (December 1966), p. 308. (Emphasis in original.)

19. See Stubbing and Mendel, *Defense Game*, pp. 279–81.

20. See Enthoven and Smith, *How Much Is Enough?*, p. 266, on the "largely negative" power of the defense secretary.

21. Enthoven and Smith, *How Much Is Enough?*, p. 263.

22. Graham T. Allison, "The F-111," based on a case study by Robert F. Coulam, in *Murphy Commission Report*, vol. 4, p. 127.

23. A study of acquisition practice during the 1960s revealed that program managers held to their original project goals even if it meant accepting higher costs and later delivery. See Robert Perry and others, *System Acquisition Strategies*, RM-733-PR/ARPA (Santa Monica, Calif.: Rand Corporation, 1971).

24. See Robert F. Coulam, *Illusions of Choice: The F-111 and the Problem of Weapons Acquisition Reform* (Princeton University Press, 1977), especially chap. 3.

25. Allison, "The F-111," pp. 120–21.

26. McNamara seems to have known that the specification was unachievable, at least at required weight, but the project went ahead anyway. Coulam, *Illusions of Choice*, pp. 59–60.

27. John Steinbruner and Barry Carter, "Organizational and Political Dimensions of the Strategic Posture: The Problems of Reform," *Daedalus*, vol. 104 (Summer 1975), p. 144.

28. See Robert J. Art, *The TFX Decision: McNamara and the Military* (Little, Brown and Company, 1968), pp. 94–100.

29. See Art, *The TFX Decision*, pp. 88–102; and Enthoven and Smith, *How Much Is Enough?*, p. 240, quotation on p. 98.

30. The percent of military procurement dollars awarded by cost-plus-fixed-fee contracts fell from 39.0 percent in 1960 to 14.3 percent in 1964, while dollars awarded through fixed-price and fixed-price-incentive contracts rose from 45 percent in 1960 to nearly 65 percent in 1964. See table 9 and the surrounding discussion in Frederic M. Scherer, "The Aerospace Industry," in Walter Adams, ed., *The Structure of American Industry* (MacMillan, 1971), p. 369.

31. Scherer, "Aerospace Industry," p. 351.

32. A Rand Corporation cost estimate available at the time suggested that building the F-111 would require roughly 6.0 labor hours per pound of aircraft. Boeing and General Dynamics estimated respectively that 2.0 and 3.8 hours per pound of aircraft would be required, with General Dynamics winning the contract. In 1968 it was determined that in reality it took 7.0 labor hours per pound to build the F-111. See Joseph P. Large, *Development of Parametric Cost Models for Weapon Systems*, P-6604 (Santa Monica, Calif.: Rand Corporation, 1981), p. 15.

33. Not surprisingly, engineering change proposals (ECPs) increased with incentive contracts. Coulam cites one large defense contractor whose business with the government shifted sharply away from cost-plus and toward incentive contracts after 1962. At the same time, contract changes quadrupled. See Coulam, *Illusions of Choice*, p. 378, note 70.

34. In the case of the M-16 rifle—another interservice project but of much lower priority than the F-111—an assistant secretary of defense was forced to decide on the weapon's trigger pull, since the Army and Marine Corps could not reach a decision on their own and their indecision was holding up development. In fact, decisionmaking on a host of minor technical issues was in this case the object of intense and often politically motivated debate. See McNaugher, *The M16 Controversies*, pp. 135–70. For a view that attributes still more of the M-16's performance problems to the politics of its development, see James Fallows, *National Defense* (Random House, 1981), pp. 76–95.

35. Coulam, *Illusions of Choice*, pp. 210–11.

36. Allen D. Lee, *A Strategy to Improve the Early Production Phase in Air Force Acquisition Programs*, P-6941-RGI (Santa Monica, Calif.: Rand Corporation, 1983), pp. 97, 99.

37. Enthoven and Smith, *How Much Is Enough?*, pp. 239–40, especially p. 347, note 5.

38. See Enthoven and Smith, *How Much Is Enough?*, p. 240.

39. For a detailed indictment of the C-5A contract, see A. Ernest Fitzgerald, *The High Priests of Waste* (W. W. Norton, 1972), especially pp. 198–223.

40. Soon afterward, the chief of ordnance resigned. See Thomas L. McNaugher, "Marksmanship, McNamara, and the M16 Rifle: Organizations, Analysis and Weapons Acquisition," Ph.D. dissertation, Harvard University, 1977, pp. 155–56, and 327, note 109.

41. See Thomas L. McNaugher, "Problems of Collaborative Weapons Development: The MBT-70," *Armed Forces and Society*, vol. 10 (Fall 1983), pp. 123–45. International development, however, resulted in some development problems similar to the interservice trouble that occurred in the TFX project. Eventually, participating services canceled the MBT-70 because technical and cost problems became so great.

42. The Army's M-2 Bradley infantry fighting vehicle, for example, was approved as a concept in 1964. The full specification was not available until 1970. See Daniel Joseph Kaufman, "Organizations, Technology, and Weapons Acquisition: The Development of the Infantry Fighting Vehicle," Ph.D. dissertation, Massachusetts Institute of Technology, 1983, pp. 176–229. For more on the Bradley, see chap. 5 in this volume. Another example is today's Blackhawk helicopter, which began life conceptually as the Utility Tactical Transport Aircraft System (UTTAS) in 1965 but did not enter development until 1972. See Giles K. Smith and others, *The Use of Prototypes in Weapon System Development*, R-2345-AF (Santa Monica, Calif.: Rand Corporation, 1981), p. 125.

43. Enthoven and Smith, *How Much Is Enough?*, p. 239.

44. See the several volumes under the general title *The Acquisition of Weapons Systems*, Hearings before the Subcommittee on Economy in Government of the Joint Economic Committee, 91 Cong. 1 sess. (GPO, 1970). This quotation comes from Senator William Proxmire's opening remarks, pt. 1, p. 1. (Hereafter *Acquisition of Weapons Systems*, Hearings.)

45. Blue Ribbon Defense Panel chaired by Gilbert W. Fitzhugh, *Report to the President and the Secretary of Defense on the Department of Defense* (Department of Defense, 1970), p. v.

46. See Gilbert W. Fitzhugh's testimony in *Weapon Systems Acquisition Process*, Hearings before the Senate Armed Services Committee, 92 Cong. 1 sess.(GPO, 1972), p. 13.

47. For a description of the so-called Packard Initiatives and an evaluation of their impact, see Edmund Dews and others, *Acquisition Policy Effectiveness: Department of the Defense Experience in the 1970s*, R-2516-DR&E (Santa Monica, Calif.: Rand Corporation, 1979).

48. Initiative 10 as outlined in Dews and others, *Acquisition Policy Effectiveness*, p. 2.

49. In 1977 Secretary of Defense Harold Brown instituted DSARC 0, which

required the services to justify a mission before they began the search for appropriate technologies to fulfill it. The Reagan administration, however, dropped DSARC 0 in 1981, because it was thought to lengthen unnecessarily the acquisition process. Franklin A. Long and Judith Reppy, "The Decision Process for U. S. Military R&D," in Kosta Tsipis and Penny Janeway, eds., *Review of U.S. Military Research and Development, 1984* (Pergamon-Brassey's, published in cooperation with the Program in Science and Technology for International Security, Massachusetts Institute of Technology, 1984), p. 15.

50. R. Douglas Arnold, "The Local Roots of Domestic Policy," in Thomas E. Mann and Norman J. Ornstein, eds., *The New Congress* (Washington: American Enterprise Institute for Public Policy Research, 1981), p. 285.

51. Caspar Weinberger, "Industry Craves Self-Governance," *Defense News*, December 22, 1986, p. 20; John G. Kester, "Under Siege," *Military Logistics Forum*, vol. 1 (September-October 1984), pp. 27, 30; and *Defense Organization: The Need for Change*, Committee Print, Senate Committee on Armed Services, 99 Cong. 1 sess (GPO, 1985), pp. 591–93.

52. Molly Moore, "Defense Oversight: War of the Watchdogs," *Washington Post*, October 12, 1987, p. A17.

53. War Department, Table of Organization and Equipment No. 7, "Infantry Division," Washington, January 24, 1945; and Department of the Army, Table of Organization and Equipment NR. 7R, "Infantry Division," February 23, 1955.

54. Dews and others, *Acquisition Policy Effectiveness*, p. 21, note 20. (Emphasis in original.) An earlier Rand report noted that contractors may "demonstrate some [performance] feature on a one-time basis even though the real technical capability nominally demonstrated may not be routinely or regularly achievable at all." Robert Perry and others, *System Acquisition Strategies*, R-733-PR/ARPA (Santa Monica, Calif.: Rand Corporation, 1971), p. 22.

55. Coulam, *Illusions of Choice*, p. 380. (Emphasis in original.)

56. U.S. General Accounting Office, Report to the Secretary of the Army, *The Army Needs More Comprehensive Evaluations to Make Effective Use of Its Weapon System Testing*, NSIAD-84-40 (February 24, 1984), pp. 4, 5, 14.

57. *The B-1B: A Program Review*, Report of the Panel on the B1-B, Committee Print, Subcommittee on Research and Development and Subcommittee on Procurement and Military Nuclear Systems of the House Committee on Armed Services, 100 Cong. 1 sess. (GPO, 1987), p. 11.

58. Russell Murray II (former assistant secretary of defense for program analysis and evaluation), "High-Tech Weapons: A Blessing or a Curse?" *Issues in Science and Technology*, vol. 2 (Fall 1985), p. 19.

59. Dews and others, *Acquisition Policy Effectiveness*, p. 39.

60. See the article by then-chairman of the Office of the Secretary of Defense Cost Analysis Improvement Group, Milton A. Margolis, "Improving Cost Estimating in the Department of Defense," *Concepts: The Journal of Defense Systems Acquisition Management*, vol. 4 (Spring 1981), pp. 7–17, where he notes, "CAIG's estimates have tended to be higher than either the program office or the service independent estimates" (p. 13). The program manager's estimates,

he adds, "are generally a product of industrial engineering judgements made by the contractors involved with the program, who are naturally in an advocacy role" (p. 13).

61. Dews and others, *Acquisition Policy Effectiveness*, p. 93.

62. On AMRAAM, see Congressional Budget Office, "The Advanced Medium-Range Air-to-Air Missile (AMRAAM): Current Plans and Alternatives," Staff Working Paper (Washington, August 1986), p. 1. On LANTIRN, see *Department of Defense Appropriations for Fiscal Year 1986*, Hearings before a Subcommittee of the Senate Committee on Appropriations, 99 Cong. 1 sess. (GPO, 1986), pt. 3, p. 821.

63. Colin Norman, "Stealth Bomber: Evading Flak over Cost, Mission," *Science*, December 9, 1988, pp. 1372–73.

64. Donald B. Rice, *Defense Resource Management Study, Final Report*, A report requested by the president and submitted to the secretary of defense (GPO, February 1979), p. 35.

65. See the perceptive discussion in Edwin A. Deagle, Jr., "Organization and Process in Military R&D," in Franklin A. Long and Judith Reppy, *The Genesis of New Weapons: Decision Making for Military* R&D (Pergamon Press, 1980), p. 168.

66. In a study of the use of prototyping under Packard, Rand analysts concluded that the "shift from prototype test to analysis as a basis for major management decisions has been almost total," suggesting that the organizational differences between Packard and McNamara were more apparent than real. Smith and others, *Use of Prototypes*, p. 2.

67. Allison, "The F-111," p. 127.

68. On the deliberations of the Army's Main Battle Tank Task Force, see Thomas L. McNaugher, *Collaborative Development of Main Battle Tanks: Lessons from the U. S.-German Experience, 1963–1978*, N-1680-RC (Santa Monica, Calif.: Rand Corporation, August 1981), pp. 31–36; and "XM-1," based on a case study by Arthur Alexander, edited by Frederic A. Morris, in the *Murphy Commission Report*, vol. 4, pp. 199–207.

69. Lt. Col. Larry E. Willner, "XM-1 Main Battle Tank," as abridged by Bernard S. Waterman and Duane H. Smith, based on Willner's paper, "XM-1: The Birth of a Main Battle Tank: The First Two Years" (Washington, National Defense University, 1975), p. 29.

70. *Department of Defense Appropriation Bill 1972*, H. Rept. 92–666, 92 Cong. 1 sess. (GPO, 1971), pp. 73–74.

71. Willner, "XM-1," p. 29.

72. Willner, "XM-1," p. 6.

73. Willner, "XM-1," pp. 24–26. (Emphasis in original.)

74. Willner, "XM-1," p. 31.

75. McNaugher, "Problems of Collaborative Weapons Development," pp. 134 and 144, note 28.

76. As it had in the 1960s, the Rand Corporation found that during the 1970s, too, program managers consistently preferred to sacrifice cost and schedule rather than performance during development. Clearly the increasingly

legislative character of initial requirements is only one of many forces that sustain rigidity during development. See Dews and others, *Acquisition Policy Effectiveness*, pp. 25–27, 93.

77. See McNaugher, *Collaborative Development of Main Battle Tanks*, pp. 46–62.

78. Lynn and Smith, "Can the Secretary of Defense Make a Difference?" pp. 61, 58. For more on the F-15's origins, see James Fallows, *National Defense* (Random House, 1981), pp. 100–02.

79. Even Air Force Secretary Robert Seamans expressed concern over "whether the Air Force could afford to buy the expensive F-15 in sufficient quantities" and thus favored the LWF program. See G. K. Smith, and others, *Use of Prototypes*, R-2345-AF, p. 85.

80. The F-16's early development occurred outside the Air Force's "normal" acquisition bureaucracies "not only as a result of the [LWF] advocates' efforts . . . but because the Air Force was devoting most of its attention to the F-15." See Lynn and Smith, "Can the Secretary of Defense Make a Difference?" p. 65. On the hi-lo mix, see p. 63. Lynn and Smith note that, in contrast to McNamara, Secretary of Defense Melvin Laird and Packard were seeking "opportunities to develop *less costly* systems rather than more *cost-effective* systems." (Emphasis in original.)

81. Senator William Proxmire directed an attempt to insert a fly-before-you-buy amendment into the fiscal 1971 defense authorization bill. The effort failed but less from resistance to the idea than from a sense "that the amendment was premature, too drastic, unnecessary, vague, and inflexible." Michael D. Rich, *Competition in the Acquisition of Major Weapon Systems: Legislative Perspectives*, R-2058-PR (Santa Monica, Calif.: Rand Corporation, 1976), p. 29. See pp. 25–29 for the full discussion of this amendment.

82. Earlier in the development phase the program office ran as small as four full-time personnel. See Smith and others, *Use of Prototypes*, pp. 90, 92, 104.

83. Smith and others, *Use of Prototypes*, pp. 64–65.

84. Lynn and Smith, "Can the Secretary of Defense Make a Difference?" p. 65. See also Fallows, *National Defense*, p. 106.

85. Bill Keller, "A Familiar Face, a Familiar Problem," *New York Times*, June 20, 1985, p. B12.

86. The most prominent document in the overall congressional effort to reorganize the Defense Department was *Defense Organization: The Need for Change*. Although it was mentioned in this document, acquisition reform was left principally to certain subcommittees. While broad organizational reforms were mandated in the Department of Defense Reorganization Act of 1986 (see Senate Report 99-280, 99 Cong. 2 sess. [GPO: 1986]), acquisition reforms were outlined in the Defense Acquisition Improvement Act of 1986 (P.L. 99-661, sections 901–63).

87. See *Defense Organization*, especially chap. 4. For a survey of these problems and also a document important in shaping the Defense Reorganization Act of 1986, see Center for Strategic and International Studies, *Toward a More*

Effective Defense: The Final Report of the CSIS Defense Organization Project (Washington: Georgetown University, 1985), especially pp. 11–22.

88. President's Blue Ribbon Commission on Defense Management, *A Quest for Excellence: Final Report to the President* (GPO, 1986), p. 53. (Hereafter *Quest for Excellence*.) To some extent, this comment is a thinly veiled critique of Reagan administration policy, which sought to limit the Office of the Secretary of Defense's influence while turning policy responsibilities over to the services. But the complaint is hardly new and transcends the policies of any particular administration.

89. The House Armed Services Committee report on the B-1B was prompted by this request. See Tim Carrington, "Air Force Supplemental '87 Budget Asks $600 Million for Further Work on B-1," *Wall Street Journal*, January 8, 1987, p. 11. See also Rowan Scarborough, "The B-1's Problem? The Air Force," *Defense Week*, April 6, 1987, p. 2.

90. After resisting this charge for over a year, Secretary of Defense Caspar W. Weinberger filled the new post late in 1984. See Michael R. Gordon, "Help Wanted in Weapons Testing Office but Pentagon Slow to Fill Top Job," *National Journal*, October 13, 1984, pp. 1914–17.

91. "In short," the Packard report says, "the prototype program should allow us to fly—and know how much it will cost—before we buy." *Quest for Excellence*, p. 57.

92. *Quest for Excellence*, p. 47.

93. See "Washington Roundup," *Aviation Week and Space Technology*, April 27, 1987, p. 31.

94. Early reports suggest this assessment is correct. See Fred Kaplan, "Watchdog's Reports Lack Bite: Weapons Review Not Independent, GAO Says," *Washington Post*, March 27, 1987, p. 21; and Debra Polsky, "Former Top DARPA Official Says Increased Funding Reflects Confidence in Agency," *Defense News*, May 9, 1988, p. 28.

95. *Quest for Excellence*, p. 58.

96. GAO, *Defense Management: Status of Recommendations by Blue Ribbon Commission on Defense Management*, NSIAD-89-19FS (November 1988), p. 22.

97. See Andrew Mayer, *The Competition in Contracting Act: Its Application to the Department of Defense*, 85-115F (Washington: Congressional Research Service, 1985).

98. See especially David E. Kaun, *Where Have All the Profits Gone? An Analysis of the Major U.S. Defense Contractors, 1950–1985*, Research Paper 4 (La Jolla: University of California Institute on Global Conflict and Cooperation, 1988).

99. Three government profit studies came to markedly different conclusions about profits. See the discussion in Fred Kaplan, "Defense Profits Are Double Commercial Profits, Study Says," *Boston Globe*, May 13, 1987, p. 9.

100. Mayer, *Competition in Contracting Act*, p. CRS-3.

101. *Department of Defense Appropriations for 1987*, Hearings before a subcommittee of the House Committee on Appropriations, 99 Cong. 2 sess. (GPO, 1986), pt. 6, p. 11.

102. See Jacques S. Gansler, "Needed: A U.S. Defense Industrial Strategy," *International Security*, vol. 12 (Fall 1987), p. 45.

103. A term first used by Merton J. Peck and Frederic M. Scherer, *The Weapons Acquisition Process: An Economic Analysis* (Harvard University, Graduate School of Business Administration, 1962), p. 583. The authors argued that given "the uncertainties and risks that pervade weapons acquisition, the development of such a nonmarket system was inevitable."

NOTES TO CHAPTER FOUR

1. President's Blue Ribbon Commission on Defense Management, *A Quest for Excellence: Final Report to the President* (GPO, 1986), p. 47. (Hereafter *Quest for Excellence*.)

2. Jacques S. Gansler, "Concurrency after Divad," *Military Logistics Forum*, vol. 2 (November-December 1985), p. 48.

3. Richard N. Foster, *Innovation: The Attacker's Advantage* (Summit Books, 1986), p. 31. For an extended discussion of the S-curve, see pp. 89–111.

4. Devendra Sahal, "Technological Guideposts and Innovation Avenues," *Research Policy*, vol. 14 (April 1985), pp. 68–70.

5. William L. Stanley and Michael D. Miller, *Measuring Technological Change in Jet Fighter Aircraft*, R-2249-AF (Santa Monica, Calif.: Rand Corporation, 1979), p. 47.

6. See "The Maverick Case for 'Total Package,' " *Business Week*, October 21, 1972, pp. 60W-Z.

7. See Morton Mintz, "The Maverick Missile: If At First You Don't Succeed," in Dina Rasor, ed., *More Bucks, Less Bang: How the Pentagon Buys Ineffective Weapons* (Washington: Fund for Constitutional Government, 1983), pp. 135–85.

8. Mintz, "Maverick Missile," pp. 136, 163.

9. "Interview: Richard DeLauer on Defense," *Technology Review*, vol. 89 (July 1986), p. 58.

10. One Pentagon official has argued that "[delivering] an imaging infrared Maverick missile is suicide." David M. North and Brendan M. Greeley, *Aviation Week and Space Technology*, December 19, 1988, p. 23. See also Franklin C. Spinney, *Defense Facts of Life: The Plans/Reality Mismatch* (Westview Press, 1985), p. 88.

11. *Report of the Defense Science Board 1981 Summer Study Panel on Operational Readiness with High Performance Systems* (Department of Defense, Office of the Secretary of Defense for Research and Engineering, 1982), pp. 6–9. (Hereafter *Study Panel on Operational Readiness*.)

12. Problems with BITE in the F-15 are well documented in Spinney, *Defense Facts of Life*, pp. 32–36. For a survey of BITE's disappointing performance and serious readiness implications, see Martin Binkin, *Military Technology and Defense Manpower* (Brookings, 1986), pp. 58–65.

13. General William E. DePuy, U.S. Army (ret.), "Technology and Manpower: Army Perspective," in William Bowman, Roger Little, and G.

Thomas Sicilia, eds., *The All-Volunteer Army after a Decade: Retrospect and Prospect* (Pergamon-Brassey's, 1986), p. 130.

14. See Spinney, *Defense Facts of Life*, p. 34.

15. Robert P. F. Lauder, "Military Aircraft Don't Fight on the Ground," *Defense Electronics*, vol. 17 (May 1985), p. 112.

16. See Spinney, *Defense Facts of Life*, pp. 33–34.

17. Spinney, *Defense Facts of Life*, p. 35.

18. *Study Panel on Operational Readiness*, pp. 6–10.

19. Franklin A. Long and Judith Reppy note, for example, "a general, though not universal, bias for improvement of contemporary weapons systems rather than the development of revolutionary ones." "The Decision Process for U.S. Military R&D," in Kosta Tsipis and Penny Janeway, eds., *Review of U.S. Military Research and Development, 1984* (Pergamon-Brassey's, 1984), p. 11.

20. See Robert W. Drewes, *The Air Force and the Great Engine War* (Washington: National Defense University, 1987), p. 15.

21. Drewes, *The Air Force and the Great Engine War*, p. 38.

22. U.S. Department of Defense, "New Air Force Tactical Counter-Air Fighter (F-X)," Development Concept Paper 19 (September 15, 1968), p. 13.

23. Drewes, *The Air Force and the Great Engine War*, pp. 39–42. As he describes it, "Instead of testing the engine at Mach 2.3 and 37,000 feet, the test was run at Mach 2.2 around 40,000 feet," producing "a very substantial difference on the total pressure at the inlet face of the engine" (p. 41).

24. Spoken by Leonard Sullivan, Jr., former assistant secretary of defense and aeronautical engineer, in relation to "some of the F-18 components" as well as the F-100 engine. See Leonard Sullivan, Jr., "Q³: The Quality/Quantity Quandary," unpublished briefing, October 1981, p. 5. (Emphasis in original.)

25. Drewes, *The Air Force and the Great Engine War*, pp. 45–47.

26. J. R. Nelson, *Life-Cycle Analysis of Aircraft Turbine Engines*, R-2103-AF (Santa Monica, Calif.: Rand Corporation, 1977), p. 17.

27. Drewes, *The Air Force and the Great Engine War*, p. 53.

28. Drewes, *The Air Force and the Great Engine War*, p. 63.

29. Edmund Dews and others, *Acquisition Policy Effectiveness: Department of the Defense Experience in the 1970s*, R-2516-DR&E (Santa Monica, Calif.: Rand Corporation, 1979), p. 93.

30. James W. Canan, "The Software Crisis," *Air Force Magazine*, vol. 69 (May 1986), pp. 46–52.

31. Edward Lieblein, "The Department of Defense Software Initiative—A Status Report," *Communications of the ACM*, vol. 29 (August 1986), p. 734.

32. Captain J. Kelley, U.S. Air Force, "F-16 Radar Flight Test: A Lesson in Software Development," AIAA-86-0827 (Washington: American Institute of Aeronautics and Astronautics, April 1986), p. 2. With the aircraft's production otherwise moving on schedule, the Air Force installed APG-68s in its new aircraft, admitting that the radar did not measure up to all specifications but asserting that "existing units are superior to what we have been using." See Rowan Scarborough, "Defects Plague Westinghouse F-16 Radar," *Defense Week*, May 12, 1986, pp. 1, 12.

33. Canan, "Software Crisis," pp. 46, 49. See also J. R. Gebman and H. L. Shulman, *A Strategy for Reforming Avionics Acquisition and Support*, R-2908/2-AF (Santa Monica, Calif.: Rand Corporation, 1988), pp. 2–11.

34. As paraphrased in William Welling, "Weapons System Buying," *Defense Science and Electronics*, vol. 6 (August 1987), p. 22.

35. Robert Perry, *The Interaction of Technology and Doctrine in the USAF*, P-6281 (Santa Monica, Calif.: Rand Corporation, 1979), p. 17.

36. See William K. Greathouse, "Blending Propulsion with Airframe," *Space/Aeronautics*, vol. 50 (November 1968), pp. 59–68, quotation on p. 60.

37. Welling, "Weapons System Buying," p. 22.

38. See Thomas L. McNaugher, *The M16 Controversies: Military Organizations and Weapons Acquisition* (Praeger, 1984), pp. 135–70.

39. See *Status of Army Air Defense Planning*, Hearing before the Special Subcommittee on NATO Standardization, Interoperability, and Readiness of the House Armed Services Committee, 96 Cong. 2 sess. (Government Printing Office, 1981), pp. 19, 34.

40. Joan Timoney, "The Role of the United States Congress in the Sorry Saga of the Sergeant York Air Defense Gun," paper submitted to the Johns Hopkins School of Advanced International Studies, January 1987, p. 16.

41. Interview with Lt. Col. William Gardepe, November 20, 1986, conducted by Joan Timoney and cited in "Sorry Saga," p. 17. The General Accounting Office said much the same thing in a report published in January 1980. See U.S. General Accounting Office, *Inherent Risk in the Army's Acquisition Strategy Demands Particular Caution in Evaluating the Divad Gun System's Production Readiness* (January 31, 1980).

42. See General Maloney's testimony in *Department of Defense Authorization for Appropriations for Fiscal Year 1983*, Hearings before the House Armed Services Committee, 97 Cong. 2 sess. (GPO, 1982), pt. 3: *Procurement of Aircraft, Missiles, Tracked Combat Vehicles, Torpedoes, and Other Weapons-Title I*, p. 814. Later, when DIVAD became publicly visible and politically controversial, it was learned that "the OT (operational test) and ECM (electronic countermeasures) portions of the check test had not been presented to the DSARC. Only the results of the DT [developmental test] portion were presented, and this data was [sic] portrayed as OT data, which produced overly optimistic conclusions." See Timoney, "Sorry Saga," p. 36. See also *Management of the Department of Defense*, Hearings before the Senate Government Affairs Committee, 98 Cong. 2 sess. (GPO, 1985), pt. 9: *Oversight of the Sgt. York Air Defense Gun and DSARC Decisionmaking Process*, p. 84.

43. Timoney, "Sorry Saga," p. 27.

44. Statement by Secretary of the Army John O. Marsh, Jr., and Army Chief of Staff General John A. Wickham, Jr., as quoted by Representative Denny Smith, Republican of Oregon, in *Defense Department Authorization and Oversight Hearings on H. R. 5167, Department of Defense Authorization of Appropriations for Fiscal Year 1985 and Oversight of Previously Authorized Programs*, Hearings before the House Armed Services Committee, 98 Cong. 2 sess. (GPO, 1984), pt. 2, p. 606.

45. Military reformers took DIVAD to be another example of the military's pursuit of sophistication and complexity at any price. The most prominent critique, and one that played extensively in congressional debates on the subject, was Gregg Easterbrook, "DIVAD," *Atlantic Monthly* (October 1982), pp. 29–39.

46. As noted in U.S. General Accounting Office, *Sgt. York: Concerns about the Army's Accelerated Acquisition Strategy*, NSIAD-86-89 (1986), pp. 28, 30.

47. *Department of Defense Authorization for Fiscal Year 1983*, Hearings before the Senate Armed Services Committee, 97 Cong. 2 sess. (GPO, 1982), pt. 4, pp. 2356–57.

48. See Drewes, *The Air Force and the Great Engine War*, p. 60.

49. Drewes, *The Air Force and the Great Engine War*, p. 55.

50. *Summer Study Panel on Operational Readiness*, pp. 6–5.

51. See, for example, the three case studies in Arturo Gándara and Michael D. Rich, *Reliability Improvement Warranties for Military Procurement*, R-2264-AF (Santa Monica, Calif.: Rand Corporation, 1977), pp. 44–57.

52. *Summer Study Panel on Operational Readiness*, pp. 3–9.

53. *Summer Study Panel on Operational Readiness*, pp. 3–9.

54. Michael Rich, William Stanley, and Susan Anderson, *Improving U.S. Air Force Readiness and Sustainability*, R-3113/1AF (Santa Monica, Calif.: Rand Corporation, 1984), p. 29. (Emphasis in original.)

55. Allen D. Lee, *A Strategy to Improve the Early Production Phase in Air Force Acquisition Programs*, P-6941-RGI (Santa Monica, Calif.: Rand Corporation, 1983), p. 100.

56. Lee, *Strategy to Improve the Early Production Phase*, p. 157. Lee modeled the program at a slower initial production rate than was actually achieved. He also assumed that the Air Force placed a few early production aircraft in a "lead the fleet" unit that flew at high sortie rates in order to generate information on reliability and performance.

57. Lee, *Strategy to Improve the Early Production Phase*, p. 172.

58. See Anthony J. Feduccia, "System Design for Reliability and Maintainability," *Air Force Journal of Logistics* (Spring 1984), p. 25.

59. Inherent reliability is defined as "the value of design reliability estimated during prediction studies." See R. T. Anderson, *Reliability Design Handbook*, RDH-376 (Griffiss Air Force Base, N.Y.: Rome Air Development Center, 1976), p. 56. The author says that reliability growth will be lower under any set of test conditions to the extent that "no specific attention is given to reliability growth" in the development process. See p. 59, and p. 57, figure 2-13.

60. Lt. Gen. Marc C. Reynolds, U.S. Air Force, "Using Technology to Improve Readiness and Reduce Cost: Challenges for Contracting," *Air Force Journal of Logistics*, vol. 9 (Summer 1985), p. 3. See also GAO, "Effectiveness of U.S. Forces," PSAD-81-17 (January 29, 1981), p. 15. The authors assert that decisions made by the end of Milestone I shape 70 percent of a new system's life-cycle costs. By the end of full-scale development (Milestone III), 95 percent of life-cycle costs have been cemented in place.

61. Howard P. Gates, Jr., and others, *Electronics-X: A Study of Military Electronics with Particular Reference to Cost and Reliability*, vol. 1: *Executive Conspectus* (Arlington, Va.: Institute for Defense Analysis, 1974), p. 4.

62. Thomas A. Blanco and others, *Technology Trends and Maintenance Workload Requirements for the A-7, F-4, and F-14 Aircraft*, NPRDC TR 79-19 (San Diego, Calif.: Navy Personnel Research and Development Center, May 1979), p. viii.

63. See Binkin, *Military Technology*, pp. 45–49.

64. Theodore von Kármán, "Perfectionism or Reliability?" *Missile Design and Development* (June 1959), p. 20.

65. Feduccia, "System Design," p. 28.

66. For details on Blackhawk's development, see G. K. Smith and others, *The Use of Prototypes in Weapon System Development*, R-2345-AF (Santa Monica, Calif.: Rand Corporation, 1981), app. C, especially pp. 135–37. Initial Army plans called for more prototypes and more testing from each contractor. These plans were scuttled by Congress, however, which saw the UTTAS program as "an extreme example of unwarranted duplication." See pp. 129–30.

67. Spoken by the chief of Army Aviation's logistics office and quoted in Deborah G. Meyer, "Simplified Fleet, More Missions," *Armed Forces Journal International*, vol. 122 (October 1984), pp. 78, 80. Although more reliable than the Huey, the Blackhawk, with two engines to the Huey's one, is still more expensive to operate. See A. Rivlin, CBO director, in *Department of Defense Appropriations, Fiscal Year 1984*, Hearings before the Senate Committee on Appropriations, 98 Cong. 1 sess. (GPO, 1984), pt. 3, p. 180.

68. General Electric Aerospace Electronic Systems Department, *Research Study of Radar Reliability and Its Impact on Life-Cycle Costs for the APQ-113, -114, -120 and -144 Radars*, ASD-TR-73-22 (Alexandria, Va.: Defense Technical Information Center, April 1973), especially pp. 1–19. APQ113/114 refers to three modestly different designs of the same basic radar.

69. Smith, *Use of Prototypes*, p. 126.

70. General Electric, "Research Study of Radar Reliability," p. 10.

71. See Michael J. Fitzpatrick, "A Case Study in Weapons Acquisition: The Sidewinder Air-to-Air Missile," *Journal of International Affairs*, vol. 39 (Summer 1985), especially pp. 175–76; and Pierre Sprey, "The Case for Better and Cheaper Weapons," in Asa A. Clark IV and others, *The Defense Reform Debate: Issues and Analysis* (Johns Hopkins University Press, 1984), pp. 196–200. For the story of the missile's early development, see John J. Fialka, "After Nearly 30 Years, Sidewinder Missile Is Still Potent, Reliable," *Wall Street Journal*, February 15, 1985, pp. 1, 2. See also William B. McLean, "The Sidewinder Missile Program," in Fremont E. Kast and James E. Rosenzweig, eds., *Science, Technology, and Management* (McGraw-Hill, 1962), pp. 166–76. McLean invented the missile and managed its early development. See also the testimony of General Alton D. Slay, then Air Force deputy chief of staff for research, development, and acquisition, *Fiscal Year 1978 Department of Defense Authorization for Military Procurement, and Active Duty, Selected Reserve and*

Civilian Personnel Strengths, Hearings before the Senate Committee on Armed Services, 95 Cong. 1 sess. (GPO, 1977), pt. 7, pp. 4581–93.

72. Lon O. Nordeen, Jr., *Air Warfare in the Missile Age* (Washington: Smithsonian Institution Press, 1985), pp. 170–184; and "British Harriers Averaged Six Sorties per Day," *Aviation Week and Space Technology*, July 19, 1982, p. 20. On the same page, "Sidewinder Performance" notes that the missile scored kills in 24 of the 27 instances in which it was fired.

73. Fitzpatrick, "Case Study in Weapons Acquisition," pp. 176–82; and "Sidewinder Used in Formosa Crisis," *Aviation Week and Space Technology*, October 6, 1958, p. 35, which notes that the use of Sidewinders "enabled outnumbered Nationalist fliers in F-86s to achieve substantial victories over the Communists fliers equipped with MiG-17s, which are considered superior to the F-86."

74. Norman Friedman, *U.S. Naval Weapons: Every Gun, Missile, Mine, and Torpedo Used by the U.S. Navy from 1883 to the Present Day* (Annapolis, Md.: Naval Institute Press, 1982), p. 176; and M. G. Burns, "Sidewinder 2," *Armed Forces*, vol. 5 (November 1986), p. 514. This is the best single article on the Sidewinder's design evolution.

75. See the testimony of Peter Waterman, acting assistant secretary of the Navy for R&D, in *Department of Defense Appropriations for Fiscal Year 1974*, Hearings before the Senate Appropriations Committee, 93 Cong. 1 sess. (GPO, 1973), pt. 3, p. 1295. (Hereafter *Waterman testimony*.) See also Friedman, *U.S. Naval Weapons*, p. 176.

76. *Waterman testimony*, p. 1295.

77. Benjamin S. Lambeth, "Pitfalls in Force Planning: Structuring America's Tactical Air Arm," *International Security*, vol. 10 (Fall 1985), pp. 105–06.

78. See " 'You Fight Like You Train' and Top Gun Crews Train Hard," *Armed Forces Journal International*, vol. 111 (May 1974), pp. 25–26, 34; and Nordeen, *Air Warfare in the Missile Age*, p. 42.

79. " 'You Fight Like You Train' "; Nordeen, *Air Warfare in the Missile Age*, pp. 65–66; and Lawrence E. Lynn, Jr., and Richard I. Smith, "Can the Secretary of Defense Make a Difference?" *International Security*, vol. 7 (Summer 1982), p. 58.

80. Nordeen, *Air Warfare in the Missile Age*, p. 76.

81. Gen. William W. Momyer, U.S. Air Force (ret.), *Air Power in Three Wars: WWII, Korea, Vietnam* (GPO, 1983), p. 157.

82. *Waterman testimony*, p. 1295.

83. See the "Sidewinder Program Review," in *Fiscal Year 1978 Department of Defense Authorization*, Hearings, pp. 4581–93.

84. The AIM-9R will feature "a significant improvement in the target acquisition range and a shortened distance where countermeasures will be effective against the infrared homing missile." See "China Lake Readies Data for 1990s Sidewinder Upgrade," *Aviation Week and Space Technology*, January 20, 1986, p. 80.

85. Burns, "Sidewinder 2," p. 515.

86. See Robert R. Ropelewski, "USAF Weighs 20 Modifications to Cut AMRAAM Cost $1 Billion," *Aviation Week and Space Technology*, July 8, 1985, pp. 21–23.

87. Donald E. Fink, "Whither AMRAAM," *Aviation Week and Space Technology*, November 18, 1985, p. 9.

88. For a documented history of AMRAAM's development and cost problems, see Thomas L. McNaugher, "Buying Weapons: Bleak Prospects for Real Reform," *Brookings Review*, vol. 4 (Summer 1986), pp. 11–12. The story draws on interviews with Defense Department personnel as well as the documents cited in the article.

89. Lambeth, "Pitfalls in Force Planning," p. 89. See also Sprey, "The Case for Better and Cheaper Weapons," p. 199; and Lt. Col. Gregg Swanson, U.S. Air Force, "From Nevada to Bekaa: Air Combat in Theory and Practice," *Armed Forces Journal International*, vol. 120 (January 1983), p. 37.

90. For a description, see *Department of Defense Authorization for Appropriations for Fiscal Year 1980*, Hearings before the Senate Committee on Armed Services, 96 Cong. 1 sess. (GPO, 1979), pt. 3, p. 1110.

91. Lt. Col. Walt Kross, U.S. Air Force, "ACEVAL/AIMVAL: Abusing Atari in the Desert," *Armed Forces Journal International*, vol. 119 (January 1982), p. 52.

92. CBO, "The Advanced Medium-Range Air-To-Air Missile (AMRAAM): Current Plans and Alternatives," Staff Working Paper (Washington, August 1986), p. 39. Test results were analyzed by the Institute for Defense Analysis. Results remain classified.

93. Fink, "Whither AMRAAM," p. 9. Early tests of AMRAAM were more encouraging than Sidewinder's early tests. Those who worked on the first AIM-9 assert that the missile's failures in its first thirteen test firings "would have . . . doomed a major development program." Because Sidewinder was then being resisted by service procurement hierarchies, it was "buried" at China Lake under the title "Feasibility Study 567" and thus was not scuttled. See Fialka, "After Nearly 30 Years, Sidewinder Missile Is Still Potent, Reliable," p. 1.

94. See, for example, Alexander, *Armor Development in the Soviet Union and the United States*, pp. 44–48.

95. In 1986, for example, the director of Defense Research and Engineering noted, "Major new Soviet systems or modernization programs take about 8–15 years to develop. This is about the same time it now takes in the U.S." If the Soviets are overtaking the United States technologically, clearly it is not by rushing new systems more quickly than the United States does from laboratory to field units. *Department of Defense Appropriations, Fiscal Year 1986*, Hearings before the Senate Commitee on Armed Services, 99 Cong. 1 sess. (GPO, 1985), p. 410.

96. Michael Rich and Edmunds Dews with C. L. Batten, Jr., *Improving the Military Acquisition Process: Lessons from Rand Research*, R-3373-AF/RC (Santa Monica, Calif.: Rand Corporation, 1986), p. 22.

97. On the M-60A2, see Alexander, *Armor Development in the Soviet Union and the United States*, p. 119.

98. Daniel Joseph Kaufman, "Organizations, Technology, and Weapons Acquisition: The Development of the Infantry Fighting Vehicle," Ph.D. dissertation, Masschusetts Institute of Technology, 1983, pp. 189–90.

99. See Thomas L. McNaugher, *Collaborative Development of Main Battle Tanks: Lessons from the U.S.-German Experience, 1963–1978*, N-1680-RC (Santa Monica, Calif.: Rand Corporation, 1981), pp. 37–38.

100. "What's Wrong with the Way We Buy Weapons: A Conversation with Lawrence J. Korb and Thomas L. McNaugher," *Brookings Review*, vol. 6 (Fall 1988), p. 7.

101. See Robert Ropelewski, "Marine/Bell AH-1W Demonstrates Improved Performance, Flexibility," *Aviation Week and Space Technology*, August 25, 1986, pp. 52–59.

102. *Quest for Excellence*, p. 47.

NOTES TO CHAPTER FIVE

1. Paul O. Ballou, Jr., "Decision-Making Environment of a Program Office," *Program Manager*, vol. 14 (September-October 1985), p. 38. (Emphasis added.)

2. See Gilbert W. Fitzhugh's summary of his commission's work in *Weapon System Acquisition Process*, Hearings before the Senate Committee on Armed Services, 92 Cong. 1 sess. (Government Printing Office, 1972), p. 13.

3. Merton J. Peck and Frederic M. Scherer, *The Weapons Acquisition Process: An Economic Analysis* (Harvard University, Graduate School of Business Administration, 1962), p. 240. Peck and Scherer were writing about the "literally hundreds of individuals [who] participate directly in the typical weapon system program decision"—based on data gathered before the Office of the Secretary of Defense (OSD) achieved the size and prominence it has today and before the Armed Services Committees interjected themselves fully into the acquisition process (p. 239). In short, their conclusion is likely to be more applicable today than when they reached it.

4. See Norman R. Augustine's testimony in *Defense Procurement Process*, Hearings before the Task Force on Selected Defense Procurement Matters of the Senate Armed Services Committee, 98 Cong. 2 sess. (GPO, 1985), pt. 2, p. 152.

5. For example, Congress inserted language in the 1986 Defense Authorization Act requiring the secretary of defense to certify that the Air Force's controversial advanced medium-range air-to-air missile, then approaching production, impart "maximum cost-reduction design changes" into the missile, while nonetheless ensuring that it "met original performance specifications." See David Silverberg, "Aspin Says Air Force's AMRAAM 'Emits an Odor of Rising Costs,'" *Defense News*, July 28, 1986, p. 18.

6. President's Blue Ribbon Commission on Defense Management, *A Quest*

for Excellence: Final Report to the President (GPO, 1986), p. 46. (Hereafter *Quest for Excellence*.)

7. *Report of the Defense Science Board Task Force on Military Software*, (Department of Defense, Office of the Under Secretary of Defense for Acquisition, 1987), p. 7. (Emphasis in original.) The panel also noted that the current Defense Department directive on software development "not only does not encourage this best modern practice, it essentially forbids it," insisting instead on the "waterfall" approach "calling for formal specification, then requests for bids, then contracting, delivery, installation, and maintenance" (p. 3).

8. *Quest for Excellence*, p. 46.

9. Benjamin S. Lambeth, "Pitfalls in Force Planning: Structuring America's Tactical Air Arm," *International Security*, vol. 10 (Fall 1985), p. 90, note 10. Robert W. Drewes confirms Lambeth's point in this comment about operational practice with the aircraft. "Relatively little time was spent at full power or very high Mach number. Much more often, speed stayed below Mach 1.5." See his *The Air Force and the Great Engine War* (Washington: National Defense University Press, 1987), p. 60.

10. Based on equations found in Joseph P. Large, Harry G. Campbell, and David Cates, *Parametric Equations for Estimating Aircraft Airframe Costs*, R-1693-1-PA&E (Santa Monica, Calif.: Rand Corporation, 1976), pp. 21, 23. My thanks to Capt. Donald L. Pilling, U.S. Navy, for bringing these formulas to my attention and for performing the necessary calculations. Average cost for the 729 F-15s the Air Force originally planned to buy was $27.9 million per aircraft in 1987 dollars. Calculation is based on U.S. Congressional Budget Office, "Total Quantities and Costs of Major Weapon Systems Procured, FY 1974–1987" (Washington, April 4, 1986).

11. U.S. Department of Defense, *New Air Force Tactical Counter-Air Fighter (F-X)*, Development Concept Paper 19 (September 15, 1968), p. 9. For this reason, the service lowered its speed requirement from Mach 2.7 to "M 2.3 with a minimum M 2.5 burst capability" (p. 10). Variable air inlets were still required, however, and airframe cost models then available would have provided a reasonably accurate assessment of what they would cost.

12. Robert F. Coulam, *Illusions of Choice: The F-111 and the Problem of Weapons Acquisition Reform* (Princeton University Press, 1977), p. 341, note 5.

13. On the lessons being learned in Vietnam as the F-15 requirement was being written, see Laurence E. Lynn, Jr., and Richard I. Smith, "Can the Secretary of Defense Make a Difference?" *International Security*, vol. 7 (Summer 1982), p. 58. Boyd's "energy maneuverability theory" of air combat confirmed the crucial importance of a fighter aircraft's ability to maneuver in the so-called transonic range—around Mach 1.

14. See Lt. Col. Jerauld R. Gentry, "Evolution of the F-16 Multinational Fighter," Student Research Report 163 (Washington: Industrial College of the Armed Forces, 1976), pp. 9–20. On the amalgamation of requirements, see Lynn and Smith, "Can the Secretary of Defense Make a Difference?" p. 58.

15. Service officials were "livid" in part, apparently, because they had

unknowingly misinformed Congress on the engine's status. But they were also angry because they had not been consulted in advance of an important program decision. See Drewes, *The Air Force and the Great Engine War*, pp. 40–41.

16. The story that follows draws heavily on Daniel J. Kaufman, "Organizations, Technology, and Weapons Acquisition: The Development of the Infantry Fighting Vehicle," Ph.D. dissertation, Massachusetts Institute of Technology, May 1983, especially pp. 165–357.

17. The change forced the service to raise the required maximum weight from 20 tons to 21 tons, and required unit cost from $100,000 to $150,000 a copy. This shift seems to have come from the Army as a product of continuing debate over appropriate MICV design and doctrine. Whatever the origins of the requirements shift, the vehicle for which the Army contracted in 1972 was not, as the General Accounting Office later noted, the vehicle it had approved only two years before. U. S. General Accounting Office, "Staff Study, Mechanized Infantry Combat Vehicle" (March 1974), p. 3, quoted in Kaufman, "Organizations, Technology, and Weapons Acquisition," pp. 281–82.

18. Kaufman, "Organizations, Technology, and Weapons Acquisition," pp. 319, 259.

19. Kaufman, "Organizations, Technology, and Weapons Acquisitions," p. 330.

20. When approved for development in 1972, the Bradley was expected to cost $175,000 (1972 dollars). By 1982 its unit cost had risen to $436,000 (1972 dollars). Kaufman, "Organizations, Technology, and Weapons Acquisition," pp. 287, 439.

21. On the swimming controversy, see, for example, Steve Johnson, "New Look at Bradley Vehicle Tests," *San Jose Mercury News*, January 21, 1987, p. 1. The British Army apparently eliminated the swim requirement for its combat vehicles "because the sides and banks along the rivers and canals in central Europe are steep and the water so swift that it didn't help to have a swimming ability." See the unsigned letter to the editor, "Role of the Bradley," *Defense News*, October 6, 1986, p. 18.

22. Hugh Lucas, "The Bradley Controversy," *Jane's Defence Weekly*, May 24, 1986, p. 937. The vulnerability of infantry carriers is troubling many of the world's mechanized ground forces. For a review of the debate, see Richard Simpkin, "The Infantry Fighting Vehicle: Maid-of-All-Work or Crown Princess?" *Military Technology*, vol. 9 (1985), pp. 55–62.

23. FMC apparently asked the Army to delete the swim requirement in 1985, long after the vehicle's design was essentially frozen. See Paul Bedard, "FMC Sought to Delete Bradley Swim Requirement," *Defense Week* May 11, 1987, p. 8. Given the vehicle's vulnerability to antitank fire, future doctrine is likely to call for mechanized infantry to trail tank forces, reducing the need for a top speed paired to that of the M-1 tank. Daniel Kaufman argues that the Army's insistence on the original speed requirement was intimately linked to power train problems experienced throughout the development and early production phases of the MICV/Bradley program. See Kaufman, "Organiza-

tions, Technology, and Weapons Acquisition," pp. 390–98.

24. The CBO analysts argued that the improved M-113 would be slightly less capable than Bradley of keeping up with tanks. Given the vulnerability of both vehicles to antitank fire, however, they argued that "prudence would dictate that, when possible, armored personnel carriers should not be employed alongside main battle tanks." See CBO, *Reducing the Deficit: Spending and Revenue Options*, A report to the Senate and House Committees on the Budget, pt. 1 (Washington, March 1987), p. 51.

25. See Bruce Gudmundsson, "The Multiple Launch Rocket System: On Time and Under Budget," Case C16-87-773.0 (Harvard University, John F. Kennedy School of Government Case Program, 1987), p. 7.

26. *Department of Defense Appropriations for 1987*, Hearings before a subcommittee of the House Committee on Appropriations, 99 Cong. 2 sess. (GPO, 1986), pt. 1, p. 602.

27. Edmund Dews and others, *Acquisition Policy Effectiveness: Department of Defense Experience in the 1970s*, R-2516-DR&E (Santa Monica, Calif.: Rand Corporation, 1979), p. 48.

28. Dews and others, *Acquisition Policy Effectiveness*, p. 48.

29. See Giles K. Smith and others, *The Use of Prototypes in Weapon System Development*, R-2345-AF (Santa Monica, Calif.: Rand Corporation, 1981), pp. 119–21.

30. On current totals, see CBO, "Total Quantities and Costs of Major Weapon Systems Procured, FY 1974–1987" (Washington, April 4, 1986). Total planned purchases (the authorized acquisition objective or AAO) provided by the Department of the Air Force, Military Deputy for Acquisition, Directorate of Development and Production, telephone interview.

31. In this case it would seem that Georgia's delegation has the power to distort the nation's force posture. An alternative explanation, however, is that the Air Force wants more C-130s and knows that the Georgia delegation will supply them. Consequently the Air Force removes the C-130 from its budget request and loads the budget with higher priority items, forcing the legislature to make tough choices—or avoid them, giving the service all that it wants, including the C-130s.

32. R. Douglas Arnold, "The Local Roots of Domestic Policy," in Thomas E. Mann and Norman J. Ornstein, eds., *The New Congress* (Washington: American Enterprise Institute for Public Policy Research, 1981), p. 262.

33. Rolf Clark, "Defense Budget Instability and Weapon System Acquisition," *Public Budgeting and Finance*, vol. 7 (Summer 1987), p. 28, table 1.

34. Dews and Smith, *Acquisition Policy Effectiveness*, p. 78.

35. Dews and Smith, *Acquisition Policy Effectiveness*, p. 78.

36. Whether or not he originated the phrase "bow wave," Franklin C. Spinney certainly popularized the notion. See his *Defense Facts of Life: The Plans/Reality Mismatch* (Westview Press, 1985), p. 138. See also GAO, "Underestimation of Funding Requirements in Five Year Procurement Plans (Briefing Paper)," NSIAD-84-88 (March 12, 1984), especially pp. 003–018, and Clark, "Defense Budget Instability and Weapon System Acquisition."

37. Spinney, *Defense Facts of Life*, p. 149. (Emphasis in original.)

38. CBO, *Operation and Support Costs for the Department of Defense*, (Washington, July 1988), p. 18, fig. 2.

39. CBO, "Defense Spending: What Has Been Accomplished," Staff Working Paper (Washington, April 1985), pp. 27–28, tables A-2, A-3.

40. CBO, "Defense Spending," pp. 27–28.

41. CBO, *Effects of Weapons Procurement Stretch-Outs on Costs and Schedules* (Washington, November 1987), pp. x, 9–13.

42. CBO, *Effects of Weapons Procurement*, p. 17. An earlier study by analysts at the Rand Corporation confirmed that slower production rates would increase unit costs, largely because overhead would be apportioned across fewer units, but cautioned that "the manner in which a given [production] rate is achieved and the time allowed for achieving that rate may be more important than the rate itself." Joseph P. Large and others, *Production Rate and Production Cost*, R-1609-PA&E (Santa Monica, Calif.: Rand Corporation, 1974), pp. 43–44.

43. The F-15E was under development through this period, but the F-15s that were purchased in the interim were produced at exceptionally low rates and thus cost 25 percent more than even the Reagan administration's fiscal 1983 estimate. CBO, "Defense Spending," p. 28, table A-3.

44. Rolf Clark argues that because the services overestimated costs during the peak Reagan years, the return to optimism will lag for a period, during which the cost padding is whittled away by cost increases because of lower production rates. He contends, however, that "after two or three years of decreasing budgets, the experience of the 1970s should re-emerge." "Defense Budget Instability," p. 29.

45. For a discussion, see William W. Kaufmann, "A Defense Agenda for Fiscal Years 1990–1994," in John D. Steinbruner, ed., *Restructuring American Foreign Policy* (Brookings, 1989), pp. 59–64, 69–71, and 82–89.

46. "Tower Hints at Military Personnel Cuts," *Washington Post*, December 26, 1988, p. A26.

47. Kaufmann, "Defense Agenda," p. 67.

48. See Nick Kotz, *Wild Blue Yonder: Money, Politics, and the B-1 Bomber* (Pantheon Books, 1988), especially pp. 180–99.

49. See Melissa Healy, "Orr Presses Blue Suits On Close Air Support," *Defense Week*, April 1, 1985, p. 16.

50. Quoted in John Morrocco, "DoD Eyes New Plane to Replace Thunderbolt," *Defense News*, June 30, 1986, p. 1.

51. See David M. North, "USAF Awards ATF Contracts to Lockheed, Northrop," *Aviation Week and Space Technology*, November 10, 1986, p. 18.

NOTES TO CHAPTER SIX

1. Peck and Scherer point out that at some level the government is many buyers. See Merton J. Peck and Frederic M. Scherer, *The Weapons Acquisition Process: An Economic Analysis* (Harvard University, Graduate School of Business Administration, 1962), pp. 75–79. In regard to the industrial policy discussed

in this chapter, however, the government remains a single buyer whose policy stems from the interaction of legislative and executive branches.

2. U.S. Department of Defense, *Defense Financial and Investment Review* (June 1985), p. v-5. (Hereafter DFAIR.)

3. For a description of the weighted-guidelines approach to profit negotiations, see U.S. Department of Defense, Assistant Secretary of Defense, Installations and Logistics, *Profit 76, Summary Report: Report of the Profit Study Group* (December 7, 1976), chap. 5. (Hereafter *Profit 76*).

4. DFAIR, p. iii-18.

5. Lichtenberg's calculations suggested "that a $1 increase in competitive procurement induces a 54-cent increase in private expenditure." Frank R. Lichtenberg, "The Private R&D Investment Response to Federal Design and Technical Competitions," *American Economic Review*, vol. 78 (June 1988), p. 555.

6. David E. Kaun, *Where Have All the Profits Gone? An Analysis of the Major U.S. Defense Contractors: 1950-1985*, Research Paper 4 (La Jolla, Calif.: University of California, Institute on Global Conflict and Cooperation, 1988), p. 21.

7. Peck and Scherer, *Weapons Acquisition Process*, p. 534.

8. See Frederic M. Scherer, *The Weapons Acquisition Process: Economic Incentives* (Harvard University, Graduate School of Business Administration, 1964), p. 31.

9. Lichtenberg, "Private R&D Investment Response to Federal Design and Technical Competitions," p. 557.

10. As quoted in James Kitfield, "Packard: Contractors Must Change," *Military Logistics Forum*, vol. 3 (July-August 1986), p. 56. See also "Contractor Self-Governance: Government Initiatives on Defense Contracts," PRT Report, initially prepared by Frederick Neuman, *Program Manager*, vol. 17 (January-February 1988), pp. 34-35, for a fuller statement on the evolution of these practices.

11. See the statement of Frank C. Conahan, director of the U.S. General Accounting Office's National Security and International Affairs Division in *Problems in the Pricing of Negotiated Defense Contracts*, Hearings before a subcommittee of the House Committee on Government Operations, 99 Cong. 1 sess. (Government Printing Office, 1986), p. 41. For examples of the overhead game, see Conahan's prepared statement, pp. 34-38.

12. Fred Kaplan, "Is Industry's Image Accurate? Yes," *Military Logistics Forum*, vol. 3 (July-August 1986), p. 64.

13. James P. Bell, *Competition as an Acquisition Strategy: Impact of Competitive Research and Development on Procurement Costs*, P-1744 (Alexandria, Va.: Institute for Defense Analyses, 1983), pp. B-71, B-72. Bell also notes that besides ignoring spares prices, competitively negotiated contracts for the M-1 covered only 6.5 percent of the total planned buy, which "did permit substantial cost growth to occur" (p. 49).

14. Some 50 percent of the profit markup was based "on facilities capital and working capital use," as outlined in Defense Procurement Circular 107,

published in 1972. See DFAIR, p. iv-10. For the seminal article on this subject, see Lowell H. Goodhue, "Fair Profits from Defense Business," *Harvard Business Review*, vol. 50 (March-April 1972), pp. 97–107.

15. For a useful history of return on investment contracting, see DFAIR, pp. VI-2, VI-3.

16. Frederic M. Scherer, "The Aerospace Industry," in Walter Adams, ed., *The Structure of American Industry* (Macmillan, 1971), p. 370.

17. For a survey of the literature, see Robert F. Coulam, *Illusions of Choice: The F-111 and the Problem of Weapons Acquisition Reform* (Princeton University Press, 1977), pp. 378–79.

18. DFAIR, pp. vi-6, vi-16.

19. DFAIR, p. vi-15.

20. DFAIR, pp. vi-16, vi-17.

21. See Scherer, "Aerospace Industry," p. 374.

22. J. Ronald Fox, "Revamping the Business of National Defense," *Harvard Business Review*, vol. 62 (September-October 1984), p. 67.

23. Jeffrey G. Miller and Thomas E. Vollmann, "The Hidden Factory," *Harvard Business Review*, vol. 63 (September-October 1985), p. 146.

24. On the relationship between spare parts horror stories and acquisition reform, see Michael R. Gordon, "Data on Production Inefficiencies May Spur New Debate on Defense Contracting," *National Journal*, June 1, 1985, pp. 1283–86.

25. William Proxmire, *Report from Wasteland: America's Military Industrial Complex* (Praeger Publishers, 1970), p. xi, 17–18.

26. See, for example, Tom Riddell, "Concentration and Inefficiency in the Defense Sector: Policy Options," *Journal of Economic Issues*, vol. 19 (June 1985), pp. 451–61.

27. Quoted in Kitfield, "Packard: Contractors Must Change," p. 56.

28. The story is taken principally from two sources, Jacob Goodwin, *Brotherhood of Arms: General Dynamics and the Business of Defending America* (Times Books, 1985), chaps. 5, 6, and 11; and Patrick E. Tyler, *Running Critical*. Tyler's book was extracted in a series of articles that appeared in the *Washington Post* on September 21, 22, and 23, 1986, particularly "Striking a Bargain with the Legendary Admiral," *Washington Post*, September 22, 1986.

29. See Tyler, "Striking a Bargain," p. A10.

30. There was such a rush to build the SSN-688 that the service omitted the usual two-year delay between construction of the lead ship of the class and construction of follow-on vessels. This decision created a great deal of design uncertainty, leading in Lewis's view to "maybe . . . five thousand [design] changes that really ripped something out and replaced it with something else." Although the claim may have been self-serving, all three of the Navy's private shipyards were engaged in similar legal suits, involving similarly enormous cost overruns. Goodwin, *Brotherhood of Arms*, pp. 98, 120.

31. Goodwin, *Brotherhood of Arms*, p. 132.

32. The restructuring was carried out under P.L. 85-804, which makes

the new contract arrangements valid unless one or both houses of Congress disapprove within sixty legislative days. Goodwin, *Brotherhood of Arms*, pp. 152–53.

33. Quoted in John H. Cushman, Jr., "Cost-Cutters Target: Secret Bomber," *New York Times*, January 22, 1988, p. A24. For a defense industrialist's lament, see Hugh Vickery, "Leading Defense Supplier Says Bureaucracy Raises Arms Bill," *Washington Times*, March 27, 1986, p. 7c.

34. Jacques S. Gansler, *The Defense Industry* (MIT Press, 1980), p. 53, table 2.6. This appears to be a postwar trend paralleling the increasing differentiation between defense and commercial products. Gansler quotes personal correspondence from General Dynamics that shows "a growing wage differential (since WWII) required to obtain aircraft employees, relative to the general labor market. By the mid-1970s this differential had reached a premium of over 20 percent." See p. 291, note 42. After controlling for the skills and education levels of aerospace workers the Congressional Budget Office found that they still earn 21 percent more than the average industrial worker. CBO analysts were unable to account precisely for this differential, but speculated that it might be a premium paid "to reduce costly turnover among workers who have special skills not reflected by their observed characteristics, such as formal education." See Congressional Budget Office, "Compensation of Aerospace Workers," Staff Working Paper, September 1984, pp. 1–2.

35. Kaplan, "Is Industry's Image Accurate?" pp. 62–64. See also Gordon, "Data on Production Inefficiencies," p. 1285.

36. Peck and Scherer, *Weapons Acquisition Process*, p. 527. The authors quote a student of the era's nuclear contracting process who concluded that cost-plus contracts "have not stultified but have permitted a substantial degree of progress" in process innovation—that is, the development of improved capital. See p. 527, note 34, quoting Richard A. Tybout, *Government Contracting in Atomic Energy* (University of Michigan Press, 1956), p. 157.

37. See H. O. Stekler, "Technological Change in the Military Aircraft Industry," *Technological Forecasting and Social Change*, vol. 27 (July 1985), pp. 419–29.

38. DFAIR, p. vi-2.

39. See *The Ailing Defense Industrial Base: Unready for Crisis*, Committee Print, Report of the Defense Industrial Base Panel of the House Committee on Armed Services, 96 Cong. 2 sess. (GPO, 1980), p. 17.

40. See Edmund Dews and John Birkler, "Producing Small Quantities: Accepting a Way of Life?" *Aviation Week and Space Technology*, October 24, 1983, pp. 11, 84, for the argument that numerically controlled machinery is the best approach to efficiency in an industry marked by frequent design change.

41. Stekler, "Technological Change," pp. 424–26. In general, the use of computerized design and production facilities erodes the usefulness of work measurement, since it "is reducing the amount of 'touch labor' involved in any project, and with it the usefulness of industrial engineering." See Ellen B.

Brown, "Yesterday's Solution = Today's Defense Problem," *Wall Street Journal*, August 5, 1986, p. 30.

42. Gordon, "Data on Production Inefficiencies," p. 1285.

43. See the discussion in Peck and Scherer, *Weapons Acquisition Process*, pp. 509–10.

44. *Fiscal Year 1976 and July-September 1976 Transition Period Authorization for Military Procurement, Research and Development, and Active Duty, Selected Reserve, and Civilian Personnel Strengths*, Hearings before the Senate Committee on Armed Services, 94 Cong. 1 sess. (GPO, 1975), pt. 6, p. 3215.

45. The cost estimate omitted license fees but was for the same quantity of tanks as the XM-1 buy. FMC Corporation, "Leopard 2 (AV) Battle Tank Cost and Producibility Study: Budgetary Cost Estimate for Production Program," CDRL Sequence B003, DI-F-1203 (MOD) (San Jose, Calif.: December 1976), pp. 4–62.

46. For other tank unit cost comparisons see Capt. Gerald A. Halbert, "World Tank Production," *Armor*, vol. 90 (March-April 1981), p. 45, which lists unit costs for thirteen of the world's major tanks. The list is not well documented, nor does it make clear the precise kind of cost being compared. For what it is worth, however, the list places all three major U.S. tanks—the M60A1, M60A3, and M-1—in roughly the same range as others of the same vintage.

47. The study focused on the cost of the one hundredth aircraft to control for quantity differences. See Frederick P. Biery and Leonard Sullivan, Jr., *Assessing U.S. Weapon System Modernization Cost and Performance Trends*, TR-3997-3, report prepared for the Office of the Secretary of Defense (Arlington, Va., April 1985), pp. 2-17–2-24. The slope of the cost curve for European tactical aircraft is partially corroborated by D. L. Kirkpatrick and P. G. Pugh, who argue that the price of British combat aircraft has been rising at roughly 8 percent a year since 1910. See Kirkpatrick and Pugh, "Towards the Starship Enterprise—Are the Current Trends in Defence Unit Costs Inexorable?" *Aerospace*, vol. 10 (May 1983), p. 16.

48. The TASC study found that the Tornado cost slightly less than or just equal to comparable U.S. systems. Still, cost figures for Tornado have never been released, and there are grounds for disagreement. The British government once admitted, for example, that the Tornado program cost more than the Trident missile project, which at that point cost the United Kingdom nearly 10 billion pounds. Using this figure, one British journalist calculated what in the United States would be called a unit program cost (prorating R&D costs across the buy of 385 Tornadoes) for Tornado was roughly $45 million for each aircraft, more than the unit program cost of the F-15 or F-14. See "Cheaper Weapons: Europe Does it the Second-Best Way," *The Economist*, June 21, 1986, p. 23.

49. Gary Putka, "Britain's Troubled Nimrod Plane Shows Europe's Defense Woes," *Wall Street Journal*, February 11, 1986, p. 36.

50. George G. Daly and others, *The Effect of Price Competition on Weapon*

System Acquisition Costs, P-1435, report prepared for the Office of the Under Secretary of Defense Research and Engineering (Alexandria, Va.: Institute for Defense Analyses, 1979), p. A-4.

51. For much stronger conclusions about the positive value of competition, see Lou Kratz and others, "Competition of Defense Procurements: Evidence, Theory, and Application," The Analytic Sciences Corporation, undated ms., especially p. L-6.

52. On learning curve estimation see J. S. Cullen, "Cost Estimating from Initial Actuals," study sponsored by the Office of the Director, Planning and Evaluation, Office of the Secretary of Defense (August 20, 1976), p. 16. For the assessment of competition case studies see Capt. Donald L. Pilling, U.S. Navy, *Competition in Defense Procurement* (Brookings, forthcoming).

53. Michael Beltramo found that in six of the forty-seven cases used by the Institute for Defense Analyses (IDA) the price of the last noncompetitive buy fell far below the earlier prices, suggesting that the firm may have been trying to convince program managers that competition was not needed. Three firms, by contrast, raised their prices before competition was introduced, possibly seeking to take profits early. See Michael N. Beltramo, "A Case Study of the Sparrow AIM-7F: Findings, Theories, and Thoughts about Competition in the Procurement of Weapon Systems," *Program Manager*, vol. 14 (September-October 1985), pp. 28–35.

54. Beltramo, "Case Study of the Sparrow AIM-7F," p. 35, note 5.

55. *Ailing Defense Industrial Base*, p. 14.

56. Daly and others, *Effect of Price Competition*, pp. 83–84. Note that the IDA was seeking to estimate net savings of competition, taking into the account the costs of introducing competition in the first place. Technically, the price differential, and hence waste in production, should be more pronounced than these figures indicate. However, the IDA study failed to subtract most of the costs connected with establishing competition, making their savings estimate for the net cost of competition relatively optimistic and putting their percentage figures closer to the measure of "waste" in the production process. See the critique by K. A. Archibald and others, *Factors Affecting the Use of Competition in Weapon System Acquisition*, R-2706-DR&E (Santa Monica, Calif.: Rand Corporation, 1981), p. 45.

57. For the full story of the fighter engine war, see Robert W. Drewes, *The Air Force and the Great Engine War* (Washington: National Defense University Press, 1987); and David M. Kennedy, "The Great Engine War," Case C16-85-629 (Harvard University, John F. Kennedy School of Government Case Program, 1985).

58. A careful reading of Drewes, *The Air Force and the Great Engine War*, suggests that saving money was never the goal of the program. Rather, the Air Force sought to use the threat of competition to gain leverage over Pratt and Whitney, a firm most service officials saw as arrogant and unresponsive. See especially pp. 92–111.

59. For background, see Michael R. Gordon, "Selling the F-20, or How

Northrop Corp. Turned a White Elephant into a Prize Bull," *National Journal*, July 13, 1985, pp. 1609–13.

60. From "The F-20 Proposal," Northrop Corporation, undated. Cost figures are also taken from briefing papers prepared by Lt. Col. Rich Buickerood, Headquarters of the U.S. Air Force, Programs and Resources, International Programs Directorate, Weapons Programs Division, pp. 38–48.

61. See U.S. Congressional Budget Office, "Options for an Air Force Tactical Fighter Competition," Staff Working Paper (Washington, October 1985), p. 10.

62. Dividing annual procurement cost by the number of F-16As procured between fiscal 1978 and fiscal 1982 shows that the fighter's average cost fell from $25 million in the first year of production to $13 million in the last year. Jonathon Tyson and Diane Griffith, "Total Quantities and Costs of Major Weapon Systems Procured, FY 1974–1987," table of historical data costs in constant 1987 dollars (Washington, CBO, April 1986). Not surprisingly, General Dynamics claimed that the F-16SC's low cost was the result of deleting systems from the F-16C rather than competition. Air Force cost estimates tended to verify that claim. See CBO, "Options for an Air Force Tactical Fighter Competition," p. 10.

63. For a discussion, see James Kitfield, "Cheaper Spares, But at What Price?" *Military Logistics Forum*, vol. 2 (June 1986), pp. 16–25.

64. See Jacques S. Gansler, "Needed: A U.S. Defense Industrial Strategy," *International Security*, vol. 12 (Fall 1987), p. 45, note 1. See also the pessimistic assessment of whether the services can handle the additional workload efficiently in Drewes, *The Air Force and the Great Engine War*, p. 150.

65. Perhaps this conclusion should not be so surprising. If U.S. weapons systems were exorbitantly more expensive than their European equivalents, they would not sell as well as in the international market. And even strong nationalist sentiment might not prevent the U.S. services from purchasing more European weapons if they were dramatically more cost-effective than those developed in the United States. If competition always yielded stupendous savings, the services and Congress would probably have far less trouble than they currently do in overcoming their short-term perspective and investing in more of it.

66. As quoted in Dan Beyers, "ATF Teams Disdain R&D Dollar Drain," *Defense News*, March 9, 1987, p. 26.

67. The two contractor teams—Lockheed-Boeing-General Dynamics and Northrop-McDonnell Douglas—each signed fixed-price "demonstration and validation phase" development contracts for $691 million, while observers agree that the ATF designs submitted will probably cost $1 billion each. See Beyers, "ATF Teams Disdain R&D Dollar Drain," pp. 1, 26; and David M. North, "USAF Awards ATF Contracts to Lockheed, Northrop," *Aviation Week and Space Technology*, November 10, 1986, pp. 18–19.

68. One argument holds that dependence on foreign suppliers will hobble the nation's effort to mobilize. The other argument focuses on the dangers to

the nation's technology base should foreign firms purchase American defense firms. The first argument is important to this discussion. For a discussion of the second, see Bernard L. Schwartz, *Foreign Ownership of U.S. Defense Companies: Where Do We Draw the Line?*, Foreign Policy Briefs (Johns Hopkins University, Foreign Policy Institute, School of Advanced International Studies, 1988). Clearly the broader question—should economic forces or national security concerns dominate these determinations?—is relevant in both cases.

69. This may be because the industrial base planning problem is impossibly complex. See Lawrence J. Korb, "A New Look at United States Defense Industrial Preparedness," *Defense Management Journal*, vol. 17 (Third Quarter 1981), pp. 4–5.

70. The House Industrial Base Panel found little evidence of any serious industrial base planning in the Defense Department. Instead, panel chairman Richard C. Ichord noted, "The [Defense Department's] Consolidated Guidance sizes our defense production base on the assumption that all future wars will be short wars." See *The Ailing Defense Industrial Base: Unready for Crisis*, report of the Defense Industrial Base Panel, Committee Print, House Committee on Armed Services, 96 Cong. 2 sess. (GPO, 1980), p. 20.

71. See, for example, Fred Hiatt and Rick Atkinson, "Profits Soar in Buildup: As Firms Cash In, Questions Crop Up," *Washington Post*, April 1, 1985, p. 1; and Center for Defense Information, "No Business Like War Business," *Defense Monitor*, vol. 16, no. 3 (1987).

72. The study found defense profits to be "very similar to those of comparable durable goods manufacturers for the years 1970–1979," but while profits among durable good manufacturers "deteriorated dramatically" from 1980 to 1983, defense firms "were able to maintain their profitability primarily because of the increase in defense outlays and the decline in inflation." See DFAIR, pp. E-2, IX-3.

73. See John H. Cushman, Jr., "Pentagon Revising Rules on Contractor Profits," *New York Times*, August 21, 1986, p. D2; and Financial Executives Institute, "Recent Developments in Government Profit Policy," undated pamphlet, Washington. Policy changes confirmed in interviews with personnel in the office of the Undersecretary of Defense, Acquisition.

74. The DFAIR study noted that profits as a percent of sales will remain roughly constant, but return on assets will decline since asset levels will remain static. See DFAIR, p. V-57.

75. Dan Beyers, "Air Force Plans to Limit Industry Cost Sharing in Development of New Weapons," *Defense News*, February 1, 1988, p. 13. See also Judith Kohn Brown, "Defense Spending Bill May Inspire Scrutiny of Fixed-Price Contracts," *Defense News*, January 4, 1988, p. 5.

76. Gansler, *Defense Industry*, pp. 56–57.

NOTES TO CHAPTER SEVEN

1. Charles F. Lindblom, "The Science of 'Muddling Through,'" *Public Administration Review*, vol. 19 (Spring 1959), p. 85.

2. The Packard Commission, for example, called on the Pentagon to use off-the-shelf components, relying on the development of "new or custom-made items only when it has been established that those readily available are clearly inadequate to meet military requirements." The report correctly noted that those requirements are the problem when it admitted that "excessively rigid military specifications" are chiefly responsible for preventing off-the-shelf buys. President's Blue Ribbon Commission on Defense Management, *A Quest for Excellence: Final Report to the President* (GPO, 1986), p. 60.

3. See William W. Kaufmann, *The 1985 Defense Budget* (Brookings, 1984), pp. 36–37.

4. In the initial request for proposal for the advanced tactical fighter, the Air Force called for an average unit fly-away cost of $35 million in 1985 dollars for a total buy of 750 aircraft produced at 72 aircraft a year. See "Air Force Requests Proposals For Advanced Tactical Fighter," *Aviation Week and Space Technology*, October 14, 1985, p. 24.

5. See K. A. Archibald and others, *Factors Affecting the Use of Competition in Weapon System Acquisition*, R-2706-DR&E (Santa Monica, Calif.: Rand Corporation, 1981), p. 17, note 2.

6. Merton J. Peck and Frederic M. Scherer, *The Weapons Acquisition Process: An Economic Analysis* (Harvard University, Graduate School of Business Administration, 1962), pp. 59–60.

7. Giles K. Smith and others, *The Use of Prototypes in Weapon System Development*, R-2345-AF (Santa Monica: Rand Corporation, 1981), pp. 88–89.

8. On the company's risky design features, see Smith and others, *Use of Prototypes*, p. 101.

9. An important exception was the absence of attention to reliability, maintenance, and field support. In particular, the Air Force did not supply a "support concept" until the prototype phase of the program was nearly completed. See Smith and others, *Use of Prototypes*, pp. 87, 90. This is not to say, however, that competing contractors were unaware of service support concepts, any more than they were unaware of service operational concepts and debates. Presumably the Lightweight Fighter program could have carried competition through full-scale engineering development in a way that would have encouraged Northrop and General Dynamics to pay attention to reliability and support as well as to operational performance.

10. John Newhouse, *The Sporty Game* (Alfred A. Knopf, 1982), p. 3.

11. Frederic M. Scherer, *The Weapons Acquisition Process: Economic Incentives* (Harvard University, Graduate School of Business Administration, 1964), p. 48.

12. David C. Morrison, "Pentagon Dogfighting," *National Journal*, October 8, 1988, pp. 2524–28.

13. The lightweight fighter prototypes cost the government roughly $127 million in 1975 dollars. See Smith and others, *Use of Prototypes*, p. 117.

14. See "X-29 to Explore New Flight Regime," *Defense Electronics*, vol. 19 (September 1987), p. 53.

15. See Judith Reppy and F.A. Long, "The Pentagon's Program of IR&D:

The Need for Reform," *Bulletin of the Atomic Scientists*, vol. 32 (January 1976), pp. 30–36.

16. William B. McLean, "The Sidewinder Missile Program," in Fremont E. Kast and James E. Rosenzweig, eds., *Science, Technology, and Management* (McGraw-Hill, 1963), p. 166 (Emphasis added).

17. U.S. Congressional Budget Office, *Effects of Weapons Procurement Stretch-Outs on Costs and Schedules* (Washington, 1987), p. xiv.

18. See Michael D. Rich, *Competition in the Acquisition of Major Weapon Systems: Legislative Perspectives*, R-2058-PR (Santa Monica, Calif.: Rand Corporation, 1976), pp. 29–40.

19. Michael H. Armacost, *The Politics of Weapons Innovation: The Thor-Jupiter Controversy* (Columbia University Press, 1969), pp. 16–17.

20. Alain C. Enthoven and K. Wayne Smith, *How Much Is Enough? Shaping the Defense Program, 1961–1969* (Harper and Row, 1971), p. 266.

21. General Lawrence A. Skantze, "B-1B: A Timely Lesson in Risk Management," *Aviation Week and Space Technology*, March 23, 1987, p. 11.

Index

A-*7* aircraft, 55, 66
A-*10*, 78, 147, 194
Abrams, General Creighton, and M-*1* tank project, 74
Advanced medium-range air-to-air missile (AMRAAM), 8, 80, 116–18
Advanced Research Projects Agency, 41
Advanced tactical fighter project (ATF), 175, 178, 186, 192, 194
Aerospace industry, 42; military production percentage, 32; public relations, 42; subcontractors, 42
Air Corps Act of 1926, 26–27
Aircraft: competitive bidding, 26–27; cost, 19; development speed, 21, 22, 25; technological evolution, 17, 18–19, 30; electronics components in, 30; experimental contracting for, 25; House Committee on Military Affairs hearings, 28; mass production, 20; monopoly production rights, 27; new technology, 19; pre-World War II procurement, 29; proposed procurement reforms, 28–29; sole-source contracting, 27; underbidding, 27; in World War I, 18–19, 22
Aircraft industry, 31; competition in, 24; development advantages, 23; fixed-price contract, 24; political problems, 23; role, 22–23
Air Development Center (Wright Field), 23

Air Force, 18, 30–31. *See also* Army Air Force; use of cost-plus contracts, 31; defense budget share, 30–31; development contract competition, 32–41; procurement process, 33–38; production concurrency, 34–35; prominence, 30–31; Thor-Jupiter controversy, 48; weapon system development, 33–34
Air Force Systems Command (AFSC), 63, and F-*16* development, 78, 101
Air Research and Development Command (ARDC), 31, 35–36, 38; bureaucracy, 45–46; formalism, 35–36; production concurrency, 38; subcomponent definition, 37; weapon system development, 38
AMRAAM. *See* advanced medium-range air-to-air missile
Analytic Sciences Corporation, The (TASC), 168
Apache helicopter, 120
APG-*68* radar, 101
Appropriations Committees, defense subcommittees, 40, 57
APQ-*113/114* radar, 111–12
APQ-*120* radar, 111–12
ARDC. *See* Air Research and Development Command
Armacost, Michael H., 47–48, 201
Armed Services Committees, and the acquisition process, 40–41, 56; oversight of research and development, 56–57

245